18.95

3

T73

2010

PASSINGS

SANTA
MONICA
PRESS

Published by: Santa Monica Press LLC
P.O. Box 1076
Santa Monica, CA 90406-1076
1-800-784-9553
www.santamonicapress.com
books@santamonicapress.com

Printed in the United States

Santa Monica Press books are available at special quantity discounts when purchased in bulk by corporations, organizations, or groups. Please call our Special Sales department at 1-800-784-9553.

This book is intended to provide general information. The publisher, author, distributor, and copyright owner are not engaged in rendering health, medical, legal, financial, or other professional advice or services. The publisher, author, distributor, and copyright owner are not liable or responsible to any person or group with respect to any loss, illness, or injury caused or alleged to be caused by the information found in this book.

ISBN-13 978-1-59580-048-0

Library of Congress Cataloging-in-Publication Data

Travis-Henikoff, Carole A.
 Passings : death, dying, and unexplained phenomena / by Carole A. Travis-Henikoff.
    p. cm.
 Includes bibliographical references.
 ISBN 978-1-59580-048-0
 1. Death. 2. Death–Psychological aspects. I. Title.
 HQ1073.T73 2010
 306.9–dc22
                            2009039714

Cover and interior design and production by Future Studio

PASSINGS

Death, Dying, and Unexplained Phenomena

Carole A. Travis-Henikoff

Foreword by Dr. Garniss H. Curtis

CONTENTS

For Kim

FOREWORD

by Dr. Garniss H. Curtis

I awakened with my heart pounding. "Did she call? Does she need me?" Seconds later, as I awakened more fully, the awful truth came to me: Dorette hadn't called me. She would never call to me again. Dorette was dead. To myself, I said, "Garniss, she is dead. Do you understand? Dead!" The words reverberated through my head over and over again.

I had fallen asleep in a chair several hours after my wife, Dorette, had died of cancer with our daughter, Ann, and me by her side. I had been unaware of falling asleep. I had sat down from total emotional exhaustion, thinking I could never sleep again. Now an empty, hollow feeling gripped me, "Forty-seven years together, and it's over? No, no, no, it cannot be over!"

Following Dorette's final moment, my daughter and I had held and hugged one another for a long while. Tears had come to our eyes and sobs were heard, but we were unable to really cry. We simply could not release the huge pressure of grief we both felt. In fact, I was not able to let out these pent-up emotions for several weeks, and only then at a time I least expected.

Among our friends, the author of this book, Carole Travis, was the youngest. We had been attracted to her through her love of gourmet cooking, as Carole is the author of a superb cookbook entitled *Star Food*, a collection of favorite dishes from two

famous Los Angeles restaurants, one of which belonged to her
family. Recently widowed, Carole was past the grieving stage for
her second husband, but still working through the pain caused
by the loss of many other family members when I phoned her regarding a recipe, several weeks after the death of my wife. Carole
was very familiar with the stages one goes through in the grieving
process. I was a neophyte. Until I lost Dorette, I was completely
unaware of what happens inside of you when you lose someone
very close and dear to you. Even though I had known of my
wife's impending death months before it occurred, I had not an-
ticipated all of the effects her death would have on me.

Once over the immediate and terrible shock of her
death, which lasted two or three days, I went into a phase during which I appeared outwardly calm and more or less normal.
My friends saw me laughing and joking with them and accepting their sympathies with an air of "Yes, Dorette is gone and I
feel very badly about it, but life goes on." Inside I knew it was
an act, inside I felt nothing—no pain, no sorrow, no joy, no
emotions of any kind. I felt empty, hollow. After several weeks
of this, I began to wonder if anything would ever truly give me
pleasure again. Those things that had given me so much enjoyment in the past—classical music, travel, camping, swimming,
small parties with close friends, scientific research—seemed now
to hold no meaning for me.

Carole, who had gone through the grieving process over
and over again, knew exactly where I was in that most lone-
some of processes. Moreover, she had read the same books as I
concerning death and dying and understood my negative reaction to them, and thus could help me understand that I was not
abnormal in my inability to feel anything but a vast emptiness. I
recall well how quickly Carole was able to see through the lie of
my outward calm and joviality over the phone.

"Cut the nonsense, Garniss," she exclaimed after a few
minutes of conversation. "It doesn't wash with me. Have you
been able to cry yet? I mean really cry?"

"No," I confessed. "I have not been able to."

"I didn't think so. I can hear how dead you are inside. Believe me, Garniss, you will not begin to feel again, to live again, until you really cry, and I mean cry and cry and cry. Not just once, but over and over again, today, next week, and next month. The grief that is bottled up inside of you is so intense that it is keeping you from feeling any other emotion. You can't live until you relieve the tension. Get it out. Get it all out. It's a catharsis that you must go through."

Carole's injunction broke down the monstrous dam that had been holding in my grief and I cried as I had never cried before. How long I cried I have no idea, but afterward I did feel greatly relieved, and, to my amazement, Carole was still on the phone.

"Feeling better? I hope so, but you are a long way from being out of the woods. It will be easier, though, next time."

And she was right; that first immense outpouring of grief was a beginning for me, which would lead me back to the wholeness we all need in order to be truly alive.

I learned at this time that Carole's tragic experiences had motivated her to begin a unique autobiography, which focused mainly on the deaths that had so recently punctuated her life. Surrounding these deaths were anomalous occurrences that begged for explanation. Carole, not intimidated by the opinions of scientists and psychologists, pressed forward with years of research into metaphysical and paranormal experiences that have been recorded throughout all of human history. Carole offered me parts of her manuscript. The pages she sent affected me deeply. I found myself relating fully to both the occurrences of death and the people who populated her pages, which in turn helped me through my own grief as no other book on this subject had managed to do. I'd been completely turned off by books encouraging me to join the local church or bridge club. Those books had failed to speak to the grief I was feeling. As I read through Carole's pages, I realized that her book was not as much about death as about life. And that death is a part of life, not a separate experience.

Carole, a deeply compassionate and feeling person, more so than anyone I have ever known, is like people I've met in the scientific community. As a professor and scientist for most of my 70 years, I have found great intelligence and a huge emotional capacity in all of the great scientists I have known and in all of my best students. Like them, Carole is highly motivated, imaginative, and a keen observer. From our first meeting, I was attracted to her obvious mental alacrity.

Carole knew death well. She had experienced five deaths within a span of three and a half years. Accompanying each of those deaths were metaphysical phenomena that most psychologists and skeptical scientists have, through the years, attributed to a mixture of coincidence or the highly emotional and disturbed condition of the grieving observer. Carole was fully aware of her grief and the trauma that each successive death had presented to her, yet investigation of the anomalous occurrences she had experienced stood as evidence of something real and significant as opposed to hallucinations brought on by emotional trauma. And after deep consideration, Carole rejected the plausible conclusions put forth by the soft science of psychology and the rigid refusals put forth by the hard sciences. In their place, she sought more logical and reasonable conclusions, citing the fact that many of the phenomena occurred at a time when death was not a consideration! Through her mental need for understanding, she decided on a course of logical inquiry.

Carole is neither a religious person (in the conventional meaning) nor a mystic (in any sense of the word). From the time she was a young child, she has been interested in science and has been an omnivorous reader of science throughout her life, subscribing to, and devouring, several scientific journals on a continual basis, and attending classes, symposia, and paleoanthropological digs in a consistent reaching out for knowledge.

Carole's experiences with death opened a huge collection of questions concerning the occurrence we call "death." Her immutable curiosity plagued her and she began to look for explanations for the phenomena she had observed in the regular scientific literature (phenomena that have been observed by others throughout recorded history). Nothing! The vast majority of today's scientists are not interested in precognitive dreams of death or electrical phenomena accompanying death. These phenomena cannot be weighed, measured or reproduced in the laboratory. And, as for dreams, everyone has had thousands of them that are of no consequence whatsoever. Thus, a dream that accurately predicts an event to come in minute detail *must* be coincidence—amazing coincidence, perhaps, but coincidence all the same. For many, no other explanation is acceptable. After all, scientists have *proved* that time flows only in one direction, forward, and time warps and precognition are subjects for science fiction and the tabloids, not for scientific investigation!

Carole felt differently, and as she does not have a prestigious scientific reputation to worry about, she has stepped into a field of investigation where angels (scientists) fear to tread, certain in her mind that there are time-transgressive metaphysical phenomena that are related to the very important experience we call "death."

As Carole told me, the data seemed scarce and very difficult to find, but as the scientist who finds what he is looking for, she, with her knowledge of the reality of her experiences, found more and more information as her research progressed. Many people opened up to her and added their own private experiences to an ever-growing stack of unexplainable occurrences. She told me, "It's like looking for needles in a haystack; however, it should be noted that the needles are made of steel, easily discernable against an abundance of straw."

Carole has done a remarkable job of sorting out and investigating the needles from the stacks of straw, and an even more remarkable job of trying to find explanations that either fit into the body of science we know today or into the body of science we will know tomorrow. Most of all, she has opened her eyes to death and she leads us, unafraid, to a place of understanding and acceptance of that which is the most personal experience in all of life: death.

Garniss H. Curtis, PhD
Professor Emeritus of Geology and Geophysics
University of California, Berkeley

Director Emeritus of Berkeley Geochronology Center
Berkeley, California

INTRODUCTION

Woody Allen said he didn't mind the thought of dying; he just didn't want to be there when it happened. You can put your hands down. Most of us feel the same way.

Death frightens us and fascinates us, often in proportion to belief systems, set up through a lifetime of learning and societal input. But the basic fear of death is innate within us all. That fear helps to keep us alive. It makes us look before crossing the street.

Nevertheless, death stands silently in the corners of our lives, constant, yet ignored or forgotten. For most, death (and the act of dying) is a topic to be avoided. Many view death as an option, believing modern medicine to be capable of curing and fixing all. But when we deny death with erroneous attitudes, we also shun death by finding its mention impolite or too emotionally charged to be spoken of in public. Even in the privacy of our homes death is rarely discussed with any real degree of honesty. Yet everything dies. Every known living organism dies. Mountain ranges, rivers, stars, even galaxies die. As with life, death is a natural process inherent within our universe.

Death is a deep and amazing subject surrounded by fascinating experiences and meaningful moments that touch and affect our lives. Death is also a powerful, emotional teacher that often pushes us through knotholes none would approach on his own volition. In this book, I will attempt to take you through many such narrow spaces to the serenity and understanding that lies beyond. It is not an easy ride but worth the trip.

Passings is not laid out in a preplanned, formulaic fashion so as to take the reader from part A to part B and so on. Rather, it is life as lived in its rawest form. There are no false punches or platitudes within.

Passings approaches W.C. Fields's "man in the long white nightgown" in the order directed by the Queen of Hearts: "Start at the beginning, go to the end, then stop." And so it is that the multiple deaths detailed in *Passings* are presented in chronological order. A benefit arises from this in that *Passings* takes readers back to their childhood, to the time when they first perceived death and reconciled its seeming finality in accordance with perceptions elicited by the experience and the beliefs of their society. After crawling through early memories, pondering wondrous things and examining what science can tell us, the reader can stand and walk with less trepidation through the book's often difficult labyrinth.

If my story were simply to let you know and understand more about death, the many forms it takes and the complexities of healing, I would have quite a tale to tell, but woven within the threads of every death were anomalous occurrences that my pragmatic, science-loving brain couldn't explain. And so my quest was set.

Science, with its logical, narrow paradigm, is totally incapable of looking into dimensions that appear to be contrary to the three known dimensions of our world and the fourth dimension, time, which fills the imaginations of our minds . . . and that's all right. As far as we've come, we still have a long way to go. So it is that *Passings* explores many deaths, intense human emotions and mind-bending occurrences universally experienced in proximity to death, all encompassed within a cocoon of research.

The phenomena that accompany the deaths herein work to form a braided backbone for *Passings*. As the book progresses, similarities, as well as differences, are uncovered. With science, medical data and research offering explanation and posing questions, death and its attendants are explored from every possible angle. Throughout, *Passings* flows on an undercurrent of love. Because we love, we care, and because we care, we grieve. Fortunately, we possess qualities that bring us through. We are survivors. *Passings* illuminates this global truth.

Other than the names of my family, scientists, doctors, known figures and/or quoted individuals, the names in this book have been changed so as to protect those who shared their unique experiences. I hold them all in deep appreciation for adding to this effort.

PART ONE

DEEP IMPRESSIONS

With an indescribable light, our universe began to pattern itself. Out of that initial brilliance came all we know to exist: time, space, galaxies, solar systems, black holes, matter, antimatter, particles with mass, massless particles, you and I.

CHILDHOOD LESSONS

Within each and every one of us, among myriad tracts of memories, are moments that shaped our perceptions of life and death.

I can still smell the rich batter browning on the ancient iron as each waffle puffed and oozed from the old steaming electrical device. With eagerness and never-ending questions, I would badger my mother, "Is it done yet? Is it done?" Then Mom would be lathering butter over each brown lattice and meticulously applying the syrup as I instructed, "Not too much. You missed over here." Then the two of us would settle in for some fine eating and stories about Mom's family and the times of her childhood.

I was raised in a tiny house in Brentwood, California. By the time I could recollect, World War II was raging and my mother and I were often alone since my father worked from early morning until well past my bedtime. Daddy was a master chef who had cooked for the King of Denmark prior to immigrating to America. Mom was also great in the kitchen, and my most cherished childhood mealtime memories are of waffle dinners baked for two. Mom and I would dine in the kitchen next to the long lacquered wood drain that sloped into the big old rectangular sink. I would sit perched high upon a kitchen stool with the bread board pulled out to serve as a table. Oh, the hunger and excitement. And then the stories would begin. Many were of my mother's beloved grandfather, my great-grandpa Charles Jucker, who was still alive and fast approaching the age of 90, but most of Mom's stories were about my great-grandmother Caroline Jucker, teller of fortune, medium, seer and deceased wife of Charles.

My mother, like her mother before her, had been named after the fascinating Caroline.

It was over waffles that I learned that although both of my great-grandparents had emigrated from Germany, Charles had been born to French parents in Alsace-Lorraine during a period when Alsace was controlled by Germany. Charles had clung to his French heritage, while Great-Grandmother Jucker was German through and through. Mom said that during World War I none of the tradespeople would sell to my great-grandmother because of her German accent, so my great-grandfather, with his French accent, did all of the shopping.

Once in a while, Mom would get down a black carton box embossed to look like tooled leather. In the box were tawny old photographs and tintypes. In among the litter was a picture postcard sent from Germany. On the front was a picture of a great three-storied house of white stucco plastered between dark wooden beams. It was in that house that my great-grandfather Jucker had been born in the mid-1800s. In front of the house stood many of my great-grandfather's relatives. I would stare at my ancestors as Mom told her stories. My favorite one was the time Charles went to France as a young man and got invited to an elaborate 16-course dinner. He particularly enjoyed one meat course but didn't know its origin. Finally, he worked up the courage to ask the butler what type of meat had been served. "Why, dog, monsieur," replied the man. Sickened and astonished, my great-grandfather ran from the hotel to retch in the gutter.

It was after his trip to France that Great-Grandpa went home to Germany, met Caroline and married her. Together, they had two children, Charles Jucker Jr. and my maternal grandmother, Caroline, who went by the name of Carrie.

During the first decade of the twentieth century, the family immigrated to America, where Carrie matured into a dark-haired, blue-eyed beauty and married my grandfather, Harry Lincoln Faunce, whose ancestry went back through nine generations of Philadelphians and down to the harbor and Plymouth Rock. Harry was a saloon keeper and soon squeals and squalls could be heard in the apartment over the saloon as the birth of a son, who died shortly thereafter, was soon followed by the birth of my aunt Helen, who, in turn, was followed by my mother, Caroline.

When my mother was two and a half years of age, Prohibition forced Harry to close his saloon and sell the property. That's when three generations of my family packed up and headed west over dusty, rutted roads that led all the way cross-country to Los Angeles, California, where they picked up some property in the middle of a bean field, just off a soon-to-be-paved road known as Wilshire Boulevard.

The family built several houses on what later became known as the Faunce Reservation. The front house facing onto McClellan Drive was built and inhabited by Charles Jucker Jr., my grandma Faunce's brother, while the back house, which faced onto the alley, housed my grandparents and their growing family. Attached to the back house was a four-car garage, over which sat an apartment where Caroline and Charles Jucker Sr. ended their days with Caroline hanging homemade noodles to dry over the small railing at the top of the stairs and sending Charles to eat his beloved Limburger cheese and drink his homemade wine in his workshop at the back of the garage.

Great-Grandmother Caroline would not allow Charles to bring his Limburger up to the apartment. She said its foul odor offended her clients, who arrived for psychic readings in their chauffeur-driven cars, which parked in front of the door that opened to the stairs that led up to the apartment over the garages. Up they would go, up the stairs that Caroline made her daughter Carrie scrub every single day, rain or shine, whether

she was fit, sick or eight months pregnant—and Grandma Carrie was often eight months pregnant. As the years passed Carrie
scrubbed through several layers of paint on the stairs leading
up to her parents' apartment, producing an additional five little
Faunces between scrubbings. Of course, the first was close to
grown by the time the last emerged, and by that time Caroline Jucker had died and Great-Grandpa Jucker had switched
from his homemade red to store-bought wine. I think the senior
Caroline knew she would be dead and gone long before Charles;
I see it in the stern look of her pictures and hear it in the stories
I was told as a child.

Though we lived a mile away, I did a lot of growing up
along Faunce's Alley. It was the alley onto which both Caroline's
and Carrie's doors faced, so it was the alley that saw the action
of the day. Hucksters of all types would roll down the alley in
horse-drawn carts and gasping trucks to sell their wares and gossip with the women there.

The alley boasted the vegetable and produce man, the
milkman, the knife and scissors sharpener, the junk man, the
ragman (of whom we were all afraid), the iceman and the Helms
bread man, who had great, high cream puffs snowed over with
powdered sugar, cool from his ice chest. With the sound of his
whistle, my mouth would start to salivate and I would run to
find my mother and beg for money.

But it was the iceman I loved best, with his leather leaf
thrown over his shoulder and his great muscles bulging as he
grasped giant ice tongs that bit into his large blocks of ice. I
would watch as he swung a blue-white block around to ride his
back upon a leather leaf, then run and skip along behind him as
he carried the frozen block into Grandma's house and placed it
in the old wooden icebox.

One day they moved the old icebox out and installed a
funny-looking white metal monster that hummed, even through
the night, but didn't need a block of ice.

"You can even make ice cream in it," my aunt Helen

enthused. I missed the iceman.

My mother, Caroline, was her grandmother's namesake, but the senior Caroline didn't like her. She called my mother *Zigeuna* ("gypsy") and treated her harshly. Mom ached over the favoritism the elder Caroline showed to her firstborn grandchild, Helen. Mom's sister Helen was her senior by only 18 months, but she was from another planet as far as my great-grandmother was concerned.

Caroline Jucker never owned a cookbook but her culinary skills were legendary and the aroma of rich pastries would often settle over the Faunce Reservation. It was on baking days that my great-grandmother would invite her granddaughter Helen up to join her for an elaborate tea party served on Haviland china brought all the way from Europe via tossing boat and bouncing car. My mother, Caroline, would be told to stay away. While her sister had high tea with the soothsayer, Mom would sit on the stoop at the end of the narrow stairway that led up to the apartment over the garages and cry.

Though time presented the senior Caroline with more and more grandchildren, only gentle Helen was ever invited up to tea. My mother never came to understand the attitude her grandmother had shown towards her as a child, but knew without a doubt that the woman could read the minds of others. Mom said her grandmother always knew every thought in her head, every naughty thing she had done in school or in the gully across the road, and even chastised Mom for things that no one else knew anything about.

From the memories of others, I see my great-grandmother as a harsh and demanding woman who ruled over her daughter Carrie with an iron hand padded with love. But I also see an extremely intelligent woman who seemed close to genius on many levels, particularly on subjects pertaining to the lives and emotions of her fellow man. Caroline Jucker ended up being remembered as a harsh and authoritative, yet incredibly wise and easy to listen to person who had the capacity to speak sagely on one subject after another. Last, but perhaps most important in relationship to our tale, are the claims of her paranormal expertise. Caroline Jucker was so in tune with others that she sold her talents for a goodly sum to those who could afford the price.

And so we come back to the chauffeured cars that frequented Faunce's Alley, along with the junk man, the ragman and the iceman. Great-Grandmother's clients were the wealthy and the famous, but regardless of who they were, they all had two things in common—$10 cash and a yearning to know the future or contact the other side. From tales often told, it seems clear that Caroline was telepathic and what is commonly referred to as psychic.

When a client wished to see the future, Caroline read the tarot cards or her astrological charts as a consulting physician reads an X-ray. I don't think she needed cards or physical props to tell someone what only they knew or what the future held for them. I believe she used these standard props, knowing that to simply sit across from someone and tell them what she could discern made her seem too powerful, hence too frightening. Thus she softened her innate knowledge and powers of observation with props in order to soothe her clients.

Tarot cards and all, Caroline Jucker was a normal human being with some less than desirable traits, one of them being her habit of taking the long fingernail of her right pinkie and drilling holes in the bottoms of See's chocolates so that she wouldn't inadvertently consume one she didn't like. Obviously, she was unable to read chocolates the way she read people.

As children, Aunt Helen and my mother, Caroline, would sit on their front porch next to the door leading up to their grandmother's apartment and wait for clients to come down the stairs after a reading. As clients were greeted by their chauffeur or waiting friend they would shake their heads. "She couldn't have known that." "Nobody knows that." Helen and Caroline heard it a thousand times.

Some clients requested a séance and though Caroline

Jucker knew séances to be more theatrics than substance, she also knew that it was all those $10 and $20 bills that had helped to purchase the Faunce Reservation and sustain her family through the Great Depression.

Caroline Jucker had few scruples in her pursuit of solvency and it never bothered her to have her grandchildren help in the rigging of séances. As for the children, they thought it great fun and Mom loved to tell of when they had her brother John play his trumpet into the dark corner of a closet, causing his attending sisters to clasp their hands over their mouths so as to muffle their uncontrollable laughter.

Though phony, the séances were performed with great solemnity and often incredible, reliable words would exit from Caroline's mouth as she sat in "trance." So the cars continued up the alley and Grandmom Faunce went on scrubbing her mother's stairs until Caroline died at home after a brief, but critical illness.

Years after the elder Caroline's death, a woman stopped my grandmother in a market and said, "Aren't you the daughter of Caroline Jucker?" Grandma stared at the fur-draped woman and admitted her parentage.

"My dear, I'm so glad to see you as I've wanted to tell you something. I saw your dear mother some 10 years back. She told me that in three years' time, on August fifth, my husband would die quite suddenly. She said that those about me would want me to do certain things with his money, but that I should do another." The woman waved diamond-infested fingers into my grandmother's face and then continued, "She was right my dear, dead right. I had wanted to thank her, but I heard that she had passed on."

And so she had.

And so my great-grandmother's death, her act of no longer being present, of existing only in memory, gave me my first glimmer of the thing we refer to as death.

In January 1944, British police broke into an séance and arrested Helen Duncan for witchcraft and compromising Britain's safety. During the height of World War II, the unfortunate seer had told a couple that their son had gone down on the HMS *Barham*, a ship whose 1941 loss had not been reported in hopes of keeping morale high. Ms. Duncan's list of clients is said to have included Winston Churchill and King George VI.

Was my great-grandmother Caroline Jucker—the medium, the seer, the psychic, the lover of chocolates, the great-grandmother I never knew—truly prescient, or just unusually adept in observation and the reading of others? Are psychic powers real? Can some tap into the minds of others or "see" what the future holds in store? [The word "psychic" is derived from the Greek word *psychikos* ("of the mind" or "mental").]

Joseph of the Old Testament repeatedly and correctly deciphered dreams of the future. Nostradamus, despite his naysayers, cannot be easily thrown aside and the case of Edgar Cayce scrambles the brain. Throughout history there have been shamans and seers, oracles and prophets; from religious writings and myth to aged documents and detailed histories, prescient minds have filled our communal past. Peoples of the past, whether primitive or sophisticated, along with many living today, listened to and believed the shamans, seers and psychics of their day; their words being acted upon not only by the general populace but by kings, pharaohs and chancellors.

Today, within modern societies, it is different. Anything that won't fit into a test tube and/or can't be replicated in a laboratory, or proven through equation or theory (a reasonable idea about a specific subject) is viewed to be false. Science's flat denial of anything existing beyond its realm of inquiry began in the early 1900s, when authors began writing against religion and for science. Those first writings didn't actually deny the existence of a soul, a subconscious, which suggested various levels of mental awareness and capabilities, prescient thoughts or anomalous occurrences, but those first writings did prompt others to separate science from all else, with the added dictum that nothing existed other than that which could be proven scientifically as fact. In other words, all things that stood outside the realm of science didn't exist, or were "simply of the mind," which is somewhat of a strange statement, as many scientists are reductionists who don't believe you have a "mind," just a brain. They are minimalists who reduce everything down to its base components, often excluding all data and questions that arise in the minds of others as they squeeze large subjects into short formulas. In doing so, the reductionists often leave a wake of unanswered questions begging for further exploration. Fortunately, on the other side of the scientific fence, within many fields of science there sit many dualists who believe in both the brain and the mind, who recognize that there is much we don't know and much more to learn. If you read the history of science and discovery, you will find that in every era people have claimed to have found "the truth," "the answer." One writer in the 1800s, after the electromagnetic force had been correctly (provably) set in equational form, stated, "There is nothing more to learn."

Nevertheless, current curricula continue to teach that if science can't prove it, it doesn't exist, it never happened, and furthermore, it can't happen . . . which leaves huge chunks of life in limbo. To complicate things, many anomalous occurrences have been studied, some over and over again, but things that go bump in the night don't seem to like test tubes and refuse to be replicated. That doesn't mean these things don't happen, it simply means that at this point in time we can't prove them scientifically. And, for me, that's perfectly all right. I live in a world where it is easy for me to accept what is known through scientific method, and where there are myriad things yet to be explained or understood.

Question: Why do humans want to know it all? Are we frightened children pretending to be courageous by thinking we know everything? The true scientist is a seeker of knowledge, a person who knows full well that some of what he believes today may be folly tomorrow. New findings and information may dismay him as they crumble a long-held belief, but if he's a true scientist, his feeling of dismay will be followed by "Eureka! I have found a truth!" . . . for the moment.

Concerning the word "truth," it should be carefully noted that false mediums, seers, psychics, et al., number in the hundreds of thousands and can be found in every country on planet Earth. Each one of them is after one thing—your money. Unfortunately, their gross deceptions make it easier for scientists to scoff at the unexplainable. Beware.

G reat-Grandfather Charles Jucker had the most twinkling blue eyes imaginable. He loved children, animals, gardening, stinky French cheeses, pinochle, and the making and drinking of fine wine. (Perhaps we should reverse the order.) Through his years of widowhood, he was looked after by his daughter, my wonderful grandma Faunce, and spent much of his time hiding behind the corner of her house, garden hose in hand, ready to jump out and squirt you if you didn't keep your wits about you. Fortunately, he lived to be 91, which allowed him to become one of my earliest and most favored memories.

On a fine spring day, I sat on the old cement porch that branched out from my grandma's frame house, a superstructure of heavy beams rising about it. Red-petaled bougainvillea clutched at the timbers, clinging tightly to the wood that showed through flaking paint. The eastern edge of the porch was six feet from the stoop and door that led up to my great-grandpa's apartment. The same stairs the rich and famous had once climbed to have a reading done by Caroline. I sat in my short-sleeved print dress, swinging my legs out in front of me, allowing my gleaming white Buster Brown high-topped shoes to knock against the cement side of the porch. My mother had bleached the laces of my shoes, and her nightly polishing shone in the sun as a hummingbird whirled around the honeysuckle bush growing on the other side of the alley across from me. My hair was barley white, with bangs cut sharp across my brow. Beneath the bangs, blue eyes of inquiry peered out trying to discern the events going on about me. I was five years old.

From the porch, I could watch all the comings and goings. My aunt Jackie walked by holding tight to Grandma's hand. She was only three and a half years older than I but I thought her to be much older. Our eyes met and I saw the wide-eyed apprehension of a frightened child. Then they were gone. I listened as they climbed the old stairs to the landing with its narrow railing where Great-Grandmother Jucker used to hang her noodles to dry. Bees continued to hum around the bougainvillea. Aunt Jackie and Grandma reappeared. Both of them were crying.

My mother came down the stairs, "Would you like to come up and see your great-grandpa? He would like to see you."

I held out my hand. Mother took it and helped me jump down from my perch. As we climbed the stairs, Charles Jucker's own peculiar smell bruised my nostrils. The man had always made his own wine and drank a great deal of it along with his favored Limburger cheese, but besides the wine and cheese there was the added aroma of rich, heady tobacco. For most of his adult life, Charles Jucker had smoked an antique Turkish water pipe, its carafe made of lovely cloisonné, burnished with years of use. Great-Grandpa had bought the pipe in an antique store in Paris in the year 1878. Only God knew how old it was. The original tubes and fittings had long since disintegrated, but Great-grandpa had fixed it, just as he had fixed everything else, and now it sat with garden hose and baling wire connecting its parts. Within the cloud of odor, which seemed to take on a life of its own, was the acrid smell of urine. Charles's bladder and kidneys had begun to fail following a whack of a nightstick given to him a year before by a police officer who thought he was trying to leave the scene of an automobile accident. Actually, he was trying to walk down the street to my grandma's house so she could help him communicate with the officer. So now Charles Jucker's private pungency had taken on a new and powerful meaning all its own.

My nostrils flared as Mother and I ascended the old stairs. Over the general haze that bespoke of my great-grandfather's presence, there was a hint of mildew in the kitchen, which in turn was overcome by the odor of the Turkish water pipe as we passed through the tiny living room, and then we were in the bedroom, all snowy white from the combination of sunlight and white linens. Charles had flung the bedclothes from his body in Mother's absence. He was lying on his side, facing us with his nightshirt gathered about his waist, his genitals displayed swollen and immense, level with my eyesight. My stomach knotted at the sight of them.

"Great-Grandpa's very swollen from being sick," my mother soothed as she gently covered the old man she loved so much. Mother's intense caring and gentleness calmed me as I got up the courage to look into the old man's eyes. They were beautiful—shining full of laughter and love. Why had everyone come down the stairs crying and sobbing? An old, weak hand came out to me, and though frightened, I gave up my tiny hand to the wrinkled old one. I don't recall what he said, just the warm, loving feeling of the moment and then Mother was turning me and taking me back down the old stairs so that I could once again sit on the porch.

"Don't you want to go and play?" she asked.

I shook my head in the negative and resumed my perch.

The morning wore on. When the sun was almost at its zenith, a great deal of crying came down to me from the open window of my great-grandpa's bedroom. I sat very still, conscious only of my sense of hearing. The bees continued to hum; no noise seemed to make them pause.

Everyone was upstairs when I saw it. It was coming down the alley very slowly. It was white, as white as could be, and I thought it to be one of the funniest looking cars I had ever seen. It was very long. The front end, where the driver and another man sat, looked like a normal car, but the back end, behind where the men sat, went on and on with no windows or doors breaking its length, just a big red cross painted where I thought windows and doors should exist. The man who was driving pulled right up to Great-Grandfather's door, looked out his window at me, smiled sadly and got out. The other man did the same. Both men were dressed entirely in white; even their shoes. They walked to the back of the long white car and opened up the back end. Out of it they took a long board with handles on the ends. Each man took the handles of an end and up the old stairs they went, up to my great-grandpa's apartment. I thought of the smell the men would encounter and wondered what they would think. Our house didn't smell like that; I wondered if theirs did.

I heard more crying coming down from the window and then I heard the men coming back down the stairs. They were coming down much more slowly than they had gone up and their footsteps seemed to be heavier. When they came out of the door, I noticed there was something on the board and that a big white sheet lay over it. As the men walked past me, I realized that my great-grandpa lay under the sheet. Mother had said he would go away when he died—that he would be okay but wouldn't be with us anymore. I wondered where the men were going to take him. The two men slid Great-Grandpa into their long car, shut the back doors, walked to the front end, got in, smiled sadly at me once more and drove away. As the long white car with the big red cross on its side pulled away down the alley, I noticed two small windows set into the back doors of the car at the spot where they had put my great-grandpa. As they drove off, I wondered if Great-grandpa could see out through those little windows. I raised my hand and waved goodbye—just in case.

My mother had told me Great-Grandpa would be all right after he died. I am sure I asked where he was going and I assume she said he was going to heaven. In my baby book it says that at age five I asked if we could see God and if God could see us. Whatever the answers, I believed, and because I believed I was not afraid. With my only knowledge of death being what my mother had told me, I stood by the bed of a dying man without fear of the unknown. The anguish of missing someone was something I would learn in the future, but at that moment I read the ease and peace of death through the innocent eyes of childhood as I peered into eyes of age and wisdom. I sat on my grandmother's porch unafraid. All I experienced was love.

Several years after the death of my great-grandfather, I was playing in our neighbor's enclosed garden. I loved it there for it had a big, beautiful lawn surrounded by an elaborate array of flowers and shrubs. It was summer. I was nine years old. No one was burning trash. There was no wind. There was blue sky and a young girl all alone in a big garden. Then, suddenly, there was an odor and I wasn't moving. Not until the occurrence was ending did I realize that I couldn't have moved if I had wanted to. From the start, my senses became alert and I sensed the presence of my great-grandfather. No one, nothing on Earth, could ever produce an odor like that of my great-grandfather Jucker. I saw nothing and I heard nothing, yet I was filled with an emotional warmth coupled with a tremendous feeling of being loved. I remember it well. Then there was just blue sky, grass, flowers, no odor and I could move again. How long did it last? I can't say, but the experience was singular in that it was an intimate, powerful, describable experience that stood outside the realm of everyday life and thought. In *A Book of Angels*, Sophy Burnham comments, "Like angels, ghosts can come as a thought, nudging our minds, or as a sense of their presence." Truly, as in my case, they sometimes leave nothing more than a mental stain and an indelible memory of a pungent aroma.

After sensing the presence of my great-grandfather in the garden, I walked all over the neighborhood with my nose on alert trying to find the source of the aroma that had held me spellbound on that summer's day. I was unable to find either smoke or odor—or the incredible feeling of being loved.

Most significant, perhaps, is that the experience still sits solid and unchanged in my mind. Whatever happened, the mental sensations that impressed themselves upon my psyche that summer's day were very powerful. I have never forgotten them, which always surprised me until decades later when I learned that such occurrences have been found to leave lasting memory tracks in our brains. Somehow, for reasons yet to be understood, such moments are laid down in mental cement.

Also of interest is the fact that research has shown that nothing brings forth and reproduces a memory as sharply as an odor or fragrance. Odors stimulate the brain in articulate and accurate ways that few other stimuli can emulate.

ALMOST THERE

At the age of six, I suffered a virulent case of strep throat. Months later, I was diagnosed with rheumatic fever overlaid with acute allergies that led to complications of hay fever and bronchial asthma. I was consigned to bed for a year, followed by long two-hour naps to be taken after school. During those interminable naps, I was allowed no books or radio. I was instructed to sleep, but sleep rarely found me. My boredom grew so great that I can remember learning to catch flies with my bare hands and torturing my captives by pulling off a wing, and eventually the other, before giving the poor creature over to his maker. My wingless flies mirrored my physical entrapment and, embarrassingly, I recall little remorse. But then remorse is a mature feeling rarely felt by children whose prefrontal lobes (the gray matter that sits behind your forehead) are just beginning to organize themselves. Prefrontals allow for memory retention, salient decisions, rational judgment and clear thinking, which can keep you out of harm's way and help you make wise choices. Trouble is, they don't finish maturing until you are 24 years of age. Remorse demands an understanding of one's actions and the consequences thereof.

After the nap years, my walk to and from school was the only source of exercise allowed me by my attending physician. All strenuous physical activity was curbed or curtailed. At least that was the order given; I considered dance a non-sport.

During the years of my recovery, on a hot spring day, a girl at school, my archenemy, taunted me to leave my prescribed bench and join a game of tetherball. Back and forth the ball went, whipping through the air. As we waged war on each other, our emotions bristled. The heavily charged atmosphere of mutual animosity drew other children to it as a magnet. The last thing I remember is a sea of gawking faces.

The heat of the day and overexertion had caused me to pass out. I awoke on a cot in the corner of the nurse's room. Mom came to get me and I spent the rest of the week in bed.

After that I tried to ignore my female antagonist, but my friends and I loved to play horse in vacant lots, loved to charge about whinnying like wild stallions, rearing up, pawing the air and snorting in fine animalistic style. The strain of the play may not have been good for my heart, but the weed pollen I inhaled while galloping through head-high wild grasses were the real villains. Attacks of asthma were a given after an afternoon in the field and so it was that after a particularly fine afternoon of playing horse I lay abed, two pillows at my head.

There had only been two pills left of my prescription and now they were gone. In those days there were no all-night pharmacies, nowhere to get more medicine. The night wore on—my condition worsened. I was 11 years old. The memory lingers crystal clear.

It had been four hours since the attack had begun. I lay

racked with apprehension, gasping and struggling for each inadequate breath as the congestion within my lungs simulated the act of drowning. Then, quite suddenly, a vivid truth consumed me and I knew I was about to die. Not only did I know I was going to die, but I knew that it was all right to do so. All fears connected with my mortal body vanished while my conscious mind clung to certain earthly items—my toys. With great effort, I struggled long and hard to croak out two sentences.

"Mommy, I'm going to die." (I thought she should know.) And, "Give my toys to Christie" (a younger cousin).

Then willingly, peacefully, I let go.

All pain, all apprehension dissolved, all physical discomfort ceased. I felt whole and healthy and very much "me." Most of all, I felt secure. I do not think it possible to feel as alert and secure under any circumstance here on this earthly plane as one feels at the time of death. It is indescribable.

I found myself moving down a very black passage. Many people define it as a tunnel, but I had no concept of walls, just inky blackness within the boundaries of my peripheral vision. Ahead of me was a beam of white light of incredible brightness. It seemed a long way off and the rays of the light made the space between appear misty or foggy, although things got clearer the closer I got to the light . . . and I so wanted to reach that light.

As with others who have had a near-death experience (NDE), my emotional and mental goal was to reach the light, but to the right of the light stood three people—two men and a woman. At least that was the visual impression coded back to me. I could only see their silhouettes as the light was behind and to the left of them. One of the men wore a hat and both seemed to be in overcoats. The woman was too vague to comment about in detail, though I noticed that her hair was longer than my mother's and she was taller than the men and appeared to be wearing a long, heavily draped gown. Regardless, it was apparent the three were there to prevent me from reaching the

light. In fact, they absolutely forbade it. I remember them telling me over and over again that I had to go back, that it wasn't
my time. I remember the voiceless mental communications
that seemed to get messages across in a more succinct way than
if the people had spoken. Regardless of mode, I didn't want to
listen to them. I felt a part of all knowledge, knowledge far beyond what is known on Earth. I tried to ignore what they were
telling me and continued in my effort to reach the light, but
the three sentinels repeatedly refused me passage. I whined; I
wanted to get to the light, but again and again, they told me,
"No. You have to go back. You cannot come here now. You
have to go back."

Eventually, reluctantly, I gave into the realization that
I was not going to be allowed access to the light. The instant I
accepted the fact that I had to go back, everything stopped. The
memory ends.

I awoke the following afternoon in the bedroom of our
little house. The same old dusty tree was scraping at the bedroom window screen with its gray-green leaves, just as it had
done on all the afternoons when I had taken my interminable
two-hour sleepless rests. I was thoroughly disappointed.

"Oh no, heaven's just like my old room," I said out loud
to no one.

My mother rushed into the room at the sound of my
voice. She sat on the edge of my bed and hugged me as she related what a rough time we had had the night before.

"I know," I said, "I died."

"No, no, no," my mother soothed, "you just had a really
bad attack. The doctor arrived and gave you a shot. I was so
scared, but you are here and you are better and you are going to
be all right."

"But I did die," I demanded.

"No," my mother said, again and again, "you just had a
bad attack and it scared you."

"But it wasn't scary. I wasn't scared at all."

It was of no use. Mother must have thought that I was afraid of dying or was afraid that I might die with the next attack. She kept soothing me, reassuring me that I had not died. When she ran out of steam, I asked, "Did the doctor have a hat on his head?"

"No. Why?"

The next day I went to school and told my two closest friends about dying. They told me I was crazy and walked away from me. With my mother and two best friends refusing to believe me, I tucked my experience away in a cranial closet where it replayed itself through solid memory.

More than what I saw is how I felt. I felt secure. The totality of this feeling cannot be defined. My feeling was one of total completeness, keenness of thought and security. Thoughts of fear, worry or concern were not possible. It seemed as though I had plugged into a universal source in which resides all knowledge, as though my earthly consciousness, with all its cares and worries of everyday life, had faded away but that my real mind, the real me, had melded with an all-encompassing universal mind and within that mind existed all things knowable. Out of the experience came the distinct feeling that all was right and in its proper place, that there was no right or wrong, simply what I can only refer to as the truth (that which is), and that "truth" was complete. The entire event was wondrous, but even at the age of 11, I was bewildered by the strong sense that neither right nor wrong exists—this one feature of my near-death experience remains a conundrum for me to this very day.

Ten years after my near-death experience, following years of allergy shots, at a time when asthma was a memory, my mother admitted to me that both my heart and respiration had ceased just prior to the doctor knocking on our door. If not for a shot of adrenaline I wouldn't be here today. I said nothing at the time, but deep inside I nodded and smiled . . . vindication at last, but it would be many years before I admitted to anyone that I had had a near-death experience. I cannot tell you how heart-warming it was when I finally heard and read of others who had seen the light and felt the security of death, along with the overwhelming knowledge that pervades the experience. Kubler-Ross did far more than write on a fascinating subject. She and other writers have allowed millions of people the comfort of knowing they are not alone, that near-death experiences are real occurrences that have been experienced globally over the millennia by people of every age, physical condition, religious bent and/or persuasion.

I had always told the story of Great-Grandpa Jucker visiting me in the garden with tongue in check. It is a joyous story that fulfills our fantasies about an afterlife. I knew something had happened that day, but I never gave it much thought or put much credence in the event; it was a nice little ghost story with a hint of possibility in it, but my near-death experience was different. I never once thought I had had the experience, I knew I had had the experience, though I quickly realized that those who had never had an NDE thought my elevator didn't go to the top floor. Nevertheless, it was wonderful to know that I was in good company with others from around the world. Now I proudly tell people of my experience and when they look at me with crossing eyes, I don't mind.

As years passed, I read everything I could find on NDEs and listened to others who had either had an NDE or knew well the story of a friend, relative or patient.

Near-death experiences have been reported throughout history, from the oldest of writings to oral histories and myth. In the *Epic of Gilgamesh*, written some 4,500 years ago by 12 different writers in the Akkadian language, Gilgamesh travels through the interior of a dark mountain, emerging into a land of bright light. Centuries later, Pope Saint Gregory I, known as Gregory the Great (c. AD 540–604) experienced and recorded an NDE. And a bit later in the seventh century, Taoist monks did seven years of research on near-death experiences and came to the same statistical findings in regard to memory retention, percentages of positive versus negative experience and the universal uniformity that has been recently rediscovered.

Still, humans rarely have faith in anything they have not experienced for themselves.

In regard to near-death experiences, many scientists appear to be challenged by anything they cannot understand, prove or replicate and end up working diligently to diminish or detract from the validity of near-death experiences and other anomalous occurrences. Some say, "It is all of the mind." Of course! Where else would an individual register such an event? The question is why have humans had such experiences since times prior to writing and in every part of the world, regardless of race, education, religion or belief? What wonderful trigger allows death to be so blissful, so illuminating? If one dies without resuscitation, as most did prior to modern medicine, there would be no benefit to the individual or their species, so why does nature give a gift that offers no survival or reproductive benefits? The entire arena of such events opens multiple doors to myriad questions. And it is important to keep those doors open as closed doors stop learning, research and the growth of knowledge. Without science and a hunger for knowledge, humankind will back itself into the cave of our beginnings.

Through much of the twentieth century, near-death experiences were condemned to halls of hallucinations, psychotic personalities and the world of brain chemicals. One of many efforts to label near-death experiences as illusions of the brain was through the administering of the drug ketamine, a dissociating anesthetic used in both human and veterinary medicine. Satisfied with their results, researchers claimed to have reproduced the many features common to NDEs, as described in the most cited works. But what they list as common "features" of near-death experiences, combined with what their study subjects report, contain aspects that do not correlate with actual near-death experiences. Those who participate in such experiments often describe their experience the same way a drug user describes what his drug of choice does for him, including a sense of unreality along with feelings or thoughts that, to my knowledge, are never expressed by those who have had an NDE.

Though many have tried to negate them and/or replicate them, to date no scientific experiment has convinced me or reproduced all of the components that fill a naturally occurring near-death experience.

So what produces the experience? Why does having a near-death experience influence a person psychologically and intellectually? Why is the change almost universally to the good? Do such moments occur only when death is imminent or in process? Why does this particular experience impart such a complete sense of loving security coupled with an acute alertness of mind, overlaid with a feeling of universal knowledge beyond present scope? Why do those who have had an NDE never forget the experience?

Various researchers claim that six to ten percent of NDEs are negative in nature. The classic of this category is the young suicide victim who had a terrifying NDE that changed her life forever, all to the good. She is still thankful that she was allowed to return and feels strongly that when she does die, the experience will be different. Others who have had a frightening NDE agree with her. Research and statistics also show that people who have had an NDE rarely commit suicide and that criminals have been known to completely change their ways and mental outlook on life following an NDE.

Whatever they are, however they work, near-death experiences are singular, life-changing occurrences.

The old suggestion that NDEs are hallucinations was set aside with the realization that a vast majority people who have had an NDE were psychologically healthy at the time of the occurrence, were not taking drugs, nor had they ingested any mind-altering substance. Still, many continue to report that the "molecule of happiness," serotonin, which has been connected with hallucinations, may be involved during the course of near-death experiences. (Serotonin is produced in the pineal gland, but found in greatest quantity in the gut.) Researchers also say that the production of serotonin is activated by stress coupled with the fear of death. The fact that a great many people die on operating tables while under general anesthesia prompts obvious questions.

Correctly administered, general anesthesia induces the loss of sensitivity (pain) throughout the body. At the same time, it quiets the brain to the point where emotional responses are deactivated. Hence, fear and/or stress concerning what is happening to the body, or the possibility of death, do not register while a person is "under." Also, the body's first reaction to fear is a rapid heart rate, as instinctual responses to danger flood the body with adrenaline so that it can respond with the strength and ability to either flee or fight whatever is threatening the individual. But adrenaline is not found in connection with NDEs and a positive NDE always produces calm and secure feelings rather than feelings of fear. Today, more and more patients who expire on an operating table while anesthetized are being brought back, with no reports or memories of stress or fear, though many return to tell of an NDE.

Away from operating rooms, many have been struck dead from behind or rendered unconscious from a surprise attack, such as a bomb. In such cases, there is no time for the brain to register fear. And then there are the many heart attack victims who claim to have no memory of the attack. They state that they felt fine and then the next thing they knew they were waking up in a recovery room in a hospital, some of them with stories of the late-great light show.

In 1490, Hieronymus Bosch, one of my favorite artists, painted a four-panel polyptych entitled, *Visions of the Hereafter*. One of the panels shows angels carrying aloft naked bodies of the dead to a huge tube-like tunnel, at the end of which is a bright light, its rays streaming towards the entrance. The panel is titled, *Ascent of the Blessed*. Within the tunnel, Hieronymus shows people moving towards the light unassisted by angels.

In 1490, there were no anesthetics as we know them nor man-made molecules duplicating brain chemicals.

In September of 2008, a study for "Awareness During Resuscitation," sponsored by the University of Southampton, UK, was announced by project leader Sam Parnia of New York's Presbyterian Medical Center. Twenty-five hospitals, most of them in the UK and the US, have set up protocols for doctors to monitor and interview patients who have experienced cardiac arrest and been revived. Former statistics find that 10% of such patients report a near-death experience, but this is the first time doctors will work in anticipation of such an event and look at oxygen flow to patients' brains and test for blood proteins released when brain cells die. Most importantly, they will document occurrences where the revived patient not only reports an NDE, but relates things they saw while "out of body" that are fact related. Psychiatrist C. Bruce Grayson of the University of Virginia says of the project that should the phenomenon prove real it will show "that the current understanding of brain and mind [which are needed for such occurrences] is inadequate." In other words, the reductionist view—that we possess nothing but a cellular brain, and that the concept of "mind" is fallacy—will have to be revisited.

The marvelous thing about NDEs is that they have been experienced in like fashion in every corner of the world, by people of every age and sex and from our beginnings. Only religious and/or cultural beliefs impose any variation. I often wonder if the first religions arose from near-death experiences. Think about it. Igor experiences an arrhythmia and drops dead. Gonnad runs to Igor, thrusts his fire-hardened stick-spear about in anger, then drops beside Igor and starts pounding on his chest, yelling at him not to die. A particularly well-placed whack gets Igor's heart pumping and Gonnad rejoices. Afterwards, Igor sits around the night fire and tells his clan about not being afraid (an unheard of thing in Igor's day), of feeling a hell of a lot smarter than he actually is, and about an incredible light in the midst of darkness, etc., etc. Many years later, a similar event occurs with another person, who would have died but didn't, and lives to tell a similar story. Heavy stuff. Wonderful stuff. Stuff with which to build a belief about life and death, such as a religion, or, at the very least, the formation of an idea that life doesn't end with death.

During recent decades, it was unwise, in terms of career, for academics to ponder things mysterious or seemingly spiritual, but things are changing. Researchers at Johns Hopkins University and University of California, Los Angeles, are beginning to look into mystical experiences. Recent experiments with psilocybin, an active ingredient found in hallucinogenic mud mushrooms that boosts transmission of the brain chemical serotonin, have produced some interesting results. When *carefully selected* subjects were given injections of psilocybin, many experienced events of "spiritual transcendence," including feeling free, wonderful, in touch with a higher form of knowledge and other mental sensations common to NDEs. Most interesting is that many of those who were chemically induced to experience such mental impressions were changed by the event. Their experiences appear to have left them with a better outlook on life and many felt that they could and should achieve more within the framework of their lives. The researchers are now looking into methods of boosting people's awareness of life and/or help those who suffer from depression. This would be a fine thing, but what about near-death experiences?

Though I have yet to hear or read of any "spiritual transcendence" experiences that truly relate to or replicate an NDE, the question needs be asked: does serotonin flood the brain when death draws near? Possibly, perhaps, probably. After all, we are the body electrochemical; there is no other way for our minds and bodies to react and/or function. Electrochemical processes are what allow for life. If the above tests are repeated with good success, they may offer some partial understanding of the chemical makeup of NDEs, but if serotonin and/or any other chemicals are present at the time of an NDE, did the onset of death prompt the release of this naturally occurring chemical, or is it released in reaction to the NDE itself?

In a well-known experiment, researchers worked with 15 Carmelite nuns, all of whom had had at least one mystical experience. The sisters agreed to have functional magnetic resonance imaging of their brains while doing their mental best to relive their experiences. The end results showed neural activation in dozens of areas of the brain, especially areas that involve perception, emotion and cognition. Bottom line: mystical states activate many "extremely complex" areas of the brain. Is that why such experiences are so well remembered? For those researchers who believe that a chemical, or a combination of chemicals, produces such events, the work done with the nuns suggests that it was the thoughts and memories they were asked to remember that triggered chemical responses within their brains, not vice versa.

But again, why all the wondrous feelings and mental enhancements at the time of death? What possible survival advantage could feeling fabulous do if you are not going to be around to enjoy or tell of the gifts of death? Only in very recent history have so many been "brought back." Over the course of millions of years, few returned, so what is the biological advantage of a near-death experience?

Above all others, children have changed the minds of doubting researchers concerning the reality of NDEs. With modern medicine, more and more people are being resuscitated, including children, and it is children that make the difference; it is children who convince the researchers and the doubters. Why? Because young children have no real sense or understanding of what death is, nor have they read or been told about NDEs, to say nothing of the fact that their brains are still in the process of organizing themselves. Still, the NDEs of children mirror those of adults on a global scale.

I love the story of a toddler who was learning to talk. One of the words he knew was the word "light." The child died and was revived. Afterwards, he would point to any bright light, smile, get very enthusiastic and say, "Light! Light! Light!" then clap his hands and dance around. Finally, someone asked the child if he had seen a wonderful light. The child nodded yes, laughed and said, "Light."

Author Timothy Ferris, in an article entitled "A Cosmological Event," sees early humans sensing a universal, biological belonging, an emotional bonding to life, the planet earth and the cosmos at large, which allowed them to view life and death for what they are, normal events within a continuum. Taking this thought, he extrapolates on stars and galaxies dying, only to be renewed within the natural state of cosmic flux, then returns with the thought that the bliss we feel at the time of our death is but a major chord played on the nervous system, one that speaks to our resonance with a universal, cosmic chord. Ferris sees death as being such a natural part of life's continuum, not only on our planet, but within the cosmos at large, that it is only natural for death to be experienced as a peaceful and fulfilling end to one phase of being. Nice thought. I like it a lot, but it doesn't fit with observed survival mechanisms that appear to rule the lives of all living things. Or does it?

Years of studying the subject of NDEs has proven to me what I had always known from my own experience: NDEs are never forgotten.

Eliane (not Elaine) was many years my senior, but we had a deep bond of friendship that began when we learned that we had both experienced near-death. Eliane was Swiss, and some years prior to her coming to America she had suffered a heart attack. When they got her lifeless body to the hospital, the doctors worked on her inert form in a routine fashion with little expectation of success. Meanwhile, Eliane was trying very hard to get to the light, but people she didn't know kept telling her she had to go back. Eliane's experience mirrored mine, so there is no need to relate the details. What is of interest is that as Eliane aged (she lived into her late eighties) I would ask her to relate her

NDE—just one more time. Eliane's story never changed, but as she got older she began to leave out minor details she had related in earlier tellings.

Another, younger friend was one of several women dressed in little black dresses, modeling millions of dollars worth of diamonds as they danced around a large stage in the arms of professional male dancers. The event was a high society fashion show, a charity event benefiting a major medical center. Twenty steps into the routine, Susan dropped to the floor like a stone. Her quick-thinking dance partner swooped her lifeless body up into his arms and gracefully danced offstage. I turned to my husband, a physician and the head of the medical center, and said, "She didn't fall [I used to be a dancer]. There's a real medical emergency backstage." My husband rushed to join four other doctors who were running backstage; guards were removing diamonds as Susan's lifeless body eliminated waste and convulsed. No pulse. No nothing. Someone had called 911; the doctors began CPR. Susan had been gone many minutes when the ambulance arrived. Oxygen and an IV were administered. Susan was, as far as could be discerned, DOA (dead on arrival) when they wheeled her into emergency. At the hospital, while my husband went behind closed doors to keep tabs on the outcome, I worked with Susan's family, including her beautiful young children. When my husband came out to check on the family, I looked into his eyes and knew the outlook was grim.

The doctors continued to work. Amazingly, they got a heartbeat, then another.

After months of recovery, Susan was left with a good deal of old memory loss and an extremely limited ability to lay down new memories. Everything had to be relearned, from driving a car to everyday chores. More than a year after an arrhythmia had stopped her heart in an instant, I went to lunch with Susan. She smiled and said, "You must forgive me. There is a great possibility that tomorrow I won't remember that we had lunch together today. I got here on time because I write everything down and work with my notes and my watch. It took a long time before I could drive myself someplace. The doctors were doubtful I could do it, but we got me wonderful maps and I have learned to live in the moment. I can do many things now and am actually with it mentally, moment to moment, but, as I said, I may not remember us having lunch together."

Susan cannot remember what happened yesterday and much of her past is gone to her, but there is one thing she remembers in detail—her near-death experience.

Susan said she found herself on a lonely stretch of sand dunes tufted with grass. Before her a large cliff loomed. Her son was by her side. Her son was upset, but she felt extremely calm. As they got closer to the cliff, she noticed a dark tunnel at its base. Then she saw a man in long robes standing next to the entrance of the tunnel. Susan told me it was Jesus (she was raised a Catholic) and that Jesus told her it was time for her to enter the tunnel. Turning to her son, she told him he had to stay. The boy cried, saying he didn't want her to go into the tunnel, but she knew she had to enter and tried to explain to her son that everything was fine, but that he couldn't go with her. The rest of her experience runs the usual course.

How could a person who had to relearn the layout of her own home, and cannot remember having lunch with a friend, remember having a near-death experience? Not only remember it once, but tell the same exact story a year later over another lunch—another event I am sure she doesn't remember. Why are memories of such events laid down in mental cement regardless of the condition of the brain upon which they are being imprinted?

In the book *Light and Death*, Dr. Michael Sabom tells of Pam Reymonds' NDE, which was experienced during an extreme form of brain surgery where the body is cooled, the brain is drained of blood and both heartbeat and breathing are stopped. During this type of surgical procedure, nicknamed "standstill" by its pioneering doctors, the patient is put into a state of hibernation at 15 degrees Celsius with no breathing, heartbeat, or brain activity for up to one hour; the patient is technically dead. In all ways, the body and brain are both inert and non-functioning. Regardless, Pam had a lengthy and well-remembered NDE. Her story has convinced many doubters, including doctors and researchers, that experiences of near-death are not only real, but more mysterious than ever believed. Some have gone so far as to question whether the mind (consciousness) exists outside of our mortal form.

Henry James (1843–1916) wrote of a "huge spider-web of the finest silken threads suspended in the chamber of consciousness" as catching, processing and sometimes remembering every particle of experience. Today, James' spider web can be seen in the intricate lacing of axons and dendrites that reach out to one another from 100 billion neurons that make up the average brain, all facilitated by electrochemical messengers swimming in a ubiquitous mental soup.

There are so many marvelous things to think about. For example, why, and how, do blind people, or those under general anesthesia, *see* their NDEs? Pam Reynolds, whose brain was non-functional at the time, was able to describe the unique skull cutting saw used by her surgeons (an implement she had never seen or heard described), plus many other details she could not have described were she not somehow witnessing the event with some unknown form of sight and memory-retaining consciousness.

Pam's case, above all others, provides the most profound evidence for substantiating the reality of near-death experiences. Her experience shouts out to the reality of events we have yet to comprehend. And, if the "mind" exists outside the body, does the brain act as a receiver? Far-out thought, but we are dealing with far-out experiences in far-out times. Truth is, we know far more than ever before, yet we remain standing on the very edge of all possible knowledge. Never stop exploring or questioning—ever.

PASSINGS

An Australian friend told me of an Aborigine who was a superb employee. Always there, always on time—an unusual trait for people who dwell in Dreamtime.

One day, the Aborigine stopped working and went to his boss. "I have to go now," he said.

"What's wrong?" inquired the boss.

"My father has died and I must attend to the funeral."

"Did you get a call?" asked the boss.

"No," said the Aborigine, tapping his head. "I will return in a month."

The boss thought a moment. "I'll be glad to drive you into the outback."

"No," replied the Aborigine. "It is necessary that I walk."

All societies, clans, tribes and groups of humans deal with death through the myths, beliefs and customs by which they live. Some accept death as the natural thing that it is, while others train mentally and spiritually in order to prepare for the rigors of reaching the other side following their demise. Flip the coin and you will find others for whom the mere mouthing of the word "death" produces fear—and that which is feared is loathed and shunned, leaving the individual in a place of mental anguish over the inevitable.

Around the globe, religions deal with humankind's innate fear of death by quelling qualms with promises none can substantiate. There are stories of rising from death, heavens full of peace, virgins, planets, bawdy halls of grandeur, hunting grounds, rivers to cross, judges to stand before, hells and purgatories. It is as though humankind, in its infancy, looked upon death as being final and so proceeded to build systems of belief through which they could prove that death was not the end or what they perceived it to be. . . . Or were they grasping at strands of a greater truth? When a minister was asked what lay at the bottom of his Christian belief, i.e., on what did he build his faith, and what did his faith do for him, he replied that his belief in Christ eliminated his fear of death; an honest answer that could be voiced by multitudes, though for many, Christ's name would by replaced with that of another.

If you travel through books, or by plane, to countries of the Far East, you will find religions that theoretically hold no fear of death. But where death is seen in a positive light, re-incarnation is often found sitting, waiting in the corner. Many believe we are reincarnated over and over again in order to learn our universal lessons. Not until one successfully learns his lessons on this plane of existence can he eventually gain freedom from the human form and be awarded the privilege of a permanent place on the other side—nirvana. Within such systems of belief, the death of a good person is to be celebrated since the deceased, through death, will be allowed to ascend another rung of her karmic ladder, bringing her ever closer to everlasting glory, unity with the universe and peaceful nothingness.

My good friend Kim Carlson traveled through Bali, where she stayed with locals in a small fishing village. Early one morning, a small child of seven came skipping and yelling through the grass and palm huts. The people of the village ran out to greet her, or called joyfully back to her from their win-dows. Kim asked her host what was going on. The man replied, "Oh, the child's mother died last night. She is happy that her mother has been allowed to go on. She is spreading the good news. You must stay for the funeral."

What's the old saying? "If you wish to change that which you perceive, all you have to do is change the way you perceive it."

Death, like any other condition, can be perceived in many ways. It can be seen as something to fear and anguish over, something to sublimate and outwardly accept, or something to celebrate. Every society, each religion, teaches its people to perceive death in a given way. Only the very young view death with total, unadulterated perception. Thereafter, their minds are formed in the ideas of their parents and surrounding society.

There are many religions that consider the other side of life to be far better than this earthly existence. They view death as a step in the right direction while holding that life is of supreme importance, that the way you live your life is binding to your eternal future. At the same time, they deem our natural fear of death as being healthy and wise. Both Taoists and Buddhists believe that it is only our natural fear of death that keeps us here working through our karma and living out our lives regardless of circumstances. They believe that without a fear of death, we would wish to be in the other, more peaceful, realm.

Psychologists agree with our Eastern neighbors, finding our fear of death to be a natural and healthy defense mechanism. Without it, we wouldn't take care when crossing a street, ingesting foods and chemicals, driving a car, climbing a ladder or going about our daily lives.

From infancy, we teach our children to "be careful," to know what things to be fearful of and how to protect themselves. We are not alone. Higher mammals and all primates teach their young the dangers that threaten life even though the natural fear of harming the materialistic body is profound within each and every living thing. In what man refers to as the lower animals, instinct is the teacher. This instinct is so strong that an infant rabbit will seek shelter when the shadow of a hawk or any predatory bird passes over him. Our natural fear of height, as when we look over a sheer cliff or over the roof ledge of a tall building, is a good example of our own instinctual fears, but whether taught or instinctual the fear of bodily harm keeps us safe from the myriad things that could easily erase our fragile life forms—the mere thought of losing them is unthinkable. So it is that when someone we love dies, the pain is excruciating. Mentally and emotionally, we take their demise upon ourselves. At such times, our conscious life force screams to the heavens, "No, no, no, they can't be dead." On a subconscious level, this statement translates to "No, no, no, I cannot die," for in the death of another is the reflection of the death that, in time, will come to us all.

Over the course of our life, we may suffer deaths of kin so close that we cry out, "Why not me? Why can't I go? Why was it not I?" These thoughts and feelings are not suicidal, but reflect the pain of having a vital part of our lives irretrievably taken from us.

Each death we face puts us in touch with our fear of the unknown, that which we innately fear. Man respects the fearless hero, not for his strength or bravery, but for his seeming ability to conquer man's most enduring fear, the fear of death.

As we pass through life, as we grow into the person we are constantly becoming, we inevitably meet with death through the experience of living. The vignettes of death that follow are presented here as each one affected me and touched me during my years of physical and mental growth. Just as each birth adds to our lives, so each death adds to our perceptions of life. There are lessons to be learned by each, but death is the more powerful teacher. We teach the newcomers, death teaches us. All those who leave through death's door have lived, and in living have made their mark upon those they have known, touched or loved. We are the family of man; what affects one, affects all.

(The words "man" and "mankind" do not bother me as I am well aware that, thus far, there has never been a man born without a mother. Now, if we start cloning people . . . that may be another book.)

L *ife* magazine lay on the oak-and-tile coffee table where my father often had a bite to eat after coming home from a long day's work. The atrocities of World War II were blazoned across the magazine's cover, and inside was an ad for my daddy's Camel cigarettes.

A telegram arrived from the War Department requesting that my father report to the nearest Red Cross center. My father had immigrated to America from his Danish homeland in 1924. Decades had passed since he had seen his mother. As we drove in silence to the Red Cross center, the tension in the car was strong—I remember it well, though I was but seven years of age. The center was an old white frame building with double doors in its middle. Once inside, we were led to a small cubicle where my parents and I sat in front of a woman who told us that the grandmother I had never met had died of a heart attack. Later, we would learn from Daddy's family how she had been sitting at her upstairs window when a jeepload of Germans had come down her street. With a machine gun mounted in the rear of the jeep, the Germans took revenge for deeds done by the underground. They fired randomly at whomever happened to be on the street. Several of the women who were slaughtered that day were lifelong friends of my grandmother. Three days later, my grandmother's heart gave out.

On the way home, Mom drove. Daddy cried. I had never seen my father cry, and the sight of his anguish caused my own tears to flow around thoughts of a grandmother I would never get to meet; a person I knew only from letters read to me by my mother, a silver baby cup, a silver spoon and a tawny old photograph.

A year and a half after my grandmother's death, after months of total bed rest for rheumatic fever, I returned to school. One of the first things I did was join the Blue Birds. Mom became one of our leaders and stayed on when our group graduated to Camp Fire Girls. Throughout those wondrous, struggling years, we were a group of gangly, growing girls—and then there was Audrey, dirty, unkempt, smelly and shy. I remember not wanting to sit next to her in school or at meetings. Mom said she had a bladder problem and that her family couldn't afford an operation. Well, she could at least take a bath, and her mother could comb her hair and wash her two dresses once in a while. Reluctantly, we did as our leaders instructed and forced ourselves to be nice to Audrey, whispering catty remarks whenever her back was turned. Unknowing, and without conscience, we tolerated Audrey, feeling smug in our ability to show emotional charity towards another.

It happened on a cold wintry night. Audrey was babysitting. She was 11 years old, taking care of a sleeping infant. There was an electric heater in the living room. Audrey had been told to sleep on the couch. She took off her dress and stood before the heater in her undershirt, underpants and slip; goosebumps formed on her skinny arms. As Audrey warmed herself before the heater, her mind wandered, then she felt a searing pain as the back of her slip ignited in flames. Audrey screamed as the flames enveloped her tiny body. In panic, she raced out of the house. She was three houses down when a neighbor tackled her and rolled her on the ground.

Because of Audrey's poor health due to a faulty bladder and poor nutrition, she was too weak to survive the third-degree burns that covered a large portion of her lithe little body. She died five days later.

I overheard Mom and the other Camp Fire Girl leader talking. They said that Audrey's father was a drunkard and that her mother drank, went out a lot, had strange men to the house and often beat Audrey.

How could I have said all those nasty things about poor Audrey? If I had only known, maybe I could have helped her by being a real friend. I went to bed and cried myself to sleep.

Our Camp Fire Girls' troop attended Audrey's funeral dressed in full regalia, honor beads swinging from blue vests, beanies with insignia in place. I don't remember much of the service, but I remember walking past the coffin and being totally shaken by what I saw. I stood transfixed, staring at what I couldn't believe. The people at the funeral home had given Audrey a bath, washed and curled her fine brown hair and found her a pretty, new, long-sleeved dress with a high collar. I stood and stared at Audrey; she was beautiful, more beautiful I thought, than all of us. Someone gently pushed me from behind. I walked on leaving the beautiful girl we had all known as Yucky Audrey lying in her new dress, cradled in a small satin-lined coffin.

I was 12 when my grandpa Faunce had a stroke, lay for two weeks in a hospital bed in the bedroom of his home that faced onto Faunce's alley and died in reasonable peace with his family about him.

Over the years, my mother had formed a real hatred for funerals and did not want me to attend my grandfather's funeral. I couldn't understand Mom's reasoning as I listened to her and Grandma Faunce arguing over the matter. Nevertheless, the outcome was that I was sent to school and spent an overnight with a friend on the day of my grandfather's interment. I recall little of the grieving that engulfed the family.

Perhaps Mom thought I was afraid of death because of what I had tried to tell her after my near-death experience. She had misunderstood me completely, so I had never mentioned it to her again, though I was sure she remembered the episode. As for her abhorrence of funerals, I can only say that my father's was stronger than my mother's. Together they had decided that for them funerals were out, and shortly after the death of my grandfather my parents began instructing me as to their own death wishes. The word was, "NO FUNERAL. Cremate us and throw a party."

For many years, I agreed with them, but as I found a life of my own, I developed an understanding of the psychological aid funerals give to the family and friends of the deceased. Funerals are a time to openly grieve for the person who has died, a time to say goodbye, to confirm the actuality of the death, to take stock and get your mental house in order; a time to ready yourself emotionally for the natural grieving process that will follow. Sometime during my late twenties, I silently vowed to fulfill the wishes of my parents while maintaining my own thoughts and feelings concerning funerals or some form of celebration for a life that was lived.

Great-Uncle Charlie (named after his father, Great-Grandpa Charles Jucker) was a mechanical genius. For years, he worked for Howard Hughes as his chief inspector. No engine, no plane left the plant without Charlie's okay. But all was not wonderful with Charlie. Charlie had a problem with the bottle. By the time he hit his mid-sixties, the paranoia, the depression and the emotional pain associated with alcoholism got the better of him. On a starry night, he drove to a mountaintop, connected a hose from the exhaust pipe of his car into the cab and bade farewell to a world he could no longer handle.

Grandma Faunce had been raised a Catholic, but had converted to Lutheranism in her later years. To her way of thinking, suicide was the most mortal of all sins, thus her brother's death stabbed at her from every emotional side, wounding her from the inside out.

I was 15 when Uncle Charlie died. I remember feeling pangs of embarrassment over my lack of grief. I had always been terrified of the man with his alcoholic breath, bone-shattering hugs and bellowing voice. The only decent memory I had of him was of the day he had almost died from a fall from a top branch of the huge avocado tree that graced a section of the Faunce Reservation.

We had all been trying to get at the top of the tree, where lay the most perfect fruit but Great-Grandpa Jucker's ancient telescoping picker wouldn't reach, and ladders were useless under branches that rose 20 feet and more. That's when Uncle Charlie arrived, drunk as a skunk. Hell, he could do it, he claimed, and up he went, scaling the tree like a chimpanzee. "Don't do it!" "You're too high, Charlie!" "That limb won't hold you! Come down!" Everyone shouted, but Charlie ignored them all. Soon, he was inching his way out along the last strong branch, some 20 feet up. Huge, luscious avocados hung just above his head. He reached for them. . . . Tilting his head back was his mistake. He began to fall backwards with his arms outstretched and his legs apart. He fell through the air as though lying splayed out on a bed. No sound came from his lips. Or maybe one did, but none of us could hear it as all of the women in the Faunce family were screaming at the top of their lungs. Grandma Faunce passed out cold. When the dust cleared, we revived Grandma Faunce while Charlie's wife ran to his inert form and beat on his chest. "Don't die on me, Charlie! Don't you dare die!" And Charlie didn't die. In fact, he had been so polluted that he suffered only a mild concussion and limped for a while.

Charlie and the avocado tree made for a fine family story, but for me, the rest of Charlie wasn't worth the telling.

Decades later, science would find the DNA that codes for each individual and come to understand the genetics involved in most cases of true alcoholism.

At age 16, Rob Bartlett lost his father to a heart attack. Rob was a lover of life. It had provided him with an active, affluent existence, complete with friends who enjoyed his fun-loving ways and infectious grin. Following his father's death, the change was dramatic and traumatic. Rob's grief swept over us like a hailstorm. He returned to school on a soapbox and his message was that God was dead, that there was no God, and that if there was a God, he was a bastard.

As Rob cursed God and everything around him, his torment etched its way under our skins and sickened us as we wondered what we would do, how we would feel if our fathers were to die at this time of learning and growth.

The school sent Rob home for a while. When he returned, he no longer screamed of God's nonexistence in the halls, but quietly—angrily—on lunch benches under sycamores. Rob told us that God didn't exist and never had existed. For Rob, God was dead; he had died the day his father had dropped dead of a heart attack.

It had been raining all evening. The thunder and lightning had marched up the canyon and proclaimed its power. As always, I had delighted in its strength. After dinner, Mom, Dad and I had watched a movie. As the credits began to roll, my parents rushed off to bed, leaving me to lock up the house, raid the refrigerator, close the drapes and douse the lights. As I pulled the drapes in the front alcove, I looked out to find the rain subsiding, giving way to a heavy mist. As I started to pull the drapery cord, I heard the shrill squeal of tires coming around the bend north of our house. Then an old '40s coupe burst into view, veered out of control and crashed into the cement light standard across the street from our house. There were sparks and flashes as the light standard snapped in three while the coupe flipped into the air and landed on its back, where it crumpled into a stack of metal three feet high.

Grabbing a flashlight from the kitchen drawer, I raced out the front door and into the rain-slickened street. I couldn't see anyone from the side of the car nearest me, so I walked around to the other side, next to the curb. I bent down. There was an arm and a hand visible and within reach. I tried to locate a pulse. My mother and some neighbors arrived. I looked up at Mom and said, "This one's dead."

I had a strong impression there were two people in the coupe though only one body was visible. I called out. Nothing. Ten minutes later, the police arrived. They told us to stand back. A faint moan came from the squashed, front section of the car. It was hard to believe. A fire rescue truck arrived. Then a passenger car stopped. The boy behind the wheel sat staring at the squashed coupe. I thought I recognized him and then we all heard him say, utterly agonized, "Oh my God."

It had been a teenage bash. Gilbert Alexander and Manuel Sanchez had left the party in Manuel's coupe. Gilbert was half Mexican, half Irish. Incredibly handsome, he was a fine athlete, full of fun and laughter. He was a high school classmate of mine. It was his wrist in which I had failed to find a pulse.

Gilbert had been crushed head to toe. Death had surely come instantaneously. Manuel was a shrimp of a guy. He had ended up in a ball under the dash on the passenger's side of the car. It took the firemen over an hour to cut a hole big enough to drag Manuel out of the wreckage. He suffered a broken wrist.

I was asked to go down and visit Mrs. Alexander. She wished to know every detail of the death of her child. My boyfriend and friends went with me. Everyone had loved Gilbert; he had been a class favorite.

Mrs. Alexander made me tell her the story over and over again until I couldn't handle it anymore.

"Mrs. Alexander, Gilbert had to have died within a fraction of a second. It's impossible that he felt any pain. I can't tell you anymore than that. One moment he was alive and the next moment he wasn't. We all loved your son. There's nothing more I can tell you."

There was nothing more to say.

We all drove more carefully after that.

Six days prior to my eighteenth birthday, I gave birth to a darling baby girl. I had planned on being a doctor, but had begun my study of anatomy at too close a range. When our physiology teacher warned us on Friday afternoons not to go up on Mulholland Drive and swap spit, we had laughed at his precautionary advice.

I was offered an abortion by a close and wealthy friend of the family, but refused because of an intuitive feeling that the person growing within me needed to be born. Three months after the birth of Kim Elizabeth, my husband and I divorced. Two years and nine months later, we remarried on Kim's third birthday. The minister said, "I now pronounce you man and wife . . . again."

Decades later, an older friend of mine, Meta Wilde, the love of William Faulkner for the last 17 years of his life and author of *A Loving Gentleman*, admitted to doing the same thing with her first husband—marry him twice that is. I shook my head and blushed as I thought of my youthful naiveté. In her soft southern accent, Meta comforted me, "Don't you worry your

sweet head about it. I did the same thing when I was young. I
didn't know you couldn't fry an egg twice."

A month after remarrying Kim's father, I was thrown over
a cliff by a horse of mistaken identity. I thought the horse I had
captured was a palomino I had ridden before. I was mistaken.
It was his unbroken son. My pelvic lobe was fractured and my
body felt like it had been on the rack for days. The break, pains
and bruises took weeks of recovery, during which time I came to
the realization that I was pregnant.

From the very start I knew the pregnancy was wrong. I
felt wrong, my body felt wrong and I experienced pains I knew
I shouldn't be having. As the pregnancy progressed, I realized
how different and abnormal this pregnancy was from my first.
Quietly, to myself, I prayed for the fetus to abort.

I was six months along when the labor pains began. A
feeling of tremendous relief filled me. Eight hours later, I produced a stillborn mass of fetal cells that had gone totally awry
due to the fall.

Everyone grieved for me. I tried to reassure them.

"Please, there is nothing to grieve over." "That one wasn't
meant to be." "It just wasn't right." "It couldn't have survived."
"It wasn't meant to be." "There will be others and they will be
healthy and come to us as they should."

Within the next two years, I gave birth to two wonderful
boys, healthy, normal and strong—just as it was meant to be.

Our three children were growing and life was its usual
frantic self when the phone rang. It was my mother, "Helen's
in the hospital." I hung up the phone and cried. I knew Helen
would never leave the hospital.

My mother's sister Helen was the oldest of the seven
Faunce children, the only grandchild ever invited up to high tea
by Caroline Jucker, the seer, the medium. And it was Helen who,
as soon as able, helped to hold the family together financially
through the Depression years by working as a beautician. And it
was gentle Helen who could grow anything and sew anything,

and now Helen was dying after a long and painful struggle with cancer. Her sisters attended to her in the hospital. With loving compassion, they eventually took the lead and forbade the doctor to administer any more pints of blood. "Bless you. And thank you," said the doctor, who was bound by law and the oath he had taken as a doctor. Regardless of his own thoughts or compassion, he was obliged to keep trying even when the medicine he prescribed did nothing but prolong Helen's suffering.

Death took Helen at the early age of 48. She left behind an adoring husband, two exceptional children, a son-in-law and one grandson. Grandma Faunce looked after Helen's husband and son, Joe. My grandmother cried daily and said repeatedly that there was no pain equal to the death of a child; no longer did she weep for her brother Charlie.

My father cried, then looked up and asked, "Who will cut my hair? There isn't a barber alive who can cut hair as well as Helen."

Helen had been my godmother. During the years when she lived down the street from us, her vegetable and flower garden bloomed to the bursting point, and while still a very little girl, I would go up and down our street lugging a big basket full of just picked cucumbers and sweet peas from my aunt Helen's garden. Ringing doorbells, I would inquire, "Would you like to buy some flowers or cucumbers?"

I was a shoo-in. I was tiny and polite, standing there with a huge basket full of color and goodness. To me, the pennies and nickels were a fortune. It was my first lesson in small-scale commerce, all thanks to my aunt Helen.

Following Helen's death, old memories welled up as I remembered Mom's stories of Great-Grandmother Jucker and how she treated Helen as though she was special and different from all the rest. I was glad Helen had gotten to have high tea on fine Haviland china in the little apartment over the garages. Glad she had been invited up to sip tea with the soothsayer with the prescient mind.

The deaths detailed above turned and pushed me in many ways. Audrey's death hit me hard at a tender age, causing me to form and hold firm to the idea that no child should be born unless it is wanted and loved by parents willing and able to care for it.

Rob Bartlett taught me how fragile our beliefs are. Not only is life itself fragile, but all that we perceive ourselves to be. Given any situation a person can do a 180-degree turn in two seconds flat.

The death of my father's mother didn't hit me until I was older, when I realized that I had missed knowing a part of my heritage. However, not having known my paternal grandmother left no mark on my personality other than a wish that I could have met the woman who had sent me a silver spoon and baby cup. In the end, we are no more, and no less, than the sum total of our experience.

The death of Grandpa Faunce is a blur of crying relatives that sits fuzzy in my mind, whereas Great-Uncle Charlie taught me that suicide is taboo in most quarters. I saw him as a man who was miserable and wanted out. Though I felt sorry for his wife, daughter and sister (my grandma Faunce), I knew I wouldn't miss his whiskey breath and crushing hugs.

By the time Gilbert died in the car wreck in front of our house, I had a firm impression that we all have a time to go. Manuel living through that accident was all the proof I needed. He had ended up in a space too small to curl into, yet he suffered only a broken wrist while Gilbert was crushed head to toe. It was just another example among thousands where people should or shouldn't have died and did just the opposite. None of it seemed to make any sense. Was there a scheme to things? This was not a frightening thought to me. My near-death experience, coupled with the beauty of design I had found in nature and the surrounding universe, made such thoughts acceptable to me. Everything has its season, and every season comes to an end, only to return once more.

So it was that through the first four decades of my life, I felt secure in my beliefs. Somewhere there was a dance card upon which all our names were entered.

A month after leaving for the outback, the Australian Aborigine who had received a telepathic message concerning his father's demise, walked into his place of employment with remnants of ash and white dots still to be seen on his face and body. His duties and journey having been completed, he went back to work.

PART TWO

DIFFERENT PATHS, SAME DESTINATIONS

Death is birth's reversal, "the most natural thing you will ever do."

A true and valid statement, though few hold to such an attitude. A majority of us fear death and fight against it tooth and nail with innate and emotional processes that are as natural as death itself. Because of our natural will to live, most of us see death as a life-robbing enemy. Only through understanding can we navigate its tangled web.

TWO MEN

We can hold to the words of Dylan Thomas, "Rage, rage against the dying of the light . . ." or W. C. Fields' humorous labeling of death as "the fellow in the bright nightgown." Either way, we find ourselves bound together by the ultimate reality of death.

Dick Travis wore cowboy boots through the streets of Westwood Village, California, for 17 years, then moved to Jackson Hole, Wyoming, taking me, my two sons and his boots with him. Dick was originally from Oklahoma, a soft-rock geologist, an oilman, and a wildcatter. Wildcatters do geologic research, obtain drilling rights from property owners and drill for oil—often where no one else has drilled before. True to their nature, Dick and his father consistently found drilling sites that were in close proximity to a good trout stream. Their drilling activities never polluted a single stream—no avid fisherman would do such a thing.

A longtime customer, Dick started coming into my father's restaurant for dinner by himself. Like me, his first marriage had ended in divorce. On slow evenings, we would get into long-winded discussions on everything from politics—his forte—to anthropology and paleoanthropology—my forte. Dick had a keen mind and I enjoyed our talks, but viewed them simply as moments of mental enjoyment. Then one day, when he was in for lunch, Dick got up, walked over to me and asked if I would go to dinner with him.

I wasn't dating at the time, so I replied "Yes, but I have to warn you, I'm a lousy date." I consented to the invitation figuring that going to dinner with Dick would be a pleasant, intellectual evening, something akin to dining with an older professor or friend.

On our first date, Dick announced he was going to marry me. I told him he wasn't my type. He said he was and would prove it. Over the next eight months, he did just that.

In September of '75, Dick and I married and moved to Jackson Hole, Wyoming. Then in the spring of '76, we purchased a small ranch on the western slopes of the Tetons and began a yearly migration to the ranch from mid-May to mid-September.

Our lives were full. My marriage to Dick allowed me time to study and write, and my boys to be part of a family again. I put out a cookbook honoring my father and Kenneth Hansen and their respective restaurants: Daddy's popular Carl Andersen's Chatam, in Westwood Village, and Kenneth's famous Scandia restaurant on Sunset Boulevard. I cooked on television and in department stores. I took to writing food columns for local newspapers and giving cooking seminars in the midst of winter. During the summer months, we all worked the ranch. Each meal was part of another food column. In between meals and writing, I rode fence, tended my multiple gardens and hosted our many guests. Dick, along with my sons Brett and Chris, mended fences, built and repaired things and kept the place in shape. In early '77, Dick purchased a Case backhoe (his "big-diggy") and took to digging anywhere I would let him.

Those first years on the ranch were among the best of my life. I worked from dawn to dusk, taking immense pleasure in each accomplishment, large and small. I grew to know the earth and her wild inhabitants firsthand. I learned more about the animals I loved and looked after through experience, and I finally got to play doctor for real by shooting up my horses when shots were warranted. And it was Doctor Carole who eviscerated the chickens at slaughter time, while Dick was known as Monsieur Guillotine. When night fell and the dishes were put away, the whole lot of us slept soundly in the arms of the mountains.

We all felt the same way about the ranch. The work was hard, but it made you feel good. The earth beneath our feet, the sun and storms, the trees upon the slopes, the four-legged and winged creatures—each, unto their kind, was as family and teacher.

It had been a late summer's day filled with bright sunlight, blue, blue skies and high cumulus clouds. The year was 1981. As usual, Dick had spent the day in his backhoe, waging war on a helpless hill, while I harvested the fruits of my labors, putting up pints of jam and quarts of pickles. Dick worked the whole day through, not out of necessity, but out of love for his big-diggy, which was an expensive toy for a grown-up boy. Now it was late and dark—well past nine. I sat in the den watching television as I reconciled my checkbook. The front door opened. It was Dick. He covered the few feet to the den entrance and entered into the light of the room. I looked up at him and froze in my seat. What I saw took my breath away. Though I had never seen it before, I recognized it immediately—it was the face of death, a mask that covered Dick's face, staring at me from a distance of 10 feet. From behind death's mask, Dick's physicality seemed far away, pale and gray, his eyes sunken and ancient, but the physical manifestations were insignificant compared to the distinct mask of death that cloaked my husband's face.

"I'm so tired, I can't believe it. I'm going to go upstairs and rest for a while."

I nodded in the affirmative, unable to speak.

I stared at the television, registering nothing. My mind was consumed with Dick's face and the ghostly mask that had covered it. I rationalized the event. Something had to be wrong with Dick. He must get to a doctor. It wasn't the face of death I had seen, just physical signs that something was wrong. I didn't believe my rationalization but I rehearsed it over and over again. It took me 20 minutes to get my head right, then I climbed the stairs.

Dick lay on our bed. He looked tired. The mask was gone. I sat down beside him.

"You really must go to the doctors for a check-up. You don't look well and you shouldn't be feeling so tired. Maybe it's blood pressure."

Dick put me off, saying he was fine. "Just a bit tired."

A week later, Dick surprised me with a party for our fifth wedding anniversary. There were 20 guests. When all were assembled, Dick stood, raised his glass to me and said, "If I should die tomorrow, it wouldn't matter as the last five years have been more than any man could ask for."

Five days later, Dick experienced rectal bleeding. My first thought was hemorrhoids—nothing to really worry about.

The bleeding increased through the day. Dick agreed it was time to head into town. The doctor examined Dick, asked him a lot of questions and took blood and urine samples.

Following Dick's appointment with the doctor, we traveled north to visit relatives who were vacationing at the Triangle X Ranch—a local dude ranch. It was going on eight o'clock in the evening when we returned home. Kim, my firstborn and only daughter, was there. She had just moved up from Los Angeles and was staying with us until she could find an apartment. Her face was long, her eyes filled with worry and concern.

"What's the matter?" I asked impatiently, sensing her emotions.

"Doctor Mellion has called three times. He says he must speak with Dick. He wouldn't tell me why."

My mind raced knowing that blood and urine tests had been run. Dick's face went dark and the heaviness of the moment weighed down upon us. Chris, home for the summer from college, came up from his room, "Has Dick called the doctor yet?"

"No, I'm just going to do that," said Dick, using his business voice.

Myologenous leukemia; prognosis: six months to five years. With Dick's blood smear and count, probably six months to a year.

Bleeding caused by a polyp on his intestinal wall: easily removed.

Now the mask of death had a name.

Dick waved me away. I went to my children and related the words of the doctor. Kim and I fell into one another's arms and cried. Chris, due to leave for his second year of college in the morning, went to his room, lay on his back, folded his arms across his chest and stayed there with tears streaming into his ears for the rest of the evening.

I went back upstairs to Dick. He was sitting at the table in the den. I asked if I could sit with him and watched as he went through all of the classic phases of impending death in a matter of 30 minutes. From denial to anger and self-pity, he journeyed on into philosophy, then rolled into bargaining and depression, ending with the classical, but seldom achieved, state of acceptance. It was an emotional tour de force and I sat watching—stunned, in grievous turmoil. I wondered if I had witnessed a superhuman feat or a preview of the torments that lay ahead.

Late that same evening, Dick sat cracking wry jokes concerning his impending death as the numbness of shock mercifully enshrouded me.

After the trauma of telling loved ones, after a doctor's appointment in Salt Lake City, after the removal of the polyp, after the initial cascade of tears, after the first round of chemotherapy had taken effect, we started down a long, twisted road marked death.

In the spring of '83, the phone rang. It was my aunt Marion calling from Los Angeles. "Carole, get a plane reservation, then call your mother. She's a basket case. Your father won't go to dialysis."

Two hours later, I sat staring out the window of a Frontier Airlines plane with tears streaming down my face. Mom was right; Daddy and I were Mike and Ike. Though heartbroken, I understood completely how my father felt about everything—even this.

Daddy and I had descended from the same pea pod and through the years he had taught me all he could. When I was confined to bed with rheumatic fever, my father spent his Sundays by my bed, building and designing houses with a marvelous set of blocks while we spoke of life and wonderful things he had read in yet another book. Aside from being a master chef and businessman, he was a constant learner, a true Renaissance man. He was a fine watercolorist and cartoonist, a woodworker and carver, a bookbinder, a jewelry maker and, most of all, a man who was always sneaking home another volume for his ever-expanding library. When I was young and money was scarce, he would tell Mom that a just-bought book was an old one that had been in the bookcase for months. And when not purchasing new books for his own library, he was busy buying me the latest on the children's best-seller list, using every conceivable occasion as an excuse for having spent some of the family's limited income in order to expand and delight the mind. During those lean years, during the war years, my father sold fat and grease from the restaurant's kitchen to munitions factories in order to buy another book or another tube of paint.

And it was my Daddy who taught me to lay a book on its spine and gently open it to the middle, allowing the two halves to open with equal, gentle pressure being exerted onto the book's spine.

"Then you can turn to the front and start reading."

While I lay abed he taught me "there's no place you can't go and nothing you can't learn to do through the pages of a book. You need not worry that you must lie here in bed. The entire world awaits you through the pages of innumerable books."

He was a forceful teacher and parent, keeping me in line

with his family-famous phrase, "You got to tink."

Through his many years as a citizen of the United States, he had never rid himself of his Danish accent. To the end he could not pronounce *th*, so Ruth was *Root* and think was *tink*.

As I grew older, "You got to tink" was often preceded by "Godt damn it!" which often produced inner smiles among those who knew and loved him. He so wanted you to understand the knowledge he was imparting or the view he was propounding that his fervor, mingled with his accent and agile mind, gathered to form a person who attracted many friends and admirers.

I was the leader of his fan club, but I also knew the other side of the man. The man who expected much from his only child and who let me know when I had strayed from the well-defined path he had planned for me.

The words, "My dear girl," gave me the shivers. During my youth, those three words spelled trouble, big emotional trouble in the pit of my stomach. When I reached adulthood, those words were a signal to listen well and mark his words.

The stewardess brought me coffee, asking if I wanted anything else. "Yes," I thought, "but you can't give it to me."

Returning to my window, I remembered the last time I had been in Los Angeles. As usual, I had taken Daddy to and from dialysis. It was obvious that his health was deteriorating rapidly. The man with a tortoise exterior and a marshmallow heart sat next to me, retching into a stack of tissues. Try as I might, I got weepy over his condition. With the first tear, he looked at me and read my mind, then scolded, "death? It's the most natural thing you'll ever do. People are born and people die every second of the day. Do you tink that because a person dies the world is going to stop? My dear girl, grow up. It's just another instant in time. Don't bother your head about it."

"Godt damn it!" It was going to be difficult without him. Very difficult.

But Daddy was 80 and had suffered enough. Four years of dialysis for failed kidneys, surgeries to enlarge the veins in his arms to accommodate the huge needles used in the process of cleansing his blood and now a body that refused to function on command. For his age, Daddy had lasted for more years on dialysis then most, but you would have expected that—he was a Viking to the core. Now he had become incontinent, and if he couldn't dress, if he couldn't take my mother out on Saturday night, if he couldn't be viable, he didn't want to be. I understood.

Mom had called Daddy's doctor, who had become a close family friend over the years. Thirty minutes after Mom's call, he stood in my parents' bedroom looking down at my father.

"Carl, you are a brilliant man and your mental faculties are intact. If I thought I could make you just a little better, I'd sit here all day and talk you out of this decision, but I can't. I respect, understand and honor your decision. Let's figure out how we can make this as comfortable as possible for you."

My grief-stricken mother had stood in the background, unable to accept what the two men realized was a proper decision for an easier passing than the one in store just down the road. Her love-man was preparing to leave her after decades of marriage and all she could feel was a sense of abandonment.

Since my father's system wouldn't tolerate drugs, the doctor suggested he drink brandy and cream to ease any discomfort the issuing poisons might cause as they took hold of the mortal frame we all loved and recognized as Carl.

Daddy refused to eat. He said he didn't want to prolong the ordeal. Of course, his Rémy Martin and cream gave him enough calories and sustenance to keep a whale alive, but he neatly skirted the thought.

On the table by his bed sat a clock, a double old-fashioned glass full of brandy and cream, his Camels (which he'd smoked for 65 years) and his porcelain ashtray with its small green pottery cigarette snuffer that eliminated the need to grind out the fire of your smoke.

Daddy often told of smoking a cigar behind the sea wall of his hometown in Denmark at the age of five and of getting violently ill. I loved his story of being chased by his brothers through the blacksmith shop, of getting kicked in the head by a freshly shod mule, and of it not being his time since he had survived, survived well enough to flip a coin at age 21. Heads—America to make a fortune. Tails—Africa to shoot lions. America won, Mom won, I won—we all won.

My aunt Marion had been right; Mom was an inch to the right of insanity. Her lover, her roommate, her dancing partner was leaving. She had always said she was going to go first as she couldn't live without my father, but her man was leaving and she couldn't stop him.

Daddy sent Mom to work, insisting that she attend to the family's business. They were of the old work ethic and he was the boss. Unable to think, my mother went blindly, faithfully, to work; a numbed and obedient partner with a broken heart.

I sat at my father's side. Too bad we didn't have the old blocks. We could have built a smashing new house. Instead, we verbally reviewed the floor plan of our lives and said "I love you" over and over again.

Each afternoon, when Mom returned from work, she took over, caring for and loving her man, pretending he wasn't leaving, pretending everything would be all right.

Dick drove down from Jackson. He came in to see Daddy. He was in total sympathy with Dad's decision. Certainly, he had a better perspective and understanding than most. He too wished to go peacefully and with dignity.

"Carl, save me a seat," quipped Dick.

"What the hell makes you tink we're going to the same place?" my father quipped back.

Humor, what a gift—a survival kit wrapped in laughter.

Dick only visited my father that once. He knew he couldn't watch the deterioration as it would be too akin to watching his own.

Daddy broke down only once when he begged Mom and me to promise that we would never take him to the hospital—

no matter what. With tears streaking his pallid face, he begged, "If my arms and legs fall off, if I lie screaming, for God's sake, don't take me to the hospital."

Mom nodded. I promised in a loud and clear voice he knew. He lay down and rested, seemingly with less effort and a real degree of calm.

As the week progressed, I realized what I had always known intuitively about my father. He possessed absolutely no fear of death. It was a normal thing to do. He really was a hero.

On the third day, he said, "You know, if I'd known then what I know now I'd never have allowed them to start me on dialysis. My time was back four years ago when my kidneys failed. I never should have allowed them to start the process."

Fifth day: extreme agitation, "How long has it been?"

"Five days."

"Oh no, oh no, oh no."

"Daddy, you have to wait your turn. You'll go when it's your time. It'll all work as it's supposed to."

Later that afternoon, when he was once again himself, he told me of a dialysis patient he'd known who had unplugged herself. Everyone thought she'd go quickly since she had other complications. She lasted six weeks.

I tried to reassure my father that he appeared to be on schedule. The doctor had said a week.

My in-laws' sixtieth anniversary celebration coincided with my father's last days. Daddy insisted we all go. He would be fine, he said. I was worried about Mother.

My oldest son, Brett, had to leave the morning of the party in order to keep his job. His farewell to his grandfather was rough. He didn't want to leave. That left Dick, my daughter Kim, son Chris and me to dress in Roaring Twenties style for the big bash. All but Dick went into the bedroom. Daddy's smiling devilish eyes twinkled as we approached his bed. He loved parties, loved to dress up. He was glad someone was having a party; glad his loved ones were attending. He beamed at the sight of us and told us how splendid we looked. As we left the room, he waved and said, "Have a good time."

It wasn't an act of courage. He truly meant it. All week long, he had said, over and over again, "Carole, have fun. Enjoy your life."

The following morning, I got up early and went into the bedroom. Mom was bleary eyed and emotionally overwrought. She said the night had been a total nightmare. That she had had no sleep, that Daddy had been half out of his head and had repeatedly wanted to get up and that she had had to struggle to keep him from hurting himself. She said Daddy had complained about everything she had tried to do for him and hadn't made sense from midnight until dawn.

I went over to my father and knelt down. His eyes lit up, "How was the party?"

"Very beautiful."

"Wonderful."

"Everyone sent their love."

"Thank you."

It was going to happen soon. The terrible night was the precursor—the struggle of the flesh, the unconscious self tearing away from its earthly plane. Daddy's voice was raspy and rough. You could hear the fluid filling the lungs.

"Mama, you go to work."

"But, Daddy . . ."

"Mama, it's better. . . . You go to work."

We all knew. Mom cried as she dressed. The children came in, gave love and tiptoed out. I sat by my father's side.

"Daddy, can I get you anything?"

"Give me a cigarette." He was too weak to reach them. I held the lighter; he barely managed to get the Camel lit. He rested, then he tried to take a puff but the lungs wouldn't let him. He tried to put the cigarette into the little green pottery butt snuffer. His hand shook, he missed. Angry, he put the Camel out in the ashtray. I had to help him.

Fifteen minutes later, he asked for another cigarette. Somehow, he managed to light it, but again he couldn't smoke it. Again he tried to place the lit end of the Camel into the pottery cylinder. Again he failed and needed my assistance.

Five minutes later, another request for a cigarette. As I held the lighter to the end of the cigarette, I looked into my father's eyes—we had always read each other well. The realization came to him that his lungs weren't going to allow him that last cigarette. With his best ever twinkle and the cutest grin in his repertoire, he looked at me and then at the cigarette; with a steady hand and the skill of Arnold Palmer he neatly made a hole-in-one as he placed the just-lit Camel squarely into the hole of the little green pottery butt snuffer.

With a grin crowding my face, I said, "I love you, Daddy."

"I love you too, Carole."

The lungs continued to fill. It was obvious there was discomfort. Daddy denied it. Mom suggested a sleeping pill to calm Daddy and ease this last phase. She said the pill she had in mind was pretty potent. The doctor had prescribed them a year ago. When Daddy had taken one the year before, it had knocked him out and he had slept twice around the clock and been drowsy for a week. The bottle was full, save one.

"How about it, Daddy?" my mother asked.

"All right, Mama, but call the doctor. If he says yes, it will be fine with me."

The doctor listened, asked a few questions, "Give him the entire bottle if he wants them."

By now, I realized that Daddy had asked us to call the doctor in order to take the onus of guilt off my mother and me. Now it was under his doctor's okay, rather than by our initiative.

Mother gave Daddy a pill. He told her he loved her and to get to work.

Fifteen minutes passed. Daddy was more awake than he

had been all week. His lungs rattled.

Five minutes more. I gave him a second pill. He insisted that Mom go to work. She left, telling him she loved him. His last words to her were, "I love you, Mama."

He asked if she was gone. I nodded yes.

I sat on the edge of the bed. Daddy began to relax. For the entire week he had remained on his left side, facing his table with his clock, Camels, Rémy Martin and cream. For the last two days, he had been incapable of rolling himself to the other side.

He looked up at me, his eyes dimming with sleepiness. I professed my love once more, as though it couldn't be said enough. He reiterated his love and then with the strength and agility of an athlete, he said, "Goodnight," and turned himself over onto his right side. Within 30 seconds, he was softly snoring.

I cleaned up a few things then climbed up on the bed and carefully placed my father's head in my lap. As I held the man who had given me so much my mind filled with the memory of my near-death experience. It wouldn't be long now.

Mom was at work. Dick and Chris were down at Dick's office. Kim was out on the window seat in the living room.

Suddenly, my mind went blank and a light mood came over me. With no thought as to what I was doing, I gently put my father's head on his pillow, checked his breathing, got up and went out to sit by Kim. The minute I sat down, I launched into conversation. Kim would later comment that it was the first time in a week that I had spoken of anything other than my father.

Five minutes passed. In the middle of a sentence I stopped. As if waking from a dream, I said, "It's over. We can go in now."

And so Carl Fredrik Sigvaard Olsen Andersen, who had claimed with a wink of his eye that as a young man he could piss his entire name in the snows of Denmark, died peacefully after 80 hardworking, fun-loving years of life.

AFTERMATH

Ann had sat by Scotty's bed for days without leaving his side. When she visited the bathroom, she left the door open so that she could watch him. On the fifth day, their daughter called from Australia, but the call couldn't be shunted into Scotty's room. A nurse came to inform Ann. She left the room to take the call. Five minutes later, she re-entered the room—Scotty was dead.

While sitting with my father's head in my lap, I had wondered if a death experience was akin to a near-death experience. If so, my father would get to reach the light. A warm glow had flowed through me as the thought came into my consciousness. There I was, holding my father, thinking calm and positive thoughts about dying, hoping the real thing was as wonderful as the near event. What made me leave? Was my father controlling me through telepathy? Did he will me out of the room or did my mind switch courses knowing it would be over soon?

The latter doesn't work. I wanted to be with my father as he crossed, just as he had sat with me for so many hours when I was a sickly child. I had been completely filled with a desire to be with him, remembering my near-death experience, hoping he would reach the light and somehow knowing he was going to be fine. I experienced no fear or apprehension. My father had been ill for several years and was dying in accordance with his wishes. He had had a wonderful life and a reasonably long one. There had been no conscious thought that would have prompted me to leave, and no subconscious thought that would have persuaded me to leave the room.

Though all seemed normal in the moment, when I look back, it is as if someone had flipped a switch in my brain, turning me into an automaton, unable to think for myself, and with no desire to fight the compulsion—the command—to leave.

When this occurrence ended and I told Kim it was over, I was as someone coming out of a hypnotic trance on the count of three and a snap of the fingers. The words, "It's over. We can go in now," didn't seem to be mine. It felt as though someone else was saying the words though they were coming out of my mouth. I recognized the words and knew them to be true, but even at the time I couldn't understand where or how the knowledge had come to me in the middle of a disassociated thought and sentence.

Though some other part of my mind seemed to be in control, I feel most strongly that I wasn't hallucinating. The event was plain and simple. I can firmly state that neither grief nor fear had managed the moment. My mind-set at the time was as my father's—"It's the most natural thing you will ever do." Kim remarked later that I seemed normal in every way, but for the fact that I wasn't talking about my father. Also, Kim hadn't made a sound or called me from the living room.

Afterwards, I thought of the many people and animals I had known, read about or heard of who wanted to die alone. It seemed as if the act of dying was so personal, so singular and apart from life as we know it, that it needs be done in private.

Did my father somehow send me from the room? And how could I possibly have known the moment of death? My father could have lasted for several hours. The two pills were not enough to bring on or hasten death.

It seemed a little thing, a person leaving, or being sent away from death, but in the years to come, I would learn again and again that many people wish to be alone in their final moments. It's a strange and rather wondrous phenomenon.

Elvis Presley made a recording of "Softly As I Leave You," on which he tells about how the song came to be written. Perhaps you remember the words:

Softly, I will leave you softly,
Long before your arms can beg me stay
For one more hour, for one more day . . .

It's said the songwriter wrote the words on his death-
bed—that he waited hours for his wife to fall asleep in the chair
next to him. When fatigue finally closed her eyes, he penciled
the words he had conjured in his mind. His song finished, he
died before his wife could wake.

Don't forget 'to tink.'. . . Godt damn it!

CANCER

My father had died after having lived a full life. Prior
to his death, his body had ceased to function prop-
erly and his days of confinement brought little joy.
Daddy had been ready to move on. He had welcomed death as
a well-deserved rest. He had walked to the end of a natural line.
His death, though grievous, can be seen as natural and right, but
Dick wasn't old or tired of life, nor was he suffering physically.
Dick had always known health and he wanted to live.

Countless books have been written over the years on the
subject of the dying cancer patient. Almost to the letter, these
volumes tell of Jack, who showed the courage of a thousand
lions, and Jill, who brought grace and wisdom to all, then died
like an angel. Bless them all, they were far better than most, but
their tales tell but one side of the story.

There is another side of cancer (and of many other ter-
minal diseases), a mean, angry, painful side that takes many a

mind to hell and back. Few will discuss this dark side because of love and allegiance, but if we are to help those stricken with this fatal disease, as well as those who must stand by while a loved one passes, then it is time for some honesty.

A physician friend once confided in me that all deaths are difficult for doctors, but that she could handle the death of the elderly fairly well, as they had lived a life, and also the death of children (as hard as that seems), since a child has little comprehension of what he or she is going to miss by leaving so soon. But the ones in-between, especially those in their prime, wounded her the most.

If death upsets doctors, imagine how much it upsets the patient. It is not normal to want to die, nor to take such a dreadful sentence in the prime of one's life with calm acceptance.

Dick was 55 when diagnosed. During the first hours of shock and multiple emotions, he said in anguish, "This can't be happening to me. I have always known myself to be indestructible. I have always believed that I would live into my nineties like my grandfather. I have so much more I want to do. I'm still in my prime." Moments later, he changed tack and spoke of how lucky he was, how he had had such a full life with three children and two wives and all the good things any man could wish for. "I shouldn't cry for myself. I have had a far better life than most."

Dick's incredible strength of character carried him through the first months of his disease, and almost through the six months it took him to write his will and get his affairs in order. When he had finished setting up his estate, he announced that he was ready—death could come and get him now. He had done his work, he had struggled through, and his things were in order. But death didn't want any part of him and Dick was left to stand alone with his cancer and what was left of his life and that is when the first signs of real trouble began to rear their ugly heads.

Dick was a brilliant, but spoiled individual who had always been capable of working, charming or buying his way out of any difficult situation that presented itself to him. But death isn't any ordinary customer or opponent. Death is as you see it—and it is often seen as a dirty bastard who takes away all that you know and desire. Whatever your faith or belief about death and a possible afterlife, you cannot truly, scientifically prove that which you hope to be true. Regardless of faith, most of us know, deep within ourselves, that we know not and that in the end we stand alone as individuals who may or may not follow in the paths laid down by our chosen deities.

While there are people who hold no fear of death, being so steeped in their beliefs that they have no doubts, nor any questions, Dick was not among them.

When you are told you are going to die, not right away, but soon, the mind has time to look back through its own mirror and chip away at the varnish it has applied.

Dick survived far longer than any of his doctors had privately predicted. Over a period of three and a half years, Dick was off chemotherapy and in complete remission for 27 months. But sadly, he negated a majority of those healthy months, managing to emotionally rejoin life and live for only six of those priceless periods of time. His mind was so filled with anger produced by inner fears that he couldn't accept the good news of remission, couldn't believe in its staying power, and besides, he didn't know how to set aside the power his imminent death had given him.

In many societies, including our own, an individual can control an entire family by threatening to kill himself. The family quakes under this horrifying threat and becomes a target for cruelty as the supposed suicide uses his death-power in order to get his way.

Many cancer patients use their forthcoming death in the same way. Statements such as, "You can do that after I'm dead," give a slim indication of the mental whippings that can be dealt by the patient. Such statements are always coupled with a demand that the caregiver do as the patient wishes, such as confine oneself to their presence and/or negate their life in order to serve the patient.

During Dick's worst times, the verbal abuse became annihilating and was doubled by his curtailing as much joy and life activities as possible. I became the proverbial bird in a gilded cage.

As the disease progressed, he wanted me more and more to himself. In time, we no longer *did* lunch and rarely had friends over. I became a prisoner in my own home. My only pleasure was my family (mostly via phone), my books and a food column I wrote for the local newspapers. Several doctors had advised me not to quit my column until the very end as it was my only real contact with the outside world and provided me with something to occupy my time. Naturally, Dick was acutely aware of what my writing meant to me, yet he repeatedly suggested that I quit the column. Even my solitary writing and research stood in his way of total domination.

Then it happened. A letter to the editor appeared in the main paper I wrote for. The letter was extremely bigoted and filled with hatred. Dick ordered me to quit my column, stating that I could not write for a paper that would print such hate-filled garbage. I explained that the letter was printed to show the public what kind of man the letter writer was, since the man in question happened to be running for public office. Dick phoned the editor who explained that that was the exact reason they had run the letter. (The tactic worked; the man received all of 12 votes.)

Dick refused to listen. He went wild. He ordered me out of the house. I refused to leave, so he left and went to the ranch. Then he returned. Then he left. In the course of 52 hours, he left me three times. Every time we made contact, I tried to rationalize the situation to him, but his anger only grew to match his blindness.

It was a showdown. I was frantic. Without my writing and research, I would go crazy. I had to touch the world, had to be part of it.

Towards the end of the ordeal, we somehow ended up at the ranch together. After another round of words, he ended up going downstairs to sleep on the couch. I passed out for a while, awakening shortly before dawn. I had to get through to him. I went downstairs and knelt down beside him. He was wide awake. I offered so much common sense in one short statement that I amazed myself. It fell on deaf ears. What he heard was, "I won't quit my column."

His words came like bullets; few of them missed. It was mouth-to-mouth combat, a knockdown, drag-out fight to the finish. Somehow we moved from the living room to the long, two-tabled dining room and there, by the desk in the far western corner of the room, he towered over me and let me have it.

He was still letting me have it when I was suddenly standing 20 feet away in an opposite corner, looking back at the two of us. My feeling was free and joyous, yet calm. My first thought was, "Oh, I'm having an out-of-body experience. This is wonderful." (I find it fascinating that during a psychic experience, one's mind is always rational and calm. You would expect to be frightened or excited, but that is rarely the case.) I quickly accepted my condition but was filled with wonder over my current non-body. Next, I became fascinated with the "me" that was standing across the room in front of Dick—fascinated at how I looked from the right, the backside. My mind (the one that was then in control) interrupted my self-appraisal and told me to get down to business. The thought seemed to be that this was a crisis and that it had to be dealt with immediately. The facts were that Dick was dying and I wasn't. Standing in the corner, the decision became obvious and as soon as it was made I drifted through the two tables and stepped back into my body.

Dick was still screaming at me, still calling me filthy names. Softly, I said, "It's all right, Dick, I'll quit my column." I had to say it twice before he realized he had won. He was so surprised at the suddenness of his victory that he became confused, then embarrassed. Half-heartedly, he yelled something totally meaningless, left the house, got in his car and drove away. When he got to the ranch gate, he stopped, turned around and came back.

"I forgot my camera."

"Why don't you stay for breakfast?"

Though it was but for a short time—I would guess 30 seconds to a minute or two—being out of my body was wonderful. I don't remember leaving my body, but have a distinct recollection of drifting back through the two tables and stepping back into my body through my back—a view I had never had before or since. During the experience, my inner self, my unconscious being, my soul, my spirit, my whatever-you-want-to-call-it, was complete, flawless and alert. While out of my body, I couldn't hear Dick yelling at me, nor could I see my *spirit* body; however, I could sense its existence. When I looked down, I seemed to exist in a completely transparent cellophane body, which, at the time, seemed perfectly fine and logical. As with my near-death experience, I felt whole and complete in every way. My first mental responses concerning the fact that I was out of my body and looking back at my physical form were both fun and marvelous. I felt deliciously free and complete. Even when my mind said I had to get down to business, that I was there for a reason, it was a calm, positive and very matter-of-fact experience. My inner self had risen to the emergency and I felt secure in the fact that I was able to bring about a solution. My higher self, unburdened by an ego, understood and knew what had to be done and gave the conscious, egotistical *me* the right message. Aside from providing me with a clear and precise picture of the situation, the occurrence filled me with the knowledge that Dick was going to die while I was going to go on living for many years. Above all, and perhaps most important, is that my out-of-body experience helped me deal with Dick's fulminating anger.

The story of an enraged cancer patient is not unusual, just seldom told. With new treatments lengthening the lives of cancer patients, many people are subjugated and mentally pulverized by the very people they are trying to help. I know many will understand that in time I visited a friend who is a therapist.

"Carole, you need to come see me more often or else you need to leave him. He is trying to take you with him. He is wearing you down. You are close to the edge and you have got to do something."

"But he's dying," I cried. "You can't leave a dying man."

"Many do. They do it every day because some of these patients become so abusive that no one can live with them without sacrificing their sanity."

"Well, others may do it, but I can't. What I am living with isn't the real Dick. What I am living with is fear, cancer, anger, resentment, chemotherapy and death. I can't leave. I know he is trying to take me with him, but I know the real Dick wouldn't do that."

"Well then, you had better do something, because he is not only wearing you down, he's winning."

I went home to my reading chair by the window in the library and thought. What if I was thrown into solitary confinement and psychologically abused on a daily basis? How would I survive? I knew the answer: if my jailers would allow me to have books I would survive, and I had lots of books, and could get more any time I wanted. I was going to survive.

That very day, I began to study in earnest. Learning had always been a passion for me and now I had a dire need to use my brain by directing it away from the dying that was taking place around me on a daily basis.

I had wanted to be a doctor and had read all I could on the subject for many years, but in time my interest had switched to the mind and psychology. Aside from piles of books on the subject, I read my monthly copy of what we jokingly referred to as *Sickology Today.* From there, I had gone onto anthropology, animal behavior, and more thoroughly, primatology. Now I dove ever deeper into the subject of paleoanthropology and, for counterpoint, one of the world's oldest subjects, religion, with a passion known only to those who are struggling for their very lives . . . and it worked. Daddy had been right. The entire world of art, science, thought, ideas, fantasy, data and knowledge can be found and experienced through the pages of books.

During the last year and a half of Dick's life, I traveled through thousands of pages. Through them I brought new thoughts, old thoughts and a great deal of lively discussion to the dinner table and in helping myself, I helped the man I loved . . . a little bit; as in the time it took to eat our dinner. But even a half hour of ersatz normality was a gift.

Then, in the spring of his last year, Dick got hold of himself for a few months and we took a marvelous trip through the Southwest and the ruins of the ancient Anasazi. While Dick drove, I read to him and for a while we were once again kindred spirits.

One night following our return, Dick and I lay in bed talking as we had done prior to his cancer. That night we cried, something we had also done before, but this time we cried for me. With few words, Dick allowed me to look into a corner of his living nightmare and there I found the fear with which he mentally whipped me. It was covering up the love I had hoped was still there. That one night he found the strength to let me know that underneath his anguish there was love. It would be many months before I saw proof of what I had perceived.

Dick's last months were the roughest, with our last Christmas being a total tragedy. Somewhere deep inside of Dick there was a voice telling him that his time was near. With incredible brutality, he wreaked havoc through emotional death throes, lashing out not only at me but at two of my children, my youngest son, Christopher, and my daughter, Kim. Brett was away at college and working a job he couldn't leave.

Kim, Chris and I grouped together to comfort one another while Dick cursed us in bellowing tones. When there was nothing left of us, he cursed Christmas and everything and everyone that came to mind.

It was the killing storm before the enlightened calm; copious, hot and bitter tears were shed—it was a living nightmare.

Then, during the first week in January, Dick came to me and said he was tired. He said it in a nice calm way and I knew at once that he was laying down the sword. Looking into his eyes, I summoned the courage to say what I had noticed for more than a week. "You are quite pale. I think we should go down and see the doctor in Salt Lake."

Dick nodded and went to make the appointment.

While our first years on the ranch had been the best of all times, the years of Dick's cancer were our worst, but with the coming of the end the storm abated and the sun streamed through our clouds of pain.

On that last drive down to Salt Lake, I noticed an easing of tension in Dick. He knew and I knew. Now my mind tried to steel itself against the enemy that had been knocking for so long at our door. I recalled the hilarious tombstone that reads, "I told you I was sick," and cried.

The doctor informed us that the leukemia had gone blastic: the leukemic white cells were multiplying, running rampant, pervading Dick's body, crowding out his very life. Twenty minutes after the doctor spoke his fateful words, Dick's entire mental and emotional attitude changed. It was like turning over a record. On one side was mind-shattering acid rock, on the other, Debussy's Claire de lune. Before our very eyes, Dick reverted to the man I had originally fallen in love with. He had told the truth. Through the years, he had insisted he was afraid not of death, but of the wait. It was the never knowing that had haunted him. Now the end was near and he could handle it. Once again he felt in control, once again he felt in charge of his own destiny.

The doctor said death would come within one to six weeks.

Prior to death, when the body and mind take note of

the circumstances, there often comes to the patient what I refer to as near-death sight. It is sight full of love, without prejudice, and clear, clearer than one can imagine. With near-death sight, the patient sees everything and everyone exactly as they are. This amazing sight opens up as the ego leaves. It seems to do so when an individual, who had clutched his ego tenaciously to his breast throughout his life, realizes he no longer needs it. And when the ego leaves, all that remains is pure honesty. This sight, this clear perception, sees all but judges not. One cannot pretend or lie to such a sight for it goes through all and everything as it sees through to reality, which it accepts unconditionally without prejudice or emotion. The most wonderful thing about near-death sight is its love. It is like being bathed in the sight of a deity that in looking at you recognizes your every fault, but loves you nonetheless. With such love and perception, one is cleansed, mentally and emotionally.

Dick worked within the realm of near-death sight for close to three weeks. During that time, he apologized to me three times for trying to take me with him. He said that the worst part of his ordeal was that on some mental level he recognized that he was trying to take me with him, but for reasons he didn't understand, he couldn't stop his annihilating behavior. He said the greatest pain of his ordeal was in watching himself lash out at the very person he loved and needed.

In the wake of Dick's apologies, my anger, fear and resentment fled and as the end drew near we were as lovers once more—our hearts and minds mingling through understanding and mutual caring. My heart pulsed with sorrow for times lost, for months on end when we could have been sharing and growing, months when the face of death had canceled the party as we stood trapped in a wasteland of fear.

It may be time for doctors to think more of a person's psyche than his physical body, for without hope, without the ability to experience the joy of life, life has little going for it. Shouting "hooray" simply because you have extended the life of the body does nothing for a mind that is shattered.

After two weeks of weakness, visits from children, final arrangements, letters and such, Dick entered our bedroom and remained there, bedridden, for the last six days of his life.

Once, three days prior to his death, I went in to check on him. I arrived just as he was awakening from slumber. His eyes were large and luminous. "Sandy's very near," he said. I agreed, telling him that I was sure that was the case.

Sandy had been Dick's orphaned cousin. Adopted by Dick's parents, he became the person Dick looked up to and idolized as a child. Emotionally, Sandy became the older brother Dick had never had. When Sandy was 16, and Dick was 11, an accident occurred on a certain Saturday.

Dick's paternal grandfather, D.R. was an orthodox Jew who followed his faith to the letter, refusing to ride in any wheeled conveyance on the Sabbath—Saturday.

For their summer holiday, Dick, his mother, one of her sisters and her sister's twins, along with Sandy, traveled a state away to visit Dick's maternal grandmother and two of her daughters. On a Friday evening the phone rang. It was Dick's grandfather, D.R.; he was frantic. "I have had a telling dream— I have had a vision. None of you should get in a car tomorrow. You must not drive or ride in any wheeled vehicle. Please, you must promise me."

My, my, what religion will do. Silly old man!

The following day, on Saturday, Dick, Sandy, the twins, their mutual maternal grandmother, plus the two aunts who lived with her, all climbed into the family's big sedan and headed out for a picnic by the river. They didn't see the speeding train until it was upon them. Sandy was decapitated. Dick found himself in a ditch. The only other survivor was one of the twins; all others were killed at the time of impact. . . . Silly old man!

Now, 48 years later, Sandy was near, and Dick, who formerly would have scoffed at the idea of a dead relative being "near," was at peace.

During those last days, Dick wanted no one in the room other than myself. Unfortunately, there were things I couldn't manage alone. My son Brett, who had missed the torture of Dick's last Christmas, managed to come home for the final curtain. Dick allowed him to come in and help me pick him up to go to the bathroom or to move him when necessary. The last time Brett and I hauled Dick's body into the bathroom was an ordeal. Dick couldn't lift a finger let alone a hand. Brett and I knew he didn't really need to go, but Dick had tried his best to talk and had made his wishes known. Now we were two short people using all possible strength to keep a six-foot rag doll from falling off the commode. Brett and I were both struggling. We both knew that Dick's sensations were false, but that Dick felt them to be real. I looked at Dick. He could no longer speak or move his facial muscles but his eyes told me everything. "Pretend you're reading *Time* magazine," I said. It was his last big laugh, but it was inaudible. With miraculous strength, he managed a wave of his head, and we hauled him back to bed. As I settled him in, his eyes were still laughing. I laughed with him knowing all the raucous things that were going through his head.

The last time the doctor checked on Dick, he drew blood but could detect neither pulse nor blood pressure. Dick tried to talk, but couldn't. Only slurred and garbled sounds broke the air and Dick eventually gave up.

Weeks later, the doctor confided in me that he couldn't believe Dick had lasted another 27 hours. It seemed a physical impossibility.

The following night was Dick's last. I thought of my mother and her description of my father's last night. Dick had been incapable of movement or speech for close to two days. As evening fell, he went into a mild coma, unable to open his eyes, though obviously agitated mentally. Then the inert form that was my husband tried to sit up. Not only did he manage to sit bolt upright, but out of nowhere came his voice, loud and clear, telling me that he wanted to get up. It took all of my strength to hold him down as I explained to him that he couldn't get up because he would only fall down and that he was sick and all the other crazy nonsense you say when the impossible seems to be happening.

Each time he tried to get up, he asked, "Why won't you let me get up?" It was a good question. I wish I could go back and allow him to get up just to see how much strength there was in a body that had been close to death for more than 24 hours. Why did I think he had to stay in bed? What life schooling demanded that I reject his request?

The night was mostly spent when Dick tried once more to get up. But this fourth and last time was different. He began to cry and whine like a little boy. When he opened his mouth to speak, the voice of a child filled the air and whined, "If my mommy and daddy were here, they would let me get up." He was right, they would have. They had spoiled him his whole life through.

Snow fell. Dick calmed. The night was waning. I felt his agile, adult consciousness return. No more words creased the air. The torrent of torment—the mind's wrestling to loose free its bonds to the body was over, but Dick still seemed to be struggling. I felt the presence of death—could feel Dick fighting it. We had spoken many times of my near-death experience and he had said repeatedly that he wasn't afraid of death. Now he stood on the diving board unable to take the plunge. The body was long gone, but the mind clung with a strength and determination equal to the personality Dick had exhibited throughout his life.

I scooted up next to the man who had invited me to dinner so many years before. I kissed him on the forehead. "Dick, I love you so very much but you are very, very sick now. If you will simply relax everything will be all right." I could sense his mind, listening, understanding. Dick stopped breathing for many seconds, then took a deep breath and relaxed for the first time in many hours. All tension left his body and his breathing returned to normal. It was 5:17 AM. I crawled up onto the bed from my side, and in kneeling position, lay my head on his chest in order to listen to his heartbeat. Instantly, I was in a deep sleep. I want to scream as I write this, for I know that no one will believe I didn't simply fall asleep from fatigue, but it wasn't sleep that befell me. Dick, or my own mind, or which removed my consciousness from the scene of death and Dick, who, as so many before him, slipped away alone. One second I was listening to his heart and timing his breathing, the next second my mind, my consciousness, my spirit, left, perhaps to wing off with him momentarily, or simply to allow him his time of passage.

Forty-five minutes later, I was awake, suddenly, completely, and in the exact kneeling position I had been in when I went to "sleep." I was at once alert, clear-headed and refreshed. Even before my eyes flashed open, I knew Dick was gone. He, too, had followed the fellow's song, "Softly, I will leave you softly. . . ."

Something caused me to leave through sleep's door, allowing Dick to slip away softly, silently, peacefully, in his own bed, just the way he had wanted. And I, who had promised to be there to the very end, had found cause to escape while birth's reversal took place. Or was that, too, the way Dick wanted it to be?

Brett was in his bedroom downstairs. Kim had come up from her apartment every day from seven in the morning until well past midnight. When I awoke from my mysterious slumber to find Dick gone, I got Brett up and called Kim, then I called Dick's parents and my mother. Brett did the rest of the calling. After Dick had been picked up and taken to the mortuary, the children and I, plus my close friends Beth Overcast and Mary Mead, who had arrived to care for us, cook for us and answer the phone (bless them both), stood around the kitchen drinking coffee, crying, laughing and talking over Dick's final hours.

In the midst of the chatter and a tenth cup of coffee, Kim looked at me with a quizzical expression and asked, "Mom? Why did you call me at 5:30 and tell me to be ready to come up in forty-five minutes?"

"What are you talking about? I never called you until it was over."

"Mom, you're just tired. You called me just before 5:30, but I couldn't understand why you didn't want me right then."

"Kim, you must believe me. Dick seems to have put me to sleep, just as your grandfather sent me from the room. I never called you until after I awoke and it was all over. Honest!"

Our minds are so mysterious. Did the man who wrote the song "Softly As I Leave You" put his wife to sleep or did he simply wait until she dozed off? Did my father actually send me from the room? Did Dick, in some way, send me away? And who called my daughter? Could I have functioned as in a dream state and actually have called my daughter, then put myself back in the exact position with my head on Dick's chest?

In going over the phone call with Kim, she said that in retrospect she couldn't swear to the fact that it was my voice on the phone. Whoever it was didn't sound sleepy or sluggish but gave the facts very matter-of-factly, then just hung up without a "Love ya" or anything.

Could Kim have dreamed the call? If so, how could she have known the proper time for the call or the fact that within 45 minutes of the call, Dick would be dead? If, on the other hand, I did indeed make the call (which I truly do not think was the case) how could I have known that my husband was going to last for another 45 minutes, or that I was going to be out for the next 45 minutes? When I awoke, Dick had a normal body temperature and appeared to have just passed.

There is no way to prove what actually happened; I can only relate how it sits firmly in my mind and that Kim said that the voice on the phone didn't sound like mine. Whatever happened, both Kim and I seemed to know the timing of Dick's departure. The bizarreness of the entire affair enhanced my belief that many wish to pass in private.

ANOTHER PIECE OF THE PUZZLE

When cancer or other long-suffering diseases strike, both the patient and family are forced into an ordeal of immense proportions. The road can be extremely difficult but all things in life offer multiple sides. To complete the picture of Dick's ordeal, I wish to offer a few bittersweet notes. We may or may not be immortal, but it is a goal humanity has been striving to achieve for a very long time.

Dick had always been a planner and an organizer. As soon as he finished setting up his estate, he began planning for his death. One day, about five months after diagnosis, his dedication to details failed as a frightening load of depression fell upon him. His emotional state became so acute that I kept him talking far into the night.

Somewhere around 3:00 AM, he asked if it was selfish for him to want to die at home with only me in attendance.

"No! For heaven's sake, I will finally get to do something for you. I don't know how to remove the cancer, but I can at least try to fulfill your last wishes."

"I know, but you'll have to fly my body to Los Angeles."

"Don't worry," I quipped, "I'll give you the window seat."

We laughed clear through to the dawn and from that day forward, whenever we traveled, he *took* the window seat.

Whenever Dick was in good form, we would talk about everything, just as we had done prior to his cancer. Because of the circumstances surrounding us, we now spoke more and more often about our species and death. Both of us were archae-

ology nuts and we soon came to the conclusion that few people
are buried properly in this day of jets and overpopulation. We
recalled the great pyramids of Egypt, the tombs of the Incas
and the ocher-covered body of a Neanderthal lying in his grave,
dug within a cave, his body curled and bound in fetal position,
blanketed with a array of flowers, many of which possessed the
power of both beauty and healing. We talked of jewelry, jars
and jade, of papyrus, parchment and pendant, of foodstuffs,
flagons and flowers, of slaves, silver and song, of goblets, gar-
ments and gold. We spoke of us, we humans, and the ways
in which we honor our dead in accordance with our beliefs.
Then we discussed what you would find if you dug up any of
the modern-day cemeteries. Other than knowing a person's sex,
name, age, and height, the knowledge gained from each coffin
would be slim. A good lab and bone man could tell you which
bones had been broken and some of the diseases that had attacked the victim, but other than remnants of material or pieces
of jewelry, little would be known of the life that had been lived.
We noted also that people of today are constantly being buried
in clothes they seldom wear. Take the farmer or mechanic: he
gets married and buried in a suit. The clothing business must
love it. Over the course of many talks, we established desired
plans for Dick's burial, remembering the tombstone that reads,
"Here I lie, all dressed up with no place to go."

When finalized, Dick relayed the details to the mortician, who later said that Dick had changed his way of thinking
in regard to his own burial.

Dick lies in a fine coffin dressed in the type of clothing
he wore 95% of the time. Cowboy boots, dress jeans, brown
belt with pewter buckle and a plaid, wool Pendleton shirt—
his handsome gray-blue one. We tried to squeeze in one of his
cowboy hats but the archaeologists would have never been able
to block it back into shape.

Besides his everyday clothes, Dick has all of his daily
needs with him. Every morning, he would pack his pockets

with all of the accoutrements he deemed necessary for survival in this madcap world. It's all there in his pockets: his pipe, tobacco, pipe cleaners, and matches, his favorite pens and pencil, a small notepad, a handkerchief, the pocketknife his daughter had given him, plus his wallet, drivers license and other documents no longer needed on this side.

Dick's hands are folded over a ziplock bag that contains his autobiography, the foreign policy he worked long and hard on (he once spoke before the UN), a photograph of him in his healthy days and a small plaster of paris plaque of the Ten Commandments, which had belonged to his cousin Sandy.

Also tucked inside the ziplock bag is a special item, one Dick never traveled without. It is an Eagle bar of Ghirardelli chocolate (one they no longer make), lying there in its white wrapper with black and gold design, its delicious, bittersweet chocolate permeating the other contents with its deep aroma. After all, kings of old always entered their tombs with a goodly supply of foodstuffs to nourish them on their journey—it is only fitting that Dick should have his favorite chocolate bar in remembrance of the thousands of salivating mouthfuls he knew on this side of the line.

Over Dick's legs lies an old blanket of Sandy's. We decided that none of the upcoming generations could ever know what that old piece of wool represented, so Dick took it with him. It may be the only article to confuse the archaeologists. But then, it's important to leave them something to hypothesize and argue about.

I had promised Dick that I would be with him every step of the way when we transported his body out to California for burial.

The day after Dick died, his father and cousin, Larry Travis, flew up from Los Angeles to help me in following Dick's last wishes. That night we viewed Dick's appropriately dressed and furnished body. George, Dick's father, faltered; Larry caught him and helped him to a chair. The next morning started with an early breakfast with a friend who had arrived to drive us all to the airport. On the way, she dropped Larry and me off at the mortician's. The mortician had Dick all packaged for the trip and loaded into the hearse. His casket was sealed inside the largest carton box I had ever seen. Larry and I slid into the front seat next to the mortician and we took off. Looking over my shoulder into the back of the hearse, I told Dick that he looked ready for UPS.

During Dick's long struggle with cancer, we had flown numerous times down to Salt Lake to see his oncologist. During those tortuous years, Frontier Airlines was the major carrier servicing Jackson and we had come to know many of their personnel. When we got to the airport, I told them of my promise to Dick. Shortly after our plane landed in Jackson, the captain came and got me, walked me through the ticket counter and out back to where the hearse was parked. Then we drove Dick to the plane. I was then allowed to walk with the gurney, from hearse to plane, where the coffin traveled the ramp up into the hold, the procedure being reversed as Dick was transported from plane to plane in Salt Lake. Prior to landing in Los Angeles, the captain came to me and asked that I remain on the plane after landing until he came for me. Once again I was allowed to hold the rim of the carton from plane to hearse. It was difficult when the awaiting hearse pulled away but I had fulfilled my promise. I will never forget Frontier's graciousness and the way in which they honored Dick. Their kindness would have overwhelmed him. (Obviously, this beautiful and emotional occurrence took place pre-9/11.)

Dick's funeral was orchestrated by his mother. It was a lovely funeral, however, Dick didn't attend. Yes, you read right. We buried Dick's body, but Dick wasn't there.

I flew back to Jackson with great trepidation of entering our home. There had been three and a half troubled years there, topped off with three weeks of total understanding and love that ended with Dick's death. I wasn't sure what I would find when I returned. I didn't know how the house would feel after all that had transpired.

Tense and nervous, I pulled into the turnaround and backed down the driveway. By the time I turned off the motor, I was completely relaxed and smiling. As I got out of the car, I felt Dick's big old arms wrapping around me, and as I entered the house I was consumed with a feeling of love. It was nice to be home; Dick was still there.

A year later, I thought it would be proper to visit my husband's grave. After all, within the heavy emotions that swirl around funerals I could have misread my feelings. As I journeyed nervously to the gravesite, I recalled the many who believe that the dead actually inhabit their gravesites. Through time, the tombs of many have become shrines. People have flocked to them by the millions, even unto this day, like St. Peter's in Rome and Mohammed in Medina. In ancient times, people traveled on foot to Saqqara in Egypt to stand before the place of burial of the great Imhotep. I, myself, have stood before two of the aforementioned—and now I journeyed forth to visit the grave of my husband.

First I sat reverently by Dick's grave. It was a beautiful day—nothing—no feelings—almost a void. I sat *on* Dick's grave. It was still a beautiful day. I sprawled, spread-eagle, over Dick's grave. I tried to meditate. Then I started to laugh. I could almost hear Dick laughing with me.

My feelings had been correct. Beneath me lay a well-buried body, worthy of any archaeologist's spade, but Dick was gone and I rejoiced.

Even as a child I felt our bodies were but temples we reside in during this life experience. They should be looked after and cared for as one would care for a fine and costly home. But that's all they are: a home for yourself, a place to put your mind in, a place to leave when it wears out.

There are few today not touched by cancer or a long drawn-out disease that slowly takes away a loved one or friend.

I believe it's important to remember something about deaths that come over a period of years. You, the survivor, start to grieve, not at the time of death, but the day the doctor lowers his eyes and tells you that your loved one has XYZ and that the disease will eventually win. That day, that instant, when you receive the horrible news, is when your period of grieving begins. Thus, when the patient dies, you are halfway home as you have already survived much of your suffering. What's left is dealing with the final loss.

It is important to remind yourself that your loved one, in a healthy state, would want you to go on. If you feel he or she wouldn't, that they would actually want you to suffer, then you have to come to grips with the fact that he or she had more wrong with them than just a physical malady and get yourself some professional help.

As humans, we possess an incredible attribute: it's called hope. It is a torch none can afford to put down. Hold it high and believe in it. Without it, our species would cease to exist.

It is important to note that Dick never showed me anything but love, respect and kindness prior to his illness. Verbal abusiveness was never a part of his pattern or our marriage. Until the fear of death clutched at his very being, Dick treated me as a queen. On the morning of his death, I said to no one in particular, "Who will spoil me?" at which time my dear friend, Mary Mead, announced the sentiments of all present, "You've been spoiled enough."

ENDINGS

I would like to go back to some of the words written above: "Now the end was near and he could handle it. Once again he felt in control, once again he felt in charge of his own destiny."

In this day and age of modern medicine, with its "miracles" and life-extending capabilities, many seem to view death as an option, while others fear death with an intensity that is palpable. Add to that the fact that children often move away, families scatter and, for many, parents are seen only on occasion, thus deepening a chasm that is naturally formed by distance.

In the course of writing this book, I sat on two boards that related to death and dying: the Rush Hospice Board and a two-year research board that investigated alternative medicine. I also lectured on death and dying at conferences, in libraries, and to nurses and first- and second-year medical students. On a more personal level, I worked with cancer patients and those in the process of dying. Out of those multiple experiences came some bottom lines that everyone should know and come to understand deep within.

Dick hadn't lied: he wasn't afraid of death, he was terrified of the unknown—not what lies beyond—but of not knowing when his time would come, and most of all, of losing the control he had always maintained. That terror produced anger, resentment and dread.

We all come into life with an innate sense of invincibility that wanes, to some extent, as we age. But it's still there, it's always there—until a doctor says, "You have XYZ and I'm afraid it's incurable." The doctor's following words about treatment and the extra time modern medicine can offer usually go unheard. The first sentence spelled doom and even if modern

medicine can offer you some additional years, the bastard in the
long white nightshirt is going to get you. The ball of life has
been taken out of your hands, you are no longer in control and
your ego and giant intellect can't do a damn thing to change
your ultimate fate. And that is when all hell breaks loose as the
brain scrambles and, more often than not, fails to find the door
marked acceptance.

But that is only the tip of the iceberg I wish to expose.

In time, especially towards the end, the body's ailments
allow a person insights and emotional feelings that enable natural release. However, there are situations where the caregiver, or
children seldom seen, or a closely related individual who possesses an inordinate fear of death, barge through emotional doors,
uninvited, and that's when the healthy have been known to *kill*
what is left of the dying.

Allow me to tell you a story that happened in a major teaching hospital. Let's call the father "Mike" and his son
"Mark."

Mike had battled cancer for five years and now his time
was near. Mike had had the usual ups and downs, both physical
and emotional, but he had eventually put his affairs in order and
come to mentally accept the inevitable. Being of sound mind he
signed a DNR (do not resuscitate) order.

Mike's son, Mark, had left home with his parents' encouragement and money to go to a prestigious university. After graduation, Mark hit the Big Apple and made it his own.
Through diligence, Mark made a great deal of money over the
years. During those years, he had been too busy to return home
to see his good old, middle-class mom and dad.

So it was that when Mark got the news of his dad's impending death he caught a plane and walked into the hospital as
if he owned it. No flunky doctors were going to allow his dad to
die! The bottom line is that Mark told the doctors that his father
had signed the DNR under duress and then went on to threaten
them and the hospital with huge lawsuits if they didn't hook

his father up to every machine available and keep his dying and agonizing flesh alive for every second possible. Mark's actions reflected his inner guilt over being one of the worst of sons. But guilt does not excuse such actions. Mark's ego was so inflated that it blinded him to his father's suffering and desires. But the most horrible of Mark's actions was that of taking away his father's right to end his days as he wished, of taking the ball of life, which Mike had finally regained control over, and snatching it out of his hands. In doing so, Mark took away his father's power and dignity, leaving him with nothing. After five years of cancer and fear, Mike had come to terms and didn't want to die hooked up to machines, lying in a hospital bed where pain would be his constant companion in a room he didn't like. By interfering with his father's wishes, Mark made the last few weeks of his father's life a living hell. The doctors were horrified and deeply saddened, but in this most litigious of times they were over a barrel. Mike died in agony; even morphine couldn't erase his pain.

There is another side to this. Institutions are constantly being threatened with lawsuits that force them to do things they do not wish to do, but they do, even if it is not in the full interest of the patient. I'm speaking of times when a DNR order is ignored.

There have been many cases where a patient signed a DNR that was duly posted on the chart at the end of his bed. Then in the middle of the night, the patient goes into cardiac arrest. A housekeeper walks by the room, recognizes trouble and pushes the emergency button. It's three in the morning; the emergency night crew is on duty. They don't know the patient and they don't know that a DNR has been signed. All they know is that it's an emergency and every second counts. They intubate the patient and put him on life support.

In other cases, it's a health provider who believes that no matter the condition of the patient, no matter his wishes, or the fact that he has signed a DNR, or that the treatment forced upon him will offer nothing more than a few hours or days of discomfort and pain, "they" are going to save a life; in their minds their personal beliefs supercede those of all others. And, of course, there are people such as Mark, a wonderful family member who steps in and threatens the hospital with a lawsuit, usually with comments such as, "My mother would have never signed that! The doctor talked her into it." Whatever the case, the patient's wishes for a peaceful death have been denied; it is a problem that needs solving.

It is important to let your loved ones know your desires and that you will haunt them if they go against your wishes. I'm being facetious—or maybe I'm not; surely they will remember your words for the rest of their days. Let the hospital know that you expect your wishes to be followed. If the end is near and you are the patient's mate or advocate, stay in the room with the patient. Many hospitals allow this and provide reclining bed chairs that allow for a bit of sleep.

An important part of this discussion may be the fact that many people don't know the difference between a DNR and an end-of-life directive, which is a document that lists your desires as to what kind of treatment and medical procedures you would wish to have when you are nearing the end of your life. For example, would your wish be to be put on dialysis, a breathing machine, or be resuscitated. Do you wish to be an organ or tissue donor, etc.

However, when death is imminent and modern medicine has done all it can do for your condition, a DNR order is a sane and reasonable thing to sign. On the other hand, if someone has a heart attack and there is a real possibility of recovery, you should never sign a DNR. Do-not-resuscitate orders should be signed only when a person is in an end-stage situation and recovery and a return to health is not a possibility. When death is inevitable, when all that medicine can do is prolong the processes of dying, then a DNR order is very much in order so as not to bruise those last precious hours or days.

In the January 20, 2009, edition of the *New York Times*

Science section, Dr. Robert L. Martensen, retired emergency doctor, professor of medicine and author of *A Life Worth Living*, covers the many adverse ways in which death is handled in our American hospitals. He speaks of situations where people have signed DNR directives and the hospitals still resuscitate them. He also addresses some of the terrible ways in which the elderly are treated during their last days, weeks and months. I will list but a few pertinent facts noted in his book.

The motto in most nursing homes is, "No one dies here."

Result: elderly patients are rushed to the nearest emergency room without a medical history or an advocate. Many elderly patients are shipped to an emergency room six to ten times during the last months of their lives. On each visit, they are subjected to numerous expensive, and often unnecessary, tests and interventions, including being placed on life support. It's not a gentle ending.

As Dr. Martensen notes, many doctors in America seem incapable of saying the simple truth, "Your mother is dying," then goes on to tell of an elderly woman who went from a serious neurological problem to end-stage renal (kidney) failure. Her condition was absolutely hopeless yet the hospital hooked her up to life support and put her into an intensive care unit for months. No one told the family the true condition of their mother. When someone finally told them, they were furious and rightly so.

Martensen quotes a doctor who said, "I can't take away a person's hope." Martensen's response: "It is as if doctors were bestowing life" as opposed to prolonging the process of dying.

We select medical students for their pragmatic, science-based take on life, then train them to view death as a failure. Many admit that once death is imminent, they feel defeated and leave the arena either emotionally, physically or both, right when the patient needs them most.

A close friend of ours, Dr. Jose Velasco, is a marvelous

surgeon, head of his department and a magnanimous, caring man. His reading of this book during its formative years has produced many discussions. The last time I spoke with him, he explained an amazingly kind and gentle way of handling end-of-life issues; it is as wise and compassionate as the man himself.

One of Jose's patients was in end-stage cancer. Then another complication arose that could be relieved through an extensive operation, but wouldn't save or extend the man's life. In private, the man let Jose know that he didn't want a useless surgery under the circumstances, but that his children were having a hard time and wanted him to have the operation. In looking over the situation of this particular case, Jose had a stroke of genius. He stayed at the hospital and waited for the man's family to arrive for their nightly visit. He approached the family and invited them into his office. He then explained that children are frequently placed in a difficult situation when a parent is near death. He told them how children often feel that it is imperative that they make final decisions on behalf of the parent, but that what is most important is that they listen to the desires of their loved one. He then walked with them to their father's room. After greetings, Jose took the patient's hand and spoke to him of his condition, saying that he wanted to explain everything with his family there as such situations are usually difficult for loved ones to understand and accept. Then he told the man what he already knew. First, he spoke about the operation, how extensive it would be and the painful recovery period. Then he addressed the man's current condition and what could be expected, ending his discussion with, "Knowing all that, as your physician, I feel that the decision must be yours. I wanted your family here so they could become aware of all aspects concerning your situation and hear what it is that you want under the circumstances. I will do anything and everything I can for you. Be it all or nothing. It's your body and your life. You have full mental and emotional facilities; it's your decision. I will follow your wishes." The man squeezed Jose's hand, then he thanked him and said that he didn't want the surgery, that he had suffered long enough and that the trauma of surgery, on top of his cancer, would be too much. He said he wished to be made as comfortable as possible, have his family about him and die in peace.

Jose promised to fulfill his wishes, shook hands and gave hugs to the man's children and left as the family crowded around their father with love and understanding . . . and that's what it's all about.

Another close friend, Dr. Sam Spivak, a retired oncologist, always asked his patients if they would like him to record his words whenever he had to give a patient the bad—as well as the good—news. Many accepted his offer. When the appointment was over, he would hand the tape to the patient and/or caregiver (if present) so that they could listen to his words at home, after the shock and tears had subsided, at a time when they could hear the positive, as well as the negative, side of the situation. The tape also served as a sound library, in that they could go back and listen to it again and again so as to make sure they had a full understanding of the circumstances. Another wise and compassionate idea.

In Martensen's article, he describes his own father's death. It mirrors that of my father. "He didn't have an extended period of dying because he avoided being put on a ventilator. My father died comfortably, surrounded by people he loved. He was lucid till about five minutes before his death." Martensen adds that he hopes he will have the courage and understanding exhibited by his father.

I agree with Dr. Martensen in that my mind is at peace concerning the deaths of my father and Dick. Both men wished to die at home with no excessive measures. Both died according to their wishes, in control, with dignity, with those they loved in attendance. There can be no better death.

However, if either my father or my husband had changed his mind and wished to be taken to the hospital and wanted all possible procedures performed, his wishes would have been followed.

Should your loved one be mentally incapacitated, and never wrote an end-of-life directive, sit down with your family and the doctors in attendance and discuss the true condition and outlook of the situation and what the dying patient would have wanted when he was mentally sound. Fight to put your own desires aside. Think only of the person and what he probably would have said—or did say—then do the right thing.

With all that said, there are some on the planet who know how to go out kicking. A year and a half prior to Dick's death, we traveled to New Zealand for two weeks, during which time we covered both islands stem to stern. Dick had some bad days, but otherwise it was a marvelous trip. As we were booking into a lovely hotel in Wellington on the southern tip of the South Island, a large handsome tour bus pulled up. The doors opened and people began to get off. It was a hard task for most and some were carried off and placed into wheelchairs that had been unloaded from a cargo bay. With canes and helping arms, they ambled happily into the hotel.

Later that evening, we went down to dinner, after which Dick said he wanted to go rest, suggesting that I stay and finish my wine and enjoy the pianist. Knowing he needed some alone time, I did so and got to talking with the bus driver. What I learned was wonderful. All of the people on the bus were in the process of dying. There were helpers and a registered nurse who saw to it that everyone took their medications or received needed injections.

"What if one of them dies?" I asked.

"Happens all the time. Everyone who signs on boards the bus knowing they may return home in a box."

"But, some are far from their homes. What do you do?"

"We know all of the funeral homes and we carry a temporary coffin to get them to the mortuary. They all have their desires written down. . . ." and on and on he went.

I looked over at the elderly group. They were telling tales of younger days, laughing and having a great time. "When someone dies on the trip, do the others get depressed?"

"Heavens, no. We throw a party for the departed and everyone tells a story about the deceased; tears are frowned upon. They have chosen to take the risk and enjoy their last days seeing the sights rather than lie at home and wait. Of course, there are many people who would like to take one of these trips but are too incapacitated for us to handle, but you'd be surprised if you knew how sick some of these people are."

I looked over at the animated group whose journey was almost over, taking a trip and enjoying the world. As I watched them my mind took in another slant on life; I liked what I saw. I looked back at the bus driver and commented on the wonderful work he was doing. "I love my work," he said. "These people are the best. They accept life and want to live it to their last. I've learned a great deal from them."

I hope such busses are still traveling the roads of New Zealand.

To paraphrase a favorite e-mail, "Life isn't a contest in which the aim is go out fit and beautiful, but a journey that should end with you having used up everything ever given to you, having done everything possible, with a favorite beverage in one hand, a chocolate bar in the other and a grin on your face as you slide in under the finish line totally spent, yelling, 'Yahoo! What a ride!'"

PART THREE

MOTHERS AND DAUGHTERS

Each and every death is unique, be it from sudden death due to heart attack, accident, stroke or war, to long, slow deaths brought on by myriad diseases or starvation or sheer entropy.

THE STAIR SCRUBBER

My grandma Faunce was the original Earth Mother. She birthed eight babies, seven of which survived. She raised her one son and six daughters as individuals, treating each in turn according to his or her abilities and personality.

I was Grandma's first grandchild and spent a great deal of my youth on the Faunce Reservation. My father worked long, hard hours in those days and many days of the week found my mother and me driving over to Grandma's for dinner. My mother, being the second eldest, would help with the cooking while enjoying the gathering of family.

It was a big family and when dinnertime came, my youngest aunt, Jackie, and I had to sit on two precarious stools at the end of the dining table, which so filled my grandparents' little dining room that my grandfather was forced to sit with his chair halfway into the bathroom. He did it with dignity, though, and you may not have wanted to be present if one of the girls came to the table in curlers or a robe. You dressed for dinner and you minded your manners . . . or else.

By the time I can remember sitting at the end of the Faunce table, Grandfather's son John was no longer living at home, leaving Grandfather in charge of a table lined with females. As is usual at family dinners, subjects would sometimes arise that caused consternation—especially to my grandfather.

After law and order was restored to the table, Grandfather would settle in to eat his meal while rapid-fire discussions took off between the girls. I would get caught up in all this and begin to tip back on my stool. Eventually, I would tip back to where I was balancing the little stool on two of its legs.

BAM! Down I would go, as the little stool slipped out from under me.

"Carole! Get up and sit up proper at the table," my grandfather would command, as my aunts began to giggle. In my haste to obey, I would always stand up too fast and bang my head on the underside of the table. More giggles. By the time I got myself reseated, I was red in the face and crying. Aunt Jackie, three and half years my senior, would look at me from her stool with disdain, then someone would suggest that I be put out in the night air to eat with the worms. Mom would tell me to sit up and behave, Grandfather would tell the other girls to stop their giggling and my grandmother would comfort me. When you needed love and understanding, Grandma Faunce was always there to make it all better again.

My mother's mother was goodness through and through, but she loved to tease or tug at the emotions. Little tugs were fun, but she preferred long, drawn-out tales where she could milk the emotions. One of her favorites was to sit me on her knee and tell me the story of how I had almost lost my mommy. She would go through the whole story about the doctor leaving me and the afterbirth to the nurses so he could leave on a fishing trip, telling me of how the hospital had let Mom and me go home two days later, but wouldn't re-admit me when Mom had to return due to an acute case of blood poisoning, caused by the decaying afterbirth that the nurses had failed to remove from her uterus.

On and on my grandma would go, telling me how my father had called to say the hospital wouldn't re-admit me and how she had taken the bus down Wilshire Boulevard to the hospital—how they had wrapped me in my blue blanket (Mom had hoped for a boy), and how she and I had sat on the bus bench with all those noisy, smoky old cars going by, and how we had to go home on the bus and how I was ONLY five days old . . . oh my.

Of course, by the time she told of five doctors giving up, and my daddy crying, I was crying, too. Then she would rock me back and forth as she continued with her story, telling me how she had saved my mother's life by asking that the nurses give Mom hot vinegar douches every half hour and how my mother had miraculously recovered. . . . If my mother were within earshot she would scold, "Mom, stop teasing Carole and making her cry."

Looking back, the story seems a bit morbid, but my grandmother filled it with so much love, and the ending was so happy, that I was always eager to hear it again. Actually, it was a triumphal story of beating back the man in the long hooded robe. Way, way back, in the depths of our dark caves, we learned to thrill to the story, and the scarier the better.

Only recently have I wondered if hot vinegar douches could actually cure acute blood poisoning. I know from both my mother and father that, indeed, the doctors had given my father the dreadful news that they were saddened and sorry, but that they could do nothing more for his beautiful Caroline. But hot vinegar douches?

After reading the above, several doctors have said that the story is quite plausible, that my grandmother's prescribed treatment may well have flushed enough of the poisons out of my mother's bloodstream to allow her young, healthy body to fight off what promised to be an early death.

Grandma Faunce was full of home remedies and the art of healing. She had been born into a day and age of minimal medicine, when mothers had to learn everything they could about taking care of the sick and wounded. Modern medicine lay decades into the future.

The birthing of my oldest son was a rough go. When the two of us were released from the hospital, we went home to heal.

At the time, we were living in the front house on the Faunce Reservation; the house my great-uncle Charlie had built. Grandma still lived in her little house in back, facing onto Faunce's Alley. Each morning, she would bake up one of her marvelous sour-cream coffee cakes and brew coffee in her old aluminum coffee pot. When the coffee was ready, she would knock on her bedroom window, which looked out to my kitchen. Then the children and I would walk out of our back door and take 40 steps to enjoy great coffee, delicious cake and lots of love.

It was on such a morning that I unwrapped my two-week-old son, Brett, and began to cry. The stump of Brett's navel was black, green, dead and sick all at the same time.

"Go get my sewing box," commanded my grandmother.

"Grandma! No!" I cried.

"Carole, get me my sewing box."

Grandma lit a candle and ran the blades of her big old scissors through the flame, over and over again, then she nonchalantly snipped off the dead and putrid stump, saying, "It's dead tissue. He's felt no pain. Get me the alcohol out of the bathroom cabinet."

Brett cried when the alcohol was applied. Grandma taped a clean piece of gauze over his navel, diapered him, wrapped him in his blanket and picked him up. In a few minutes, Brett was sleeping in her arms while I served up warm cake and freshly brewed coffee.

Through my years of bearing babies, my grandma taught me with time-tested wisdom and love. She never learned to drive a car or balance a checkbook, but she was keen on life, knowing more than most with an instinctual capacity for understanding every individual that entered her life. I remember her as always being there when you needed her and always with love.

By the age of 70, many little ailments had crept over my grandmother. She obeyed her three doctors and took every pill they prescribed—every day! Finally, my mother, in total vexation, emptied Grandma's medicine cabinet into a large paper bag and took it out to the trash. Grandma's health and attitude improved almost immediately but a mild form of dementia remained, like a hangover that never went away.

I was Grandma Faunce's first grandchild so she never forgot me—even on her bad days. After Dick's death, on a visit to Los Angeles, I went to see her. She opened her arms to me. I fell on my knees, burying my body in her all encompassing love.

"Dick's dead," she said philosophically.

"I know."

"You're a widow lady now."

"Yes, Grandma."

"We women live longer. We're stronger—we live longer."

Years later, my grandmother was driven back across the country she had crossed so many decades before to live out the rest of her days with her daughter Mickey and her husband. At the age 89, Grandma Faunce began her walk towards the light. Two days prior to death, she walked into Mickey's living room and looked over at an old spittoon sitting on the hearth. Thinking it to be one of her great-grandchildren she exclaimed, "Why doll-baby! Come here to Grandma."

When the spittoon didn't respond, she got somewhat peeved, "Doll-baby, come here to Grandma."

Seeing no response, Grandma Faunce went to the spittoon, picked it up and said in total disgust, "Why you're not doll-baby." Then a strange thing happened. My grandmother acted as if she could hear something and as she became intent on listening she peered deep into the foul innards of the old spittoon.

"Is that you in there, Charlie?" She asked in a loud voice, as if the sound she was listening to was far away.

Pause . . . more listening.

"Okay," she yelled into the spittoon, "I'll see you in a couple of days." Then, as if she had ended a phone conversation, she put the spittoon back in its place and went on with her day.

Two days later, while saying her prayers in Mickey's

arms, Caroline (Carrie) Jucker Faunce left us and went to join her brother Charlie, who had committed suicide several decades before.

My wonderful grandmother died in peace, with little pain and a semblance of mental alacrity. She had had a long and loving life. As with my father and husband before her, my grandma died with dignity and love. And, as said before, no one can ask for more.

So did my great-uncle Charlie visit my grandmother so as to cushion her journey?

For many years I sat on the Rush Hospice Board. Hospices, around the world, help people die with dignity and, if everyone does their job, with a sense of peace and acceptance. Most important is that the patient is relieved of pain to the best of medicine's ability.

Hospice workers and nurses deal with all kinds of death as they care for people of both sexes and all ages. Many of them witness occurrences they usually keep to themselves. In talking with a great many of them I was told of many patients talking to a deceased loved one. In one case, an Italian woman started talking to her sister, who had died some years earlier. In attendance were the woman's three daughters and a hospice nurse who had cared for the woman for several weeks.

"Mama! Who are you talking to?" asked one daughter.

"I'm talking to your aunt Paola!" said the mother of the three girls. "She's standing right there! Can't you see her?"

"No, Mama. We can't see her. There's nothing there."

In Italian, the mother told her sister that her daughters were more or less off their rockers, and then continued on to other subjects.

One of the daughters spoke fluent Italian and realized that her mother truly believed that her deceased sister was in the room. The Italian-speaking daughter had been very close to her aunt. Remembering something that had happened when she was a little girl and her aunt had taken her to the beach, she asked, "Mama? Would you ask Aunt Paola if she can remember what happened when she and I went to the beach?"

Mama asked the question, listened for a while, then turned to her daughter and told her exactly what had happened many decades before.

All stood mute in disbelief.

Mama died two days later.

I looked up from my writing pad into the face of the nurse who told me the story just related with a "You're not kidding, are you?" look on my face. Nonchalantly, she said that the story was but one of hundreds, that many dying patients tell of seeing a departed relative or of someone visiting them in a dream. After relating whatever type of occurrence they had experienced, many would add that they would be leaving soon . . . and they always did.

Over the ensuing years, I spoke with more and more people who dealt with the dying on a daily basis and came to accept the fact that many things we can't explain occur within the arena of death.

I sat at my grandmother's funeral smiling over the full life she had led, happy that she had been a part of my experience, glad that she had gone so peacefully. No pain, no tubes or machines, just a natural passing.

As the funeral service progressed, my mind wandered, taking me back three years to Houston. Dick and I had joined his family there in order to stand by while his mother was operated on for an aortic aneurysm. Normally, an aneurysm can be operated on and the patient can return to health, but my mother-in-law was in her eighties and had been knocking on death's door for close to 50 years. She had been in Houston previously when she had received some of the first Dacron arteries from Dr. Michael DeBakey, who was once again in attendance. At that time, the doctors thought the new arteries would last 10 years or so. Now, 28 years later, after running the life of others from her daybed, she was about to undergo an operation that was imperative, yet would probably end her life. The situation was a total catch-22. The doctors were damned if they did and damned if they didn't. The one thing they knew for certain was that if they didn't fix the bulging aneurysm, my mother in-law would die. They had to operate.

On the night prior to operating, the doctors met us in my mother-in-law's room on the top floor of the Houston Medical Center. They were not hopeful. In hushed tones, they let us know that this would probably be her last night. My mother-in-law, though sedated, heard it all and claimed she didn't care.

That night, when we got back to our hotel room, I told Dick (himself in the process of dying of cancer) that his mother was going to pull through.

"You're out of your mind. Didn't you hear the doctors!? Even DeBakey was drawing his hand across his throat." Dick was exaggerating, but the words had been pretty fatalistic.

"I know it looks grim, but I know she's going to pull through."

"You're crazy."

"Look, you once teased that I was a witch and lately you've been pooh-poohing me when I say I knew that was going to happen after the fact. Well, this time I'm giving you fair warning. Your mother is going to make it through this surgery and go on living for many years."

The next day, six of us sat in one of the large waiting rooms reserved for the families of patients undergoing surgery. The room, which sat about a hundred people, was standing room only.

The family had found a group of seats in a corner. We sat for hours, each with his own thoughts. I sat calmly, knowing that my mother-in-law was our bionic woman, the woman I had referred to as the iron lady and the alien. Even a tough surgery couldn't get the best of this woman. I knew she would pull through regardless of the odds. Her inner strength was phenomenal.

With my sense of security, boredom set in and I looked around at the members of her family. They were all deep in thought and their thoughts were quite visible. What were they going to do once she was gone? How soon could they hold the funeral? They would have to ship her body back to Los Angeles. What was Dick's father going to do? I watched as worries, funeral arrangements, eulogies and inheritances danced in their heads.

When our last name was called, the family was so deep in thought, they didn't respond. When they heard it called again, they awoke from their reveries, but seemed unable to react. I offered encouragement, "Come on everyone. We should go up and talk to the doctor." They looked at me and slowly rose, following me to where doctors give you the good or bad news.

The doctor was beaming, "I can't believe that woman. None of us gave her any chance at all, but she fooled us. She came through like a champ." I smiled, expecting tears of gratitude and relief from my husband's family, but they had believed the doctors and had already buried her in their minds. I prompted them, "Isn't it wonderful? I told you she would make it." The shock wore off, smiles replaced grieving frowns; the group became joyous, animated . . . and hungry. We went to lunch.

My mother-in-law lived for many more years, dying four years and three months after the death of her only son. She went peacefully in her sleep after consuming a large portion of strawberry shortcake and a cup of tea.

I came back from the land of memories and found myself still seated in my grandmother's church on the day of her funeral. The young minister was telling us how wonderful she had been. The words weren't right; he hadn't known her. At the beginning of the service, he had asked that anyone who wished to speak do so after the initial sermon. I did so. It was easy. Easy to get up and voice what everyone in the church (save for the poor minister) already knew. My grandma had been an innately wise woman; a great big bundle of love who often commented that our loved ones and friends are only loaned to us and we to them. Forrest Gump's mother told her son that death was a part of life, while Garp's mother looked out over the Atlantic and said, "We all die. The thing is to have a life before we go."

MY MOTHER CAROLINE

A female is far more receptive to sexual advances when ovulating than at other times of the month. Once pregnant, the brain cascades her body with chemicals that code for mothering. At other times, chemicals of depression can take hold.

Following Dick's death, the ranch, science symposia and a paleoanthropological dig kept my mind occupied and I began to heal. My mother did just the opposite following the death of my father. She and Daddy had known he couldn't go on indefinitely, yet never once had they spoken of death. Never once did they voice their fears or share their tears. Instead, they had lived in a sea of denial and when Daddy pulled the plug Mom simply couldn't see the rightness of it; in her mind, her man was walking out on her.

Looking back at my mother during the years following my father's death, it is hard to believe she was the same person who had raised me. I have to think back to the wonderful, loving wife and mother she had been for decades; the helpmate, entertainer, and dance partner, the person who had loved horses, the beach and water, the one who, in her youth, loved to swim all the way around the original Santa Monica Pier, the girl who, in high school, borrowed a boyfriend's four-foot garter snake and wore it home wrapped around her neck, causing Grandma Faunce to pass out cold (ladies used to do that—it wasn't uncommon).

As time went by, I had to force myself to remember the woman who taught our Camp Fire troop how to sing as she drove us all to camp:

> Skidda-mer-rink a dink a dink, skidda-mer-rink a do
> We love you.
> Skidda-mer-rink a dink a dink, skidda-mer-rink a do
> We love you.
> We love you in the morning and in the afternoon,
> We love you in the evening and underneath the moon.
> Oh, skidda-mer-rink a dink a dink, skidda-mer-rink a do,
> We LOOOOVE you.

At the age of eighteen and seven months, Caroline swallowed the castor oil and quinine her doctor had ordered to induce labor, kicked her right leg over her head—grazing the chandelier in her parents' living room—winked at her father, told him she had never felt better in her life and then allowed him to drive her to the hospital where I soon came forth into the light of day. But the doctor had hastened the delivery so that he could go fishing and, as soon as the cord was tied and he had discerned that I was in good condition, he turned the situation over to his attendants and headed north to a favored trout stream. Thanks to her mother's advice and wisdom, my mother miraculously recovered from a horrid case of blood poisoning to be my mother, mentor and friend.

Caroline Faunce Andersen was a marvelous person, a magnificent mother, and without a doubt, the most truthful person I have ever known. But after Daddy died, I had to struggle to remember the good as she began to slip away before our eyes. On the day of my father's death, Mom went from a state of numbing shock into a harsh depression. We put it to the fact that Daddy had been the only man she had ever known—the fact that he had been her everything. And then there was her bad back of many, many years . . . and the bourbon she drank to ease the pain. Many thought little of her drinking. She had always handled it extremely well and never drank until evening. The only time I can remember my mother being visibly drunk was the Christmas Eve she threw herself into the trash box. It was a great flying leap that landed her ass first into the huge carton box filled with discarded Christmas wrap. It was hilarious. She brought the house down with laughter.

Now the laughter had subsided and her depression weighed upon us all. I had stayed with Mom for a month after Daddy's death. Then I returned to Dick and his cancer. From a distance, I pushed and shoved, and with the help of one of her sisters, we got Mom to a psychologist. Four sessions later she quit. "That girl's too young to know anything. She doesn't understand. Your father and I had a love that few people ever know."

I knew Mom was skirting the hard issues, knew she was afraid to look within, knew she was too miserable to help herself.

As depressed as my mother was, she still went to work every day. She claimed she couldn't live without her work. Rather than grief, she tended to show anger and resentment over my father's death. In her anger, she stripped the house of many of my father's things, giving precious heirlooms to strangers. Mom's distribution of my father's things, coupled with her violent response to his death, distressed both me and my children. It was not only unfeeling and cruel, especially for my children, but was completely out of character. Mom had always handled the deaths of friends and relatives better than most.

Mom had wanted to be a nurse, but the Great Depression had kept her from advanced studies. Of course, that didn't change who she perceived herself to be, and throughout her years she played nurse to family, friends and customers. And she was pretty good at it.

One particular customer stands out from her ranks of patients. His name was Jeff. He had been an ace test pilot until he crashed his Porsche in the desert. The doctors saved Jeff, but he had to live as a quadriplegic strapped into a wheelchair, cared for by others.

We all made friends with Jeff, but Mother became his mentor. One day, Jeff used the one finger on his left hand that he could move at will and rolled his wheelchair and himself into a swimming pool and drowned. His mother met his body at UCLA emergency. When a doctor looked at her and shook his head, Jeff's mother began beating violently and repeatedly on Jeff's chest, screaming at him not to die on her. Jeff returned from the dead, but refused ever to see or speak with his mother from that day forth.

My mother—the pseudo-nurse—spent hours with Jeff, helping him along his bumpy road. After each visit with Jeff, she would quietly call his mother to report Jeff's condition. Then my mother, who never attended church, asked Jeff if he had read the Bible. "No," said Jeff.

Three weeks passed. Jeff called to thank Mom for her suggestion. He said reading the Bible had helped him to put himself back together emotionally. Weeks later, Jeff called again to say that he had read the Bible for a second time and that he had called his mother.

A week after the second call, the phone rang again. This time it wasn't Jeff, but a caller telling us that Jeff had again rolled his wheelchair and himself into another pool. This time he had the found the release he sought.

I cried. Mom hugged me and soothed, "It's all right. He's all right. It wasn't right the first time. He wasn't truly ready that time, but now it's all right. Jeff was never meant to spend his life in a wheelchair. He's all right now."

How could a woman of such understanding and total compassion fail so miserably in connection with her own husband's death?

The children and I discussed Mom at length and called her continuously. Meanwhile, Dick was dying. True to her beliefs, Mom didn't attend Dick's funeral. On some level, I understood. Mom had always stood by her convictions.

Shortly after Dick's death, Mom became excessively paranoid and announced she could no longer go home to an empty house. No, she didn't want to move to Jackson. No, she didn't want me moving in with her, but she couldn't be alone and that was that.

That's when my right-wing mother hired "Katrina," an illegal alien from a communist bloc country who agreed to live in the luxury of my mother's home five days and five nights a week for an exorbitant sum.

Katrina was a compulsive liar and showed open hatred towards me and the children. The entire episode became a classic scene out of a two-bit novel. For the weekends, Mom hired a fellow widow to stay with her. Her name was Julie and she was a sweet and caring person.

My daughter Kim had weathered the deadly storms that had swirled through our family with courage and wisdom. She had been remarkable throughout my father's death and even more so when Dick lay dying, always there to talk with, philosophize with and laugh with. No matter how down we were, no matter what the situation, Kim could bring forth a good thought and laughter. But now, even she could find little to laugh over in the matter of her G-mom, a name she had given my mother when she was a toddler.

I had Kim at a tender age and when my Romeo and I divorced, Kim and I lived with Mom and Dad until Romeo and I remarried. During those interim years, I ran the family's restaurant at night while Mom and Dad cared for Kim. They loved it. Kim was their smart and shining jewel. From the age of three months to the age of three years, Kim had a second Mom, her "G-mom." Over the years, Mom and Kim developed a deep and abiding love. Mom was more upset when Kim moved to Wyoming in '81 than when Dick, I and the boys moved in '75. Their love was beyond measure.

On the morning of April 22, 1986, Kim awoke with the dawn on the floor of a desert canyon in southern Utah where she and her boyfriend, Gerry, were camping. Closing her eyes, she reached back for the land of Nod, but her eyes opened wide as a feeling of agitation and restlessness filled her and thoughts of her G-mom pressed in on her from all sides. As quietly as possible, she eased herself out of her sleeping bag and struggled into her sweats, tennis shoes and jacket. As Gerry slept, Kim sat atop a large rock thinking about her grandmother. Hour gave way to hour, yet thoughts of her grandmother continued to stream through her mind. When Gerry finally climbed out of the sack, Kim was still perched on her rock.

"We've got to figure out a way to go down and see my grandmother, okay?"

On that same April morn, I awoke shortly before eight. I was in Los Angeles for the week, staying with Jim, an old friend of the family's. I would have stayed with Mom, but Katrina had taken over both my old bedroom and the middle bedroom of Mother's home. We all made jokes about it, but it really wasn't all that funny.

I awoke with suddenness and bolted out of bed. Dazed from sleep, I found myself standing in the middle of the bedroom wondering what the hell I was doing there.

Mom flooded my mind. "I'll call her," I thought, and started walking towards the phone. Something stopped me. As surely as if someone had physically moved me away from the phone, my thoughts were reversed in an instant. In a state of confusion, I told myself that if I called Mom I might awaken Jim. This, of course, was ridiculous on two counts. One, it was time to get up, and two, I could have gone downstairs to make my call.

As soon as my mind switched course, I walked back to bed, got in and closed my eyes. But rather than sleep, my brain reeled with complex images and thoughts of my mother. I was so worried about her. She had pretty much taken herself to bed three months prior with her bad back and ever-deepening depression. The same lingering depression that had started three years before when my father had died in May of '83.

Soon my mind was replaying the talk I'd had with Mom the day before. After hellos and hugs, I brought her pet parrot in to see her. The two of them had a real love affair going. The parrot went crazy with sounds and cluckings over getting the chance to be with his mistress.

"My God, Mom, Katrina might be afraid of the bird, but she could at least wheel him into you on his cart. Doesn't she know he can't bite her through the cage?"

"Oh well, we all do the best we can around here. . . . This poor bird—remember when Daddy was sick and stuck back here in the bedroom while I was at work? He didn't want the parrot in here and the bird would go nuts, screaming and calling all day long because he wanted to be with your father. Daddy kept saying he just couldn't stand it anymore, so I said I would sell the bird."

Mother continued with a long dialogue about her efforts to find a home for the parrot. She told of those she had contacted and which one she thought would be the best person to take on the responsibility of her feathered friend. As she talked, I noticed that for the first time in years my mother was talking and acting as her old self, the Caroline everyone loved and admired, the Caroline you could always rely on, the one who could outwork, out-sing and out-dance everyone else. I delighted not in her words, all of which I had heard before, but in her attitude and normalcy. Rationalizing, I attributed the change to the fact that she had sent Katrina away on a paid vacation and wasn't having to deal with her for a week, or possibly she was finally coming out of her depression . . . surely it was time.

Mom came to the end of her long story detailing what should be done with the parrot should she die before him—then she looked deep into my eyes and said, "You know, if anything should ever happen to me, everyone would understand except this dumb bird. He's too damn stupid."

We laughed in unison as my heart warmed at the naturalness that showed in my mother's eyes, but while my laughter was for real my mind pained at her obvious reference to her own demise.

Jim's phone rang. The time was 8:35 AM. Jim leapt out of bed, walked to the phone on motor-muscle control, then tried to sound awake as he gave a big "Hello" into the receiver.

I had also leapt out of bed and now watched as Jim's face twisted and paled. His eyes darting with emotion, he said, "Here, you'd better speak with Carole."

It was Mom's restaurant manager. The restaurant had been the only number Julie had been able to think of. The woman's voice was rough with emotion, "Carole, there's been an accident at your mother's house. I think she's shot herself."

"I'll be right there."

The adrenaline ran through me with incredible speed. I drove. I needed to drive. I couldn't let my mind think on an emotional level. I told Jim that if we saw an ambulance coming out of the Bel Air gate, we'd follow it to the UCLA University Hospital.

No ambulance.

On our way up the canyon, I said, "If she has shot herself in the head I pray she's gone and never felt anything."

Shock and disbelief make for dumb statements—where else would one shoot oneself?

Parked at my mother's house were two ambulances, two fire trucks and a police car. I parked across the street and ran the obstacle course through the maze of vehicles and in the front door. The neighbor ladies from either side were there, pale, drawn and tearful. They had been Mother's neighbors for more than 30 years. With wide eyes I ran past them and darted around the corner and down the hall towards my mother's bedroom. Halfway down the hall, a huge paramedic blocked my way. His massive hands took hold of my upper arms as I tried to push past him.

"I'm the daughter. I have to get to my mother."

"No. I'm sorry, you can't go in." The man's voice vibrated through me, low, calm and strong.

"I must go to my mother," I cried.

As I spoke, the man gently, but forcibly walked me backwards, back down the hall I had raced up just seconds before. I believe he had lifted me so that my shoes were riding atop his, but I couldn't swear to it. "I'm sorry, but you can't go into the room just now." He said in a firm but gentle manner.

By this time, he had me back out in the front entry where the neighbors stood with sunken heads and downcast eyes. There, too, was Jim, waiting for me. The paramedic was still holding onto me. I looked up at him, "Can you at least tell me where she shot herself?" I asked, still in denial and ever deeper in shock.

"In the head," the man said.

"Oh God, then I hope she's gone."

"She's gone. It's all over."

The paramedic released my slumping body into the waiting arms of Jim, who laid me down in a chair. I didn't pass out, but lost all control of my body.

"HOW COULD SHE DO THAT???????!!!!"

The words screeched out of me as my thoughts swam in a sea of disbelief and excruciating pain. The pain was paralyzing. Then, slowly, thoughts for Mom, rather than against her, came to me. No more anger at Daddy for dying. No more bouts of terror from paranoia. No more loneliness or twisted thoughts or paralyzing days due to depression. But how could she put a gun to her head and . . .

Mom had said to my father as far back as I could remember, "I get to die first because I couldn't live without you." And my father would say, "Mama, don't be silly, I'm 15 years older than you are." And Mom would say, "I don't care. I'm dying first."

Funny how I had never thought of what a strange statement that was for a happily married woman to make. Now I knew she had meant what she had said so many times. To her, it must have seemed that Daddy had died and left her trapped in her living form, lost and afraid. If you looked back closely, you could see that in reality she had died with him. Surely, the Caroline of the last three years had been a tragic stranger to us all.

I remembered her bright, normal-looking eyes of the day before, "If anything should happen to me, everyone would understand."

Bitter tears streaked my cheeks as my heart went past the realm of pain and sought the solace of numbness.

THE LAW

The detectives arrived in an old beat-up car. Detective Supervisor de Anda was right out of the best of pulpy paperbacks. He was good-looking, calm, and polite with antennae tuned in all directions.

While his partner headed down the hall towards Mother's bedroom, de Anda started asking questions, mostly of poor Julie, who was a basket case.

I explained that Julie couldn't possibly have had anything to do with Mother's death and that my mother's bad back had been enhanced by the horrid depression that had set in following my father's death. De Anda nodded in recognition of a familiar tale and turned to Julie, asking her to tell him what she could.

"Well, last night I fixed her fried chicken and you know, she had just started letting us cook for her, and she told me that it was the finest chicken she had ever eaten. She even ate more than she's eaten in a long time. After dinner, I helped her into the shower. She sat there on her shower seat and scrubbed her hair and just had the best time. I stood right by, just in case. It was the first real shower she had taken in more than three weeks. I was so thrilled for her. I knew it had to feel just as good as she said it did.

"Then some time after she was back in bed and she asked me how I prayed. You know, I'm a southern Baptist, just an old holy roller and I just told her that I just talk to God. I know he can hear me no matter how I talk to him and I just tell him everything. I told her to just talk to him. She said she always said the Lord's Prayer before going to sleep and I told her that was just fine.

"Then this morning, when she got up to go to the bathroom, her back slipped out again and she cried like a baby. She had been in so much pain for so long and I just hurt all over for her. She said she just couldn't take it any more. I got her back into bed and she seemed all right. She even ate her cereal, drank her milk and took her vitamin pill with her grapefruit juice—just like any other morning. Then she read the funnies, just like always. I think it was about 8:15 when I thought I heard a noise and went back to the bedroom. She was getting back into bed and seemed quite upset. I asked her what in the world she was doing up. She said she had had to get something out of the desk. I got really mad at her and told her she could have called me. Heavens, that's what I'm here for. I don't remember what we said after that, just little things and then I took her dishes and came out here to wash up. It was just a few minutes after that. . . . I was standing at the sink washing the breakfast dishes when I heard a bang. It wasn't very loud. I thought the dog had run through the house and knocked over a lamp. I dried my hands and went looking through the house to see what had fallen."

Looking over at me, Julie continued, "Your mom often fell back asleep after reading the paper so when I looked down the hall into her bedroom I just thought she was asleep. I'd seen her sleep with her head back and mouth open before and I just thought she was asleep, I'm sorry. After I finished the dishes, I had this strange feeling and wondered why Caroline hadn't called about the noise, so I went back to her bedroom. When I went in, I still thought she was asleep. I didn't even notice the blood and mess on the table, bed and rug, but then I saw the gun in her hand. (Here Julie broke down completely.) I did the most stupid thing. I took the gun out of her hand, away from her so she couldn't hurt herself. Sir, I know that was stupid, but I didn't know what to do. I didn't do it, but now my fingerprints are all over the gun."

Poor Julie wept with fear, confusion and pain. She had truly loved my mother and had always been kind to her. I felt so sorry for her. She was out of a job, and had lost her meal ticket to the horrors of a suicide while serving in the capacity of caregiver to the deceased. Guilt clung to her like a wet blanket. I went to her and hugged her as I tried to reassure her that it wasn't her fault.

De Anda stepped in, "I want both of you women to know something. I deal with at least a dozen suicides per month. There's nothing either of you could have done. Your mother's suicide had nothing to do with you. If you had sat by her side every minute of every day for a year and then left the room for 15 minutes the result would have been the same. From what you have told me of her condition since your father's death, I can assure you that what your mother did had nothing to do with you."

The doorbell rang. It seemed a horrid intrusion. It was Inger, one of our longtime employees. The day before, Mom had arranged for her to stop by on her way to work to pick up the dog and take her to the groomers. It was a new dog; the last one had followed my father to the grave. Mom knew the dog would be given back to her nephew, Alan, who had trained it. And Mom knew Alan hated un-trimmed schnauzers.

As Inger was leaving, Julie said Mom had also arranged for the Gloria House Cleaners to clean the house on Thursday. Mom hadn't used the Gloria House Cleaners since she had hired her live-ins.

In Mom's purse was an envelope with the words, "For Julie," scrawled across it. They were the last words my mother ever wrote. To this day, I can't look at the handwriting on that envelope. You don't have to be a handwriting expert to know that within five minutes' time the pen was going to be replaced with a gun.

The envelope contained two weeks' pay—in cash. Mother was always taking care of other people.

The coroner arrived with his modern-day wagon. (It wasn't white, but still rather funny looking.) Prior to his arrival, I had asked the detective if I could go and get something out of my mother's bathroom. He answered in the affirmative.

I headed down the hall, my head hung low, then for some reason I raised it. There was Mom, her head tilted back, mouth open. She really didn't look too bad from a distance and what I could see of her, but her hand—her right hand—was hanging down from beneath the sheet. It was white and ghostly. There was something about her hand that was unbearably painful to look at. I stood transfixed, my stomach knotting.

The other detective appeared in the doorway of mother's room. He looked at me, "Oh, I'm sorry, I thought I'd shut this," he said, as he gently closed the door.

Detective de Anda asked if he could do anything for me while we waited for the due process of the law. (Only now do I realize that in some government file there are pictures of my mother from all angles, plus pictures of the gun. After all, committing suicide is a crime and, at the time of my mother's suicide, treated as such. My mother hated having her picture taken.) I told de Anda that I would rather not see them take Mother's body from the house. That seeing my great-grandfather, my father and my husband carried out had been bearable;

this wasn't. The detective left for a minute, then returned, shutting all doors and curtains into the kitchen area where we sat, stood, paced and spoke as we consumed one pot of coffee after another.

Twenty minutes later, I asked when he thought they would be taking her out. "They've already left. They'll release her body from the morgue in three days."

They must have carried Mom out as there had been no sound of wheels, let alone footsteps, and they must have simply released the brake on the coroner's wagon, then started the engine someplace down the canyon as there had been no sound of a motor starting up.

When everyone had left, Jim went back to Mother's bedroom. When he came back he was pale. He ordered a bucket of water, rubber gloves and a stack of rags. Then he ordered me to stay put and not to move until he said so. It took him an hour to clean up the remains. He brought out the linens. They were very fine linens. "These are going in the trash, as is the mattress." He looked at me, reading my thoughts as they crossed my face. "Forget it," he said, "even the poorest man doesn't need these."

I helped Jim carry out the king-size mattress and box springs as Julie stood by crying. She was too old for such burdens; her tears were heavy enough. As we set the bloodstained mattress among the garbage cans, I looked at Jim and said, "She knew it was trash day tomorrow. She thought of everything."

With humor and sorrow, Jim replied, "If I'd known 30 years ago that one day I'd have to clean up your mother's brains, I never would have shaken her hand."

In Mom's bedroom, on her desk, sat the books and ledgers from the business. When I picked them up, the fold-down desktop was absolutely clear except for an old manila file folder. In her own way, Mom had left me a letter. A letter that asked me to remember her as she had been, not as she had become. Inside the folder was an old college paper done by a psychology student. The subject was a family, our family. The young student had used us as a model family, using me as her focal point.

I sat on the floor, now empty and spacious without the bed, and read the paper through. Even in my anguish, I laughed as I read about a 12-year-old me, realizing that I still carried the same faults I had brandished about at the age of 12. Towards the end of the paper, the psychology student wrote her analysis of my parents. She concentrated on my mother, whom she categorized as a loving, devoted parent with an uncommon sense of fairness and openness about her. She told of how my mother always took the time to explain things to me, how she rarely scolded me but sat down and talked things over with me, always giving me the opportunity of changing my ways. She noted that I was asked to sit in on all family discussions, including those concerning the business and that for a 12-year-old I seemed very comfortable with serious matters.

The psychology student had put down in black and white what I had always known: my mother had treated me as an adult, supported me in every way and loved me completely.

I closed the file, tears dripping from my chin. Throughout the year prior to her death, my mother had never called me without singing, "I just called to say I love you," instead of saying the usual "hello." I got up from the floor and replaced the file folder in the desk. In one of the left-hand cubbyholes lay the holster of a gun.

A man called from the morgue. He represented an organ donation group. Mother's corneas were still intact, still capable of giving someone the gift of sight. "She would love it," I sobbed, knowing the truth of my words. "She always carried her little card with her. She would be so honored, so pleased."

The man asked me to answer questions that would be recorded since there wasn't time for signatures through the mails. I answered the questions, hung up and wept. Mom was still playing nurse, still helping the sick and handicapped. Even in death, she was going to help someone.

I called Mom's doctor, Dr. David, the one who had so revered my father, the one who had tried so hard to help mother in her grief.

"Carole, I can't tell you how sorry I am, but I can't say I'm surprised. I think she's thought of this since the day your father died. I've never had a patient who so wanted to die. That last CAT scan proved there was no hope of her dying soon of natural causes. For all she drank and all she smoked, she had the strongest heart and cleanest lungs I've ever seen. You know we all tried, and I know how hard you tried. Bless you."

I called the doctor who had given Mom the CAT scan, the last doctor to see her. "God, I'm sorry. I really liked your mom, she was a hell of a gal. Sure could see the depression though. The first day she walked into my office I could read it."

The doctor and I talked. I wasn't going to try and hide this from close friends. I felt that with half the city's police and fire department parked in front of the house, a lie wouldn't cover much. A gunshot reverberates through a neighborhood rapidly. The truth is always the easiest.

The doctor warmed up to me when he realized I wasn't going for the usual, "Mom had a heart attack," routine. We talked some more. One of his final statements to me was, "I'll tell you something. Your jaw would fall if you ever found out how many people do this. Everyday, doctors write down 'heart attack' or 'stroke' or 'undetermined' and allow the family to dispose of the medicine bottle. You wouldn't believe the numbers."

In Mom's case, there were no medicine bottles.

Months later, I admitted the circumstances of my mother's death to an old friend. He bowed his head and stood in silence for some time, then he looked out to the far horizon and said, "My mother did the same, but with pills. It was easy to say it was her heart. I'm still not over it."

I too studied the horizon. "You haven't lied," I said. "They both died of the heart."

With four deaths in just under three years, I had experienced great emotional pain, but nothing came close to the horror of having to tell my three children about their grandmother. There is no way I can describe the pain, the hurt, the gut-wrenching agony of hearing their voices, their screams, the rending of their minds.

It was two days before I could reach Kim, just back from her camping trip. Her croaking screams of anguish, her mind-bending cries of despair shattered me beyond all explanation. Through her pain, she choked out the telepathic/psychic feelings she had experienced on the morning of Mom's death. Then she lamented in wailing tones, "Why couldn't she have waited for me? She didn't even wait for me to give her a great-grand baby!"

For months, I was afraid of sleep, afraid of dreaming the vision of Mom putting the gun to her head, but the vision never haunted my sleep. Instead, it would run before my eyes as I traveled down Sunset Boulevard each morning on my way to Mother's work. I have always felt that everyone in Los Angeles drives alone because the exclusive confines of their car offers them the only place they ever get to be completely alone with their thoughts—the reflections of their minds. Now, alone in my car, I screamed over the realities of my life.

As it turned out, there had been no need to fear the night. All (the entire family) of our dreams about my mother were good dreams, but for one. Months after Mom's death, Kim had a dream in which she felt Mom's pain, loneliness, fear, anxiety and despair. She awoke crying and shaking from having stood for a mental moment in her grandmother's moccasins.

SUICIDE

A ccording to official statistics, a million people a year commit suicide, a number that exceeds those murdered or killed in war. Data show that suicides in the United States outnumber homicides by nearly two to one and rank as the eleventh leading cause of death in the country.

Kim booked flights to Los Angeles. On the final leg of her journey, she met a young woman (I will call her Angel), from Washington, D.C.; an artist like Kim. It was obvious to Angel that Kim was under considerable distress and soon the two young women were talking. As Kim told of her grandmother's suicide, Angel showed great empathy. She herself had attempted suicide after learning that the love of her life had four other "loves," all with the same first name, and that for each of the five he had purchased identical diamond necklaces and many other enticements. On the day of Angel's attempted suicide, an old roommate happened into town. Seeing Angel's car in the carport, she went up for a surprise visit. When there was no answer to her knocks, she decided to leave Angel a note; by using her old key, she let herself in. Finding Angel comatose, she rushed her to a hospital where she was saved.

"When I awoke, there were two policemen standing by to arrest me for attempted suicide. If not for my mother, I would have been placed in a horrid, state-run mental hospital for a term of one year." Kim listened, clinging to Angel's words. "I think you need to know that when I tried to kill myself, I had no thought whatsoever of anyone but myself. Nobody loves their family more than I do, and I love life and my friends, but they had nothing to do with my desire to stop living. The only things running through my mind were the unbearable pain and humiliation that were annihilating me. It was pure luck that my friend came by that day, that she hadn't taken the key off her key ring, and that she found me in time. Of course, now I'm forever grateful that she found me."

Suicide has shattered the framework of many families. As written in the introduction, this book was begun many years ago. Over those years, I have shared my life with others; in many instances, doing so has opened long locked doors. A year ago, a friend of mine read parts of this book. When she got to the part above where I detail Mother's suicide, she pasted a sticky note over my comment, "Where else would one shoot oneself?" The sticky note read, "In the chest, the way my dad did." I stand humbly corrected.

Who was the first suicide? And how did the act affect those around him?

From archaeological evidence found in a cave in the Burgos Mountains of Spain, dated at 300,000 years ago, shows that man cared enough about others of his own kind to bury his dead, but what about a suicide? Was the act of killing yourself taboo from the beginning? And who was the first suicide? Was she a rejected woman? A man who'd failed his troop? A terrified boy, unable to bear the difficulty and pain of initiation? Did they leap, drown, allow a poisonous snake or spider to help them on their way or did they consume poisonous mushrooms? Perhaps it was an old man, racked with cancer who calmly walked out into the night to go peacefully through the oblivion of hypothermia, or in warmer climes, walk to the place of the lion, the leopard or crocodile.

When all peoples of the earth lived in small nomadic bands that followed migrating herds and traveled to various areas where specific foodstuffs were seasonally available, there was no way of transporting the frail or dying. In most cases, the elderly, wounded or infirm gave the sign to be left by the trail, and in areas where wolves, hyenas, wild dogs, bears or large cats were about, the person was killed so as not to be attacked and devoured prior to death.

Naturalist Margaret Murie, the late grande dame of the Tetons, told me of a poignant occurrence attended by her deceased husband, anthropologist Olaus Murie, on the isle of St. Lawrence. Olaus lived with and studied the St. Lawrence Eskimos in the early 1900s, learning their language, their myths and their ways. His adventures set some old beliefs on their heels.

The evening meal had been prepared and all had gathered to eat, but the old woman was unable to partake, even though her daughter-in-law had chewed the seal meat and blubber for her before depositing it in her bowl. When mealtime was over and all were back to their separate projects of making clothes, carving ivory, working with leather or making rope and tools, the old woman signaled to her son. "It's time," she said. Carefully and calmly, the old woman's son donned his parka and lifted her fragile frame in his arms, then walked from their hut into the cool night air. He looked straight ahead as he ascended a glacial moraine that ran along the back of the community. Midway up the slope, there was a shelf-like depression and it was here that he laid his mother down, said goodbye, then quickly and deftly strangled her.

Suicide? Murder? Altruism? Strength? Courage? Necessity? Reality?

Yes, and yet again, yes.

Within some African tribes where suicide is considered taboo, family members are deathly afraid of touching the body of a suicide for fear of contamination or contagion as they believe that contact with the corpse will cause further suicides to occur within the family. And should a man hang himself from a tree, his body is disposed of far from his village, the tree is burned to the ground and the place of the tree becomes taboo until the memory of the man has been lost. Within such tribes, the family of the suicide is shunned as it is believed that suicide is contagious. Modern studies of modern peoples tell us that those touched by the suicide of a close relative have a greater statistical chance of committing suicide. As with all things in life, it is about what you have been taught to believe. If your brother commits suicide when you are 12, and your tribe shuns your family, looks down on you, and treats you as a contagious person, the psychological possibility of you committing suicide will be greatly enhanced. The same holds true in modern societies, where major religions will not allow the body of a suicide to be buried in consecrated ground or receive the benefit of formalities performed by a person of the "cloth." The loss of face and self-worth can foment sad statistics.

On the Pacific island of Tikopia, suicide at sea was condoned. If a man paddled out to sea never to return, or if a woman swam out past the reef where ocean currents would sweep her away, the act was accepted in good grace. But should a person hang himself on land, it was considered the worst possible offense. Obviously, the Tikopians didn't like dealing with the body. It was all right to leave, so long as you took your body with you.

Suicide wears many faces: the soldier who falls on a live grenade gives his life for his brothers in arms while performing an extreme act of altruism. Such sacrifices are commended and rewarded by all societies as being true acts of altruism. But then there are works of poetry, plays, myths and myriad books that speak well of those who have destroyed themselves as a consequence of unrequited love. Mohammed held such deaths to be the most beautiful, especially if the lover took his or her own life as opposed to simply pining away. Through psychological studies and research on brain chemistry, it has been well established that grievous despair brings on a cascade of chemicals that spirals the brain into a pit in which suicide can often be found sitting in the corner. There is no romance or beauty in that, only the futile loss of someone who loved another. My mother was such a someone, as was the girl Kim met on the plane.

One day, as I sat working at my mother's desk, a woman stopped and bluntly announced to me, "Suicide is the most selfish act known to man." Then she strode into the ladies' room leaving me sitting dumbfounded by her audacity and lack of tack. However, her words prompted me to do what I have always done with anything that bothers my mind—I studied it.

Going past my earlier anthropological readings, I soon found that from the time of the earliest writings, suicide has either been culturally accepted, ordered as punishment for a crime, or outlawed. In the case of ordered punishment, the guilty party was not executed by the "state" but by his own hand. Four hundred years before Christ, Socrates wrote that a person's life was the property of the gods, and therefore an individual did not have the right to take that which belonged to the gods. Ironically, he himself was accused of impiety and forced to take his own life by drinking hemlock.

Today, more than 12 centuries after the Catholic Church made suicide a cardinal sin, the old and borrowed religious law has become public law, and in most states, it's against the law to take your own life. Should you fail in an attempt, they won't take you to jail, but they can commit you to a psych ward if they choose to. In other words, not only your life, but your death as well, is ruled by your government; they are not your own.

The Norse god Odin found runic wisdom by hanging himself. What was the thinking behind such an act? Was it an early act of self-inflicted asphyxiation, as performed by teenagers of today when they hang themselves in order to experience a mind-bending sensation, only to end up hanging themselves by mistake? Why does the legend say that in hanging himself Odin found wisdom? What wisdom?

Through the myth of Odin's suicide came a law that demanded the hanging of all sacrifices made in his honor. More than a millennium later, Hitler would delve into the Nordic mythologies and use Odin (Wotan in Germany) as an example of self-sacrifice for his special forces, who vowed to fight to the death in defense of der Führer and the Fatherland.

The Greek leader Epicurus encouraged suicide when life failed to offer happiness, while the Romans offered technicians trained to assist clients who desired to die. For many centuries, one could go before the senate, state his reason for wishing to end his life, and more often than not, be given a written prescription for poison. The same senate would, like the Greeks before them, condemn a person to death via his own hand. Later, when slaves took to suicide rather than serving their masters, the Romans outlawed the act, as all things commercial are safeguarded within all societies.

In ancient Egypt suicide was viewed as a respectable way of ending unbearable physical or emotional suffering. Likewise, martyrdom was condoned.

During the early years of Christianity, when the vast majority of new Christians were Jews who had accepted Christ as the chosen one, a self-chosen death was looked upon as being pious. But in time the number of Christian martyrs, mass murders and suicides rose to the point that the ruling Jewish faction forbade eulogies and public mourning for those who took their own lives. And it was Jewish leaders who first refused burial of suicides in hallowed ground.

Later, St. Augustine in the fourth century AD denounced suicide to all Christians. The Council of Guadix, in AD 305, purged the names of those who had taken their own lives from the list of martyrs while other councils came up with every conceivable reason for condemnation. Then, in the eighth century, the plague swept across Europe, killing millions. People, burdened with grief, coupled with the real possibility of dying, began taking their own lives. Between those lost to the plague and those taking their own lives, whole towns were threatened with extinction. That's when the Catholic Church took a phrase from the Koran that reads, "suicide is worse than homicide," and made suicide a cardinal sin—even though five people in the Bible commit suicide without condemnation. The borrowed religious law against suicide was passed and ordained, but people continued in their self-destruction. And that's when church leaders began taking the corpses of suicide victims, stripping them and hanging them in the square where they were mutilated for their "sin." And that's when the suicides of the eighth century began to taper off.

The Japanese outlawed seppuku (ritual suicide) in 1868, but the practice continued and is still seen by some as being honorable. However, common suicide has never been technically outlawed and is still considered a demonstration of courage and self-sacrifice, which is why an outcry went up when a California court put a Japanese mother on trial for murder. Her husband had betrayed her and abandoned her. Having been totally dishonored, the woman did what would have been accepted in her native country. She took her two small children and walked into the ocean to end their lives as well as her own. Unfortunately, the children had already drowned when a beach boy spotted her as she was going under, dove through the waves and rescued the mother.

One must weep for the woman who had lost everything: her honor, which to a Japanese equals life itself; her children; and her right to die. Guarded against her own hand, she was judged by a foreign culture she couldn't comprehend, which in turn, was incapable of understanding hers.

Following the death of the Japanese emperor in 1912, General Nogi and his wife killed themselves ritualistically, as did author Yukio Mishima in 1970, in public, after a failed coup attempt. And in 1999, when forced to retire by the company he worked for, Masaharu Nonaka committed seppuku, creating a new movement: *risutora seppuku* (seppuku due to corporate restructuring). More recent news reports have commented on the rising suicide rates in Japan. Many sociological reasons have been theorized.

In India, the suicide of wives who allowed themselves to be placed on their husband's funeral pyres were looked upon as being romantic and honorable, but in many cases, wives—many being mere teenagers who had been given in marriage to men decades their senior—were drugged and placed on funeral pyres with or without their consent. In one case a young wife jumped and ran from her husband's burning funeral pyre only to be chased down by the village people, dragged back and thrown into the flames.

As with seppuku, suttee (also known as sati—named after the wife of Shiva, who killed herself in like manner) was outlawed in India in 1829, but the practice continued in many remote rural areas. Customs, along with systems of belief, die hard.

In Western cultures, many believe that the soul of a suicide wanders for eternity. This theme was well demonstrated in the play *Outward Bound,* in which all suicides were forced to work aboard ships that carried the dead from this life to the next, insinuating that suicides live in perpetual limbo, sailing the seas of the cosmos, which is better than religions that assure their believers that all suicides go directly to hell. Such threats were created a very long time ago in order to intimidate people into keeping with the codes of their religious community.

It is important for those who grieve a suicide to understand that what a loved one or family member did should not mold or adversely affect one's life or the lives of their children. If, as a loving survivor, you find yourself in emotional turmoil, get professional help, but don't allow ancient taboos or current misunderstandings ruin your life or the lives of those you love. You have a life—live it. If the person who took his life could return, he would tell you the same. You were not the impetus for your loved one's suicide even if he left a note claiming that you were. Any good psychologist, bookstore owner or librarian can give you a list of books to read so that you can understand the words I have just written. Help take the taboo out of an overwhelming, exceedingly sad event.

Since Mother's demise, I have known others who took their own lives. One was a marvelous individual suffering from an extremely painful cancer. I understand the reasons behind his decision to take his own life on his own terms; one was religious, another was unbearable pain. I honor his courage and strength. Not all suicides are brought on by depression. There are many other reasons for choosing to leave life as we know it. Of the people I have known who ended their own lives, none would want others to suffer, especially those they loved.

As with all issues, there are various sides. When someone is in horrid agony and death is imminent, that person should be allowed to leave if he so desires. Those who speak out against allowing for a more peaceful death should lie in a sufferer's bed for an hour or two. It is well to remember that in this day and age modern medicine has learned how to extend lives. This is a true blessing until grievous pain and death approach. If all that can be done has been done, if there is no possibility of returning the patient to health, and only extreme measures will offer a few more hours, days or weeks, the prolonging of life must be examined from all perspectives. As mentioned before, if you don't have an end-of-life directive, write one up (you can find a form on the Web), and give copies to your family, your lawyer and your doctor(s). And do remember that you can change it anytime you wish.

Concerning the words above, I would be remiss if I didn't discuss the reason why many lawmakers refuse to allow for assisted suicide. I have often referred to our species as "greedy monkeys," and, indeed, greed is evident within every society. Lawmakers know there are those who would promote the assisted suicide of a relative for personal gain, i.e., inheritance. But if we can send telescopes into the far reaches of the universe, land robots on Mars and walk the face of the moon, we should be capable of writing a law that would protect the dying under all possible circumstances. For the time being, there is a gentler, kinder way—it's called hospice, where medications, other than those that relieve pain, and all medical procedures are stopped and the patient is cared for with love coupled with many known methods of easing one through the transition from life unto death.

Because of what I perceived during my near-death experience, I believe that whatever a suicide may have suffered in life was negated at death. If you loved them in life, hold on to that love. The rest, in the long run, is incredibly sad but meaningless in regard to the overall worth of the individual—let it go.

As to my mother Caroline . . . you would have loved her; everybody did.

I took care of the parrot. He is alive and living happily with others of his kind.

PART FOUR

A PRESCIENT LIFE

While each and every science is in the process of incredible growth, we continue to stand in huddled masses at the entrance to our timeless cave. Some— those of great courage, wonder and thought—are standing out in the sunshine looking up to see if the sky is falling, as our destinies swing silently in the balance.

MY FIRSTBORN

There is nothing so fragile, so malleable, so honest, so deceiving, so full of fantasy or so full of potential as a child. Given love, nourishment and intellectual challenge, he or she will grow to amaze you.

Portion of a letter written by my daughter, Kim, on August 26, 1986, to a friend in England:

"I apologize for not writing for so long, but it was not due to laziness this time. Spring and summer have been difficult for me emotionally due to a family tragedy.

"In April, my grandmother, who had NEVER come out of the depression she'd gone into when my grandfather died three years ago, committed suicide (gun). I can't even tell you what it's been like. She was only 67, with no gray hair. She was more my second mom than grandmother. . . . Basically, I was with her every day until I moved up to Jackson. . . . Although we NEVER saw it coming, we now can see, 20/20 hindsight, that she'd obviously planned to do this for some time, probably a year or more. It's so strange to think of someone you love quietly planning to leave you all forever. She bought me extra special Xmas gifts this year; also had a gift for me at her house at the time of her suicide. That stuff really gets to me. Our last phone call together was so strange, and of course I didn't know why at the time. I'd been to San Francisco visiting a friend and she really listened about the trip and was so sincerely happy that

I'd had a good time and that all was well with me, and the way she said 'I Love You' at the end of the call was so intense—not the usual 'Love ya, talk to you later.' And in the middle of the conversation, out of nowhere, she quietly said, 'You know, I just don't feel I have a reason to live anymore.' At that, all I felt was irritation, like, damn it, when will she snap out of this? Later I went through so much guilt, wishing I'd said something like, 'I'm a good reason for wanting to live, and Mom and my brothers!' I realized after a week of terrible guilt that she wasn't calling for help. She'd made up her mind long ago. She was only explaining herself to me ahead of time.

"That week (the week of her death) we were camping down in the desert. The morning she did it, I could NOT stop thinking of her, obsessively, to where I was wondering why. I was already feeling tremendous guilt (about no longer living near her and being with her) and kept imagining running my hands through her dark brown hair. I have no doubt that she visited me on her way out, and that somehow I connected with that level we don't understand. Subconsciously, I knew what had happened that morning. I've had other experiences like that, with deaths close to me. It really makes me wonder. I didn't actually find out till we got home 2 nights later at midnight."

KIM ELIZABETH BURROUGHS

In an Old Norse tale, Balder, son of Odin, dreamt of his own death. To protect him from his prophesy, the goddess Frigg made him impervious to all weapons until the wicked god Loki discovered that Balder was vulnerable to mistletoe, at which time he had the blind god Hother run him through with a branch of mistletoe, whereby Balder fell dead.

Kim was exceptional from the beginning. By the age of two, she possessed a large vocabulary and was a great conversationalist. At the age of three, I asked her if she would like to learn the alphabet so she could learn to read. "Yes," she replied. So we got out a big sheet of paper and her crayons. First, I wrote the alphabet across the top of the paper in big capital letters. Then I put the crayon in her hand and guided her hand over the markings of each letter several times, sounding out the letters as we traced them over and over again. Then it was playtime, lunchtime and a nap. After her nap, I asked Kim if she would like to see if she could remember any of the letters we had learned that morning. With great enthusiasm, Kim climbed up to the table. I gave her a clean sheet of paper and her crayons. To my astonishment, she wrote out the entire alphabet accurately but for inverting three letters and omitting one. By the time she entered kindergarten, she was reading books on her own.

Kim displayed my father's artistic talent and by her teens she was selling every painting she produced. I called her the Andrew Wyeth of animals. Using a dry-brush watercolor technique, she produced likenesses of animals whose fur you could mentally run your hands through. But Kim did more than paint those of the animal kingdom; she studied her subjects through text and observation. And when she wasn't painting or studying animals, she was saving their lives. All lost, wounded, or abandoned babies were brought to Kim's healing hands. Though she had an affinity for all animals, her passion was ornithology. Her first paying job was as an assistant in a private oology (bird egg) museum. The museum housed an amazing collection of bird eggs and bird skins from around the world. Through her work, Kim came to know leading ornithologists, which led to middle-of-the-night phone calls with some professor explaining that a rare species of bird had been blown off course in a storm and was sitting on some beach to the north. On such nights, Kim would suit up in warm sweats and tennis shoes, grab a bag, stuff it with binoculars, camera, sketchpad, extra clothing and food, then wait by the front door for a group of ornithologists to pick her up. Then she was off for a five-hour drive through the darkness of night to observe a tired bird from another continent that had been blown off course by nasty weather.

Her obsession with birds had begun long before Kim got the job at the egg museum. During her early teens, I would go into her room for something and there on her desk, laid out on a piece of construction paper, all in orderly fashion, would be the bones of mice, lizards and the like, all picked from the regurgitated castings of great horned owls. When an owl devours a mouse, or vole, or whatever, he swallows it whole. The owl's digestive system then takes all nourishment from the meal, wrapping the unused portions in neat bundles of fur called castings. Kim would collect these from beneath owl nests and pull them apart with tweezers and probes. It was after one of her forays down the mountain in back of our house that I would find piles of fur and line-ups of various bones on the top of her desk. She was an intriguing teenager. My only consternation was that she wore her skirts too short and she had to be constantly cautioned about breaking valuables in the living room, where she insisted on practicing her gymnastics.

After college and a failed marriage, Kim moved to Jackson, where the family had relocated. It was wonderful having Kim close by again, wonderful to walk the mountains with her as she explained animal and bird behavior to me—especially the behavior of bears, which can be a threat in the mountains surrounding Jackson Hole. It was Kim who got me to wear a small bell on my pack whenever I walked deep into the mountains. It is a wondrous sound, a small bell punctuating the sounds of nature, signaling one's presence, calling out to say I mean no harm, saying I respect you, please respect me—please don't devour me. Though many bears don't care a wit about a tinkling bell, as a person, Kim was like a life-bell, rippling through the air with humor, talent, wisdom and facts concerning life on planet Earth.

One day, some months after my mother's death, as I sat in my mother's chair at her desk, doing the work she had claimed she could not live without, the phone rang. It was Kim checking up on her mother. We spoke. The burdens of grief, business, lawyers and taxes weighed heavily upon me. Kim quickly recognized the grim stress moaning through my speech patterns.

"Mom, did you forget to awaken the child within you this morning?"

Tears sprang from my eyes, "Yes, I guess I did, honey. I think I have been leaving my child in bed a lot these days."

"Mom, you can't do that! You must not allow your child to die, if you do you will never feel the sand between your toes when you walk along the shore."

I wept and thanked my philosophical, well-read love child for always being there for me, for always seeing the right path and pattern to follow, for waking me up, one more time, to the joyous side of life.

Late June 1986

Mother's estate kept me in Los Angeles for weeks, then months. Finally, I made it back to Jackson.

It was an ordinary morning. I had arisen to grind and brew a thermos of Kenyan coffee, listen to the morning news and start in on my bookwork. At around 10:45 AM, the phone rang. It was Kim calling from her apartment just a few blocks away. At the sound of her voice, I became alarmed. Her hello sounded strange and different.

"Kim, what's the matter? Are you all right?" I asked.

"Yes, I'm fine, but I had a dream." Her voice had an odd quality to it that caused my mind to shift into an all-alert-bulletin mode of total absorption.

"Kim, what's wrong? What do you mean? What's happened?"

"I dreamt I died."

"My God! Are you all right?"

A controlled panic swept over me. Kim remained calm.

"I'm fine, Mom."

"Well, tell me about it, were you scared in the dream?"

"No, it wasn't scary at all, but I don't understand one part of it."

"What's that?"

"Well, I dreamt I died of a heart attack under ice water."

"You mean like an ice shelf in the Arctic?"

"No, no—ice water, like in a glass, but lots of it."

"Are you sure you died in the dream? They say your mind won't allow you to actually die in a dream. They say the shock would be too great and cause you to have a heart attack."

"Well, they're full of it, because I died. There was no doubt about it. But in the dream it was okay. It was okay that I died. . . . I just can't figure the ice."

"Look, are you sure you are all right? Do you want to come up for a cup of tea or something?"

"No, Mom, I'm fine, but I have been waiting all morning for Gerry to leave the house, 'cause you know how he believes in dreams and everything. If I told him about this dream he would freak out. He would be positive I was going to die on him."

"Yes, I remember you telling me about the death of his little sister."

"I couldn't wait to call you because the dream was so unique and powerful—so real, in fact, that I have been lying here all morning looking around my apartment and thinking about what I would like done with my things in case anything should happen to me within the next year or two."

I felt numb as I listened with unfocused eyes to my 30-year-old daughter tell me her will in a very matter of fact way.

"You are very serious, aren't you?"

"Yes, Mom. The dream was more real than life itself and completely singular. It was more real than sitting here talking to you on the phone. And no other dream entwined with it, before or after. It was just a very real happening."

"Maybe you weren't afraid because we have had so many discussions concerning my near-death experience."

"I don't think so. This was all about me. It had nothing to do with you or anyone else. There was just the heart attack, the ice water and death. It was so real I had to tell you in case anything ever happened to me."

Those are the words I remember verbatim, but I also remember what Kim said a minimum of three times. She kept repeating that in the dream it was all right that she died and that the dream was more real than life itself.

My mind didn't want to take in the words, but they etched themselves deeply into my gray matter. I kept telling myself that the dream was just part of Kim's trauma over the death of her grandmother; her grieving had been intense.

Two nights later, my friend Beth Overcast and I had dinner with Kim. During the meal, the three of us discussed Kim's dream. Three days later, I had to fly back to Los Angeles.

Late July 1986

Flying home to Jackson from Los Angeles: I have a window seat. There is no one sitting next to me. I sit in limbo, my mind whirling with myriad thoughts and worries over Mom's estate and life in general. Then my mind stops while my entire being is filled with the knowledge of death brought on by blood clots. The thought is coupled with a gross amount of fear. It is a precognitive thought—the kind that flies in through the side window and takes over the whole of one's self. I think the clots are for me. The fear is terrible. The only person I have ever known to die of a blood clot was a cousin of Dick's following knee surgery. I force myself to calm down. I push the thought away. I never connect the experience with Kim's dream.

Mid-September 1986

Again, on a flight from Jackson to Los Angeles: Window seat with no one else in my row. It hits again. This time the *knowing* of death by blood clot is so strong that perspiration pops out on my forehead and I look down to find that my hands are trembling. Though the thought of death by blood clot is not relegated to any specific person, I take the thought, the death, to be mine. I chide myself, thinking of all the times I have recanted my near-death experience. I wince at my fright. I tell myself that if I am so chicken, so afraid of death, I should give up riding, skiing and scuba diving. Forcefully, I push the thought of death by blood clot away, feeling ashamed at experiencing so much fear over the thought of death. After all, I am the one who knows that death is the most normal thing you will ever do. My fear bothers me more than anything else. I push it all away.

Mid-October 1986

Back in Jackson for a week.

Kim and I went over to the ranch on Sunday. As we left to return to Jackson I said I would like to come back to the ranch on Wednesday. Kim said that if she could make it she would like to come too.

Wednesday arrived. We pile into Big Blue (our ranch truck) and haul ourselves over Teton Pass to the ranch. On the way, we both make comments on how busy we've been, how we had each dropped everything in order to go to the ranch and how in all the years we had had the ranch we couldn't remember ever going over for no reason, i.e., the horses, the house, the gardens, company or whatever. There had always been a reason other than simple pleasure. We spoke of the uniqueness of the day, how on this day, Wednesday, we had simply felt an emotional need to go to the ranch.

Kim and I did our thing. We worked in the garden, straightened up the house and pigged out at lunchtime. After lunch, we were walking across the front lawn when, in unison, we turned and looked over at the horses in the east paddock. "Do you want to ride?" I asked without much enthusiasm. Kim looked at the horses, hesitated a moment and said, "Yes."

As we went to fetch the horses, I commented that we shouldn't ride Cocoa. He had thrown a friend two months earlier and had been acting up. I didn't trust him. But Kim had already caught the animal and she continued to put a halter on him, saying, "No, I'm going to ride him. I rode him Sunday."

"I wish you wouldn't. Let me ride him. You can ride Ebo, he's a great ride."

Kim insisted on riding Cocoa. After all, she had ridden him on Sunday.

We rode out past the pond and over the small hill to the north, then took the two-wheel track all the way around the barley crop. I dismounted to open and close a cattle gate. As I was beginning to remount my horse, Cocoa took off with Kim in the opposite direction from where I thought we were going to ride. Down a steep and narrow draw he ran. As he started up the south slope he picked up speed.

I jumped on my horse and raced after Cocoa, yelling to Kim to "Hold him back! Hold him back!" I don't think she heard me.

Ebo and I galloped up the hill chasing after Cocoa and Kim, who was flailing around in the saddle like a rag doll. Everything seemed wrong. Kim was a good rider.

Cocoa thundered up the hill. When he reached the crest, he threw his gigantic, mottled white and cocoa brown ass in the air. Kim flew wrenchingly from his back, thudding into the ground, arms back, in an all-points belly landing.

As Kim was dislodged from the saddle her name ripped from my lips, over and over again. Now I was turning her over to see the mask of death over her sweet face. I began screaming, "NO! NO! NO! *You can't have her!*" I don't know if my words were audible.

Slowly, Kim's eyes narrowly opened. They gazed into mine. I don't remember what I said, but I remember watching her coming back to me, the mask deteriorating before my eyes.

Thick blood ran from one nostril. She started to moan and then to speak. She was hurt, but nothing was busted. I dissolved inside, unable to contemplate losing her.

Cocoa had stopped as soon as he realized he had lost his rider. He raced back and bent down as if to inquire what Kim was doing on the ground. Kim was now conscious. She was in pain and she was mad. Ever so slowly, I helped her to her feet. She wanted to ride back. I said, "No, I'll go get Big Blue." Kim insisted. I got her mounted. Her discomfort was plain to see. I begged again to go and fetch Big Blue. No, she was going to ride. Slowly, we made our way back to the house. As I helped Kim across the lawn she said, "You know when we mounted up I had a feeling that one of us would be thrown today, but I don't know if I fed the idea to the horse or if I picked it up from him."

I called my doctor as Kim washed away the blood and checked her many bruises. The doctor was afraid of concussion. After answering a long list of questions, the doctor said it sounded like "just another bad horse wreck," but added that I should watch her over the next 24 hours. He felt she would be fine but very sore.

When I hung up the phone, Kim looked at me with tears in her eyes, "Now it's time to call Grandmom. She would tell us exactly what to do."

Together, we wept.

We drove home, down Pierre's Hole, over the pass and back to Jackson. I insisted Kim spend the night with me so as to observe her. The next day, after Kim had gone home to her apartment, I spoke with my aunt Marion in Los Angeles, "I can't tell you how awful it was. When I got to her I thought I had lost her."

Three days later, Kim put me on yet another plane bound for Los Angeles. She was still quite sore and limping due to a painful knee that had been injured when she hit the ground.

Nine days after the horse wreck, Kim developed horrid pains in her lungs. I heard about it when she called me in Los Angeles to tell me that one of our dear hound dogs had died the night before. We both cried long and hard over the loss of our dear canine friend. He had been a magnificent, people-loving animal. When our mutual tears abated Kim said, "But I have some news that is even worse." She then told me of her acute chest pains. I insisted she go in for X-rays and a thorough examination.

Diagnosis: Water on the lung due to horse fall. Will dissipate.

Everyone said, "Water on the lung? Most painful thing you will ever go through. You think you are going to die."

I returned to Jackson. Kim and I had planned to attend a science symposium at Berkeley. The doctor said she could travel; it might be painful, but she could travel. Kim said she didn't care what the doctor said she was going even if the trip killed her.

We were like a couple of young girls and had the time of our lives. I had never seen Kim look more beautiful as we flitted from symposium to dinner parties and back again.

Throughout that wondrous week, Kim was in extreme pain but we kept rehearsing what everyone had said about water on the lung. Then one night her agony was so great that I picked up the phone. The time was 3:15 AM.

"Mom, what are you doing?"

"I'm getting a doctor up here this minute."

"Mother, put the phone down. I will not see a doctor. I don't need one."

Through tears, I argued. I tried to get her to go with me to a hospital. I lost. My parents had always respected me, my opinions and my wishes; I had tried to do the same for my children. And then there was the fact that Kim had just turned 31. She was a grown woman, not a child. I begged some more.

"No."

By the end of the symposium, Kim was in terrible shape and I was completely distraught. We had followed one another in separate cars. Now it was time for us to leave in opposite directions. We stood in the parking lot facing each other. Once again, I pleaded with her to go to a hospital with me, "Just for X-rays."

"No."

"Then come down to Los Angeles with me. We can check you into UCLA and find out what the hell's going on. I'll bring you all your favorite foods from the restaurant."

"No. Mom, I want to get back to Jackson. I will be all right. I need to get back. I have to go home. I need to go. I have to go home."

I had never known Kim to be so adamant.

The doctors in Jackson found more fluid in the lung. Twice they extracted the wretched stuff. It showed discernible traces of blood. The process was excruciatingly painful. Kim's boyfriend, Gerry, held her hands. I called twice daily from Los Angeles. Kim insisted that I not come home, "Mom, I am fine. I don't even want you here. Besides, I'm staying up here at your house in your big old bed with all your pillows. I have the TV and my friends and everyone is treating me like royalty. We just have to wait until the water dissipates. Don't come home."

The doctors put Kim into the hospital for a few days for a battery of tests. The head doctor at our small hospital said, "It's lupus." Within a week, four other doctors dutifully mounted his bandwagon.

Kim and I said, "Baloney."

I said, "I am coming home."

She said, "Don't, Mom. And don't worry, Mom, I can take care of myself."

I called all over America to find out what the hell lupus was.

My friend Jim spoke with Kim on the phone, "Your mom is going crazy. She is worried, confused and hurt." Kim laughed, "Oh, Mom's just on one of her authority kicks. If she comes up here she will reorganize the hospital."

Sunday, November 23, 1986

Kim and I are talking on the phone. She tells me of a wonderful dream she had about her great-grandmother Faunce, my mother's mother. In the dream, Kim goes to see her great-grandmother. She finds her sitting in her chair. She looks fantastic and is younger and more mentally alert than the last time Kim saw her, and she is extremely glad to see Kim. She holds open her arms and Kim runs into them, snuggling in the warmth of her great-grandmother's love.

"Gerry thinks the dream means I am going to die. He says the fact that I could touch Grandma Faunce, and feel her touch me, indicates that she had come to get me through the mist of a dream. . . . Mom, he's actually scared."

Tuesday, November 25, 1986

Gerry calls. It's 9:45 PM. Kim's in the hospital again. My knees buckle. The next morning I'm on the early flight. As planes fly me towards Jackson, I review the words of those who said that it might indeed be lupus. I visualize caring for Kim, moving her up to my house and making her my life's work. We had always said we were going to end up as two funny old ladies, her being the new Georgia O'Keeffe and me writing books like the mama in *You Can't Take It With You*.

By 11:00 AM, I am in Kim's room. She is lying there in the new nightgown I had sent her. Rather than ask for help from the nurses she had removed her I.V. bottle from its stand, threaded it through the sleeve of the nightgown and gotten into the thing all by herself. Her heart was beating 148 times per minute. When she had first entered the hospital, they had taken her to X-ray and looked at her racing heart via sound waves. The nurses and doctors had stood and laughed at the sight of her rapidly jumping heart. They even called in others to view it (!!!).

"How do you feel?"

"If it wasn't for this heart beating so fast, I would rush outside and take a long walk in the snow."

"Kim, I'm so glad you didn't resist my coming. This time you couldn't have stopped me. I have never known such anxiety in my life. Obeying your wishes almost killed me. I felt like I was going crazy."

"It's okay, Mom, you weren't needed then, but now the time is right. I need you now and I'm so glad you are here."

We spoke of the crazy doctors and their hang-up on lupus. I stood at the foot of the bed looking at my beautiful daughter lying there with IV and oxygen.

"Does it hurt with your heart beating so rapidly?"

"No, but it causes me to feel anxious—I'm sure high blood-pressure makes you feel the same way."

A doctor came in; not the one who had diagnosed Kim with lupus. He was the only one who had questioned the head man's diagnosis. He and I had spoken on the phone several times. Now he asked that I come to his office.

"Is my daughter's life in danger?" It was a question I had

asked many times over the phone. This time he knowingly lied.

"No, but she's very ill." He went on about lupus—having been swayed by his superiors. I asked him to see about an air ambulance to get her out of there and into a large medical facility.

After speaking with the doctor, I returned to Kim's room. We talked. Her friends came by. We shared the candy I had brought and remembered funnier times. I left to buy food for Thanksgiving and then returned, staying into the evening.

Early the next morning, I hurriedly started Thanksgiving dinner then raced to the hospital. Kim was unusually quiet. She seemed down. I had seen the doctor from the day before in the hall. He said she had had a good cry that morning—mostly over the fact that they wouldn't let her go home for Thanksgiving dinner. He thought her tears to be good for her. "Lupus can be a long, hard, haul."

I put on the Macy's Thanksgiving parade. It was as a gross intrusion. I turned it off. We talked. I held her hand. I walked to the end of the bed and looked at the young woman who was so much a part of me, the child I had grown up with. She spoke of how hard she had tried. How she had meditated and sent love and healing to her lungs.

"Mom, do you remember my dream?"

Every word of her dream came back to me as if I were back in my kitchen with the phone to my ear. Stunned by the vivid memory I nodded in the affirmative. I couldn't believe that in all the weeks since her horse wreck, I had not once thought about her dream of death.

"Well, maybe I misread it." She went on, "Maybe this rapid heartbeat is the heart attack and the ice on the windows is the ice."

I looked at the ice arching up and down the lower windows of her room as a quiet, protective numbness settled over me.

The underling doctor came in. The head doctor, the "lupus doctor," was out of town, nowhere to be found. We told him that we were bringing in a huge turkey dinner later in the day and asked if he would care to stop by for pie. He asked what time, noted that Kim's heart rate was 138 beats per minute and left.

Brett and his wife, Mary, called. Kim loved her brothers completely; she had been a second mother to them as much as a loving sister. Brett and Mary were pretty sure they were pregnant. Kim laughed and giggled with glee, making them laugh and giving them love.

Kim's best friend since childhood, Megan, called. She sensed how sick Kim was and ended up in tears. Kim hung up the phone and started to cry. "I can't stand anyone crying over me. I don't want anyone to hurt or worry. I'm all right and I'll be fine. I don't want people hurting over me."

The nurses came to put in a new IV and to switch arms. First they administered a shot of anti-clotting medication.

Kim's veins had always been hard to find. It was a painful process. I knelt down by her and rubbed the middle of her forehead. She asked what the doctor had said when I had gone to his office. "Well, the good news is that you are not going to kick the bucket. The bad news is that we may be in for a long haul and we are going to have to take a very expensive plane ride."

Kim made no comment. I looked at her eyes. Beneath them, the skin showed tints of green and blue. The thought of death creased my consciousness. My mind forced it to wing off. The moment became a memory, but left my conscious thought.

Gerry, Kim's boyfriend, returned from errands and I left to fix Thanksgiving dinner.

At 2:30 PM, I called. I told Kim the food was ready and asked if she wanted us to come over early or perhaps just come and sit with her. She said she was not hungry but that it was okay if we came over, then she changed her mind. She said the night before had been terrible and she hadn't been able to sleep. She said Gerry was taking a nap on the other bed. "I think I will take a nap too. I feel tired."

Three of Kim's close friends were staying with me. They watched a movie. I puttered.

At 5:15 PM, I called back. I asked for the nurse's station in case Kim was still asleep. I wanted a cart on which to transport the feast I had fixed for my most avid chowhound.

"I'm sorry there's no one at that nurse's station."

"Then please connect me with room 132." The reply was halting and nervous, "I'm sorry but I can't connect you with . . ."

"What the hell is going on?" I screamed into the receiver. Gerry must have been standing there. I heard his voice, felt it shake, "Carole?"

"Gerry, what the hell is going on? What's happened?!"

Half crying, he replied, "I don't know but I'm really scared."

It's a seven-minute drive to the hospital. The three girls and I were there in six. We ran down the hall. At the last bend in the hall, I stopped, then walked in a daze. Nurses were running into Kim's room with huge blue bags of ice cubes.

Night, November 27 into 28, 1986

A deep guttural exhaust seemed to expel from not only my lungs but from every cell of my body. I felt a deep rasping burn that scraped at every cellular surface of my being. How such anguish could keep from producing death was incredible. The fact that I didn't die as the agony and the night wore on was unfathomable to me and yet miraculous at the same time. How could a mortal frame, a physical body, survive such pain?

I sat huddled in the corner of the library sofa swathed in afghans and trauma—shivering in the depths of despair. Rather than flowing, my tears seemed to cough themselves out of their ducts and splash downward onto my cheeks with the sensation of liquid lava. My mind reeled at the realization that my best friend, my beautiful daughter was dead—gone—lying in the mortuary never again to make me laugh or share with me the pains and joys of her life. Never to raid my refrigerator or bring me her tears, or console me when I was down. Never to create another painting or walk in the woods, never to work side by side with me in the garden or house, never to go exploring through the pages of books or journey forth on her beloved travels. Sharing, living, loving, caring, sharing . . . gone.

They had worked on Kim for close to an hour. They had put Gerry, the three girls and me in a room down the hall. I had gone to the window and screamed out to Kim, telling her to hang on, to come back—that she could come back if she wanted to. A message came back to me, filling up my senses—she couldn't come back, she had already left. Forty minutes before the distraught doctors and nurses gave up, I, and Kim's friends, knew her to be gone. Later, we would compare notes and all say the same thing: on the ride to the hospital each of us had individually felt Kim pass as we drove down a certain block, just past the last motel. So we had all known the outcome before the play had ended. Nevertheless, we went onstage.

The doctor came down the hall. Gerry had run out of the hospital. The three girls and I were rotating from the floor to the one chair the nurses had brought out to us. I was on the floor. Lizard-like, I squirmed towards the doctor's ankle, grabbed it and cried, begging for an explanation.

The doctor took me for a walk. The new snow crunched beneath our boots, stars winked above. I walked and talked in shock; the real pain stood waiting in the wings. I spoke of us as being grains of sand, of Kim's intelligence, of her talent, her ability to bring deep and total joy to people. I talked.

As we were about to re-enter the side door of the hospital, the doctor laid his head on the glass and said, "God, I hate death. I hate it so much that when my brother died I didn't even go to his funeral."

I went home to my pain.

A million loving addictions had been ripped from my psyche and I sat alone in fear and desperation. I felt as though a large blade had swiped though my being, causing most of "me" to fall away into nothingness. How could I go on? How could this be happening after the tragedies we had already suffered? How much did the man upstairs think we could take? Why this fifth and most grievous agony? What had I done wrong? Was Kim's death my fault? If only I had overridden her insistence and forced her to go to a large medical facility. Panic gripped me. She could not be dead, she was my beautiful, bright soul mate, my alter ego—the closest and best friend I had ever had, one of the most complete loves of my life. But I had seen her lying there in her hospital bed looking like a princess. Wet from melted ice, she lay sweet, serene, asleep, but she was not asleep, she was dead, gone to another realm, leaving me to shoulder the heaviest burden of my life . . . life itself.

So it was that with each breath and sob I was torn and ripped apart. Many thoughts came to me, some pragmatic, some mystical, most full of self-pity and anguish. And my heart ached for her, for what she was going to miss here on this earthly plane; the flowers she would never smell, the birdcalls she would never hear and the songs she herself would never sing. Yet deep within, I knew that Kim had smelled the roses, cried her tears and laughed from the depths of her soul. Indeed, Kim had been one of those who had had the courage to leave her mundane workaday duties to play in nature's theater, to journey over the mountains to Taggart Lake, across the deep snow flats to Jenny Lake, or up Cache Creek to stop, look and listen where the creek burst forth from under its winter mantle of ice and snow to sing in gurgling tones, "I am here, I am alive, though most of me be hidden, I am here, carrying within me, both life and death."

Earlier, on the night of Kim's death, while my brain was still rational, I ordered an autopsy. Kim's lower chest cavity was filled with blood clots, her lower left lung tissue rotted. Death came when an immense clot that had been growing for six long weeks in one of her pelvic veins broke free and traveled upwards towards her heart, where it lodged itself at the apex of the pulmonary artery, creating a saddle-block embolus, resulting in a massive and lethal heart attack.

The attending physicians had packed Kim in six large blue bags of ice cubes as they tried in vain to save her life. When all efforts failed and defeat was accepted, Kim lay beneath gallons of ice water.

"Like ice water in a glass, but lots of it."

There was no evidence of lupus.

With Kim's death, all of my beliefs, everything that had held me together over the previous years, were washed away as the dark of the night covered me and my emotions consumed me.

THE PARK

This is a fairy tale that really happened; an occurrence that continues to remind me that there is something right and wonderful about the universe.

It was a chill wintry night. A light snow was falling

Stan Wilhelmsen, county coroner and mortician, called to say that Kim was ready for viewing. He apologized for the delay. The pathologist had been away for the Thanksgiving holiday when Kim died and 17 hours had elapsed before they could perform the autopsy. Then Saturday, Stan had another funeral to take care of, so now it was Sunday, three days after Kim's death.

After receiving the call, we ate dinner, dressed and drove down to the mortuary.

Since this is a short story there is no need to elaborate on the monsters of grief that surrounded us. Suffice it to say, they were in attendance. Tears fell and pain was paramount as we stood before the coffin of our beloved Kim.

Present were my sons Brett and Chris; Brett's wife, Mary; Kim's boyfriend, Gerry; Kim's girlfriend, Lynda; my friend, Jim; and me. We had dressed for the occasion, as had Kim. She lay in the lovely lavender dress she had worn just a month earlier when we were in Berkeley for a symposium and attended a gala dinner in San Francisco at the home of Gordon and Ann Getty. I had never seen her so beautiful as that evening. She had reminded me of a princess. I'd had a camera with me (in the hotel room and later in my bag) but I never took a single picture—very unlike me.

After tears and remembrances, we placed letters we had written to Kim beneath her hands and replaced the fake roses she held with real ones.

As we left the mortuary, Lynda said she was too upset and was going to walk home to spend some time alone. The rest of us turned west and headed slowly towards the town square.

The snow had ceased to fall and our little town lay still and quiet as a Christmas card, all glistening and white. The trees in the park were frosted with snow and festooned with tiny white lights. The air was crisp and clean.

We walked in twos and threes, clinging to one another as we softly sobbed over our great loss. At the center of the park, where the war memorial stands, we stopped to comfort one another. We were a sad and troubled group standing in the fallen snow in a deserted town park surrounded by deserted streets. Not a car or human sound could be seen or heard.

Suddenly, the stillness of the night was shattered by the sound of a car racing along the south side of the park. Just as suddenly, the car pulled over against the curb and came to an abrupt halt. Three never-before-seen children—two boys and a girl—leapt from the car, scrambled over the fence and raced through the newly fallen snow. We stood huddled together, holding one another, protecting one another in our grief.

And then a hit—and another hit. Snowballs! Snowballs to the right of us, snowballs to the left of us. And children! Children laughing gaily, giggling as they scooped up the snow.

And then we too were laughing and giggling and throwing snowballs. Snowballs to the right of us, snowballs to the left of us. And the laughter—oh, the lifting of spirits!

Our pain was shed, left lying in heaps at the feet of the memorial. Screams of glee rent the chill night air and our hearts flew with every toss.

All the while, the children's parents stood as silent sentinels off in the corner of the park. No words of admonition came from them. No words of encouragement as the battle raged on. No don'ts or dos, just a silent guarding from the corner of the park.

Then, as suddenly as they had arrived, without a word from their parents, the children ran to their car and were gone.

When it was over we walked slowly from the park. Within our group existed many faiths, various attitudes, many ways of looking at life. In unison, over and over, we said as one, "That was Kim's doing."

And so it was.

A MOMENT TO REMEMBER

Light—visible energy—is but one of many forms of electromagnetic radiation that permeate our universe. The visible light we receive from the sun makes life possible. Without it, life on Earth would cease to exist. Sunlight comes to us via particles known as photons—massless wonders of the particle world—that travel at the speed of light, or 186,000 miles per second. Reflected light from the moon reaches Earth in 1.2 seconds, while the sun's rays take a whopping eight minutes.

What I am about to tell you may not seem rational and there is no way I can prove that what I witnessed actually occurred. Prior to finding corroborating evidence, I tried to tell myself it was a hallucination, a vivid dream, but such thoughts wouldn't wash. When it happened, I was wide awake, and, to this day, the event sits solid in my mind.

Kim died Thursday evening. The following day, Brett, Mary and Chris arrived from various parts of the country and faithful Jim flew up to hold my hand once more. Three of Kim's girlfriends also arrived with the crowd. The house was filled with love, flowers, anguish, tears, memories and haunting remembrances of Kim's laughter.

Chris arrived late at night, alone from Florida. When our tears subsided, he took me by the shoulders and said, "Mom, you're not going to let this break you. You're not going to let this make you old or take away your thirst for life." I have wonderful children.

It was three nights after Kim's death (the same night of the snowball fight in the park). The clock read three-something AM, but time seemed meaningless.

I had taken no drugs, nor had I drunk any alcohol. I have abhorred pills since childhood and through the many deaths that had recently assaulted my senses, I had learned that it is better to walk unaided through the line of fire than to shield oneself with drugs or alcohol, which temporarily mask the anguish but draw out the process of pain and grieving.

The house lay sound asleep. Suddenly, I awoke with a clear feeling of awareness, sensing and knowing that something had happened or was about to happen. Then I was hollow. There was nothing, only my body lying on the bed. My eyes were wide open and I was extraordinarily alert. My brain was active, but my mind wasn't functioning. My computer/brain was on, but nothing had been loaded into its memory. The screen was vacant, yet expectant. Then, five feet in front of me, between my wall closet and a desk that sits some six feet opposite, there appeared a thin crackling rod of shimmering white light. The brilliance of it I find hard to express. Minute sparks flickered from it, but the visual was pure white, as white as is possible for white to be. The rod crackled, I could hear it. The rod shimmered and then it was gone. How long did this vision last? Two seconds? Four? Eight? I don't know.

I lay still, eyes wide, my egotistical mind still absent, my brain still absorbing, still re-running that which had been. My memory says that I lay motionless for many minutes. There was no feeling of fear or awe for I was emotionally vacant. Like a snippet of film, I had simply registered the occurrence without conscious or interpretative thought.

Slowly, my conscious, ego-filled mind returned, along with my emotional baggage. I let out a long breath and said into the ether of the night, "Kim? Was that you?" No knowledgeable feelings came to me as to who or what had invaded the atmosphere of my bedroom. I lay awake for some time. Then, filled with wonder, I slipped into sleep with an all-encompassing feeling of peace.

In the morning, I awoke with an uncanny notion that everything was all right. My conscious mind fought the feeling tooth and nail. It wasn't possible for me to feel all right. Everything I had been taught, everything my society had told me said I couldn't be all right.

Throughout the day, I went about in a half-conscious state. Part of me was listening to Kim. She kept flooding my mind with words such as, "If your near-death experience and all you have experienced and believe in helped to get you through the other deaths, why isn't it working with mine? If all you believe in doesn't work with my death, then all you and I believe in is a lie."

Repeatedly, I recalled the last two-hour discussion Kim and I had had on death and the possibility of surviving it in some other form. We had gone over near-death experiences, out-of-body experiences, the Bible, Far Eastern religions and wondrous new branches of science, from particle physics and cosmology to quantum mechanics. We had done it before, and as one death followed another, we had continued to converse on these entwining subjects, each of us finding it therapeutic.

At the end of our last discourse, I had said, "Let's face it, we're never going to know for sure until we make it all the way to the other side."

With one of her most mischievous grins, Kim beamed gleefully at me and replied, "I know, but wouldn't it be fun to know before you went?"

Now, three months later, she was gone, and I walked the house hearing her voice, wondering if it could be possible that she had indeed visited me, proving that which we wish to know. It was hard to think the thought. I wanted to trounce the idea scientifically while intuition told me that science wasn't the closet in which to look. Whatever I had experienced in my bedroom fell into a basket marked inexplicable.

I felt confused. I wanted to go with the warm feelings that permeated my very being, the feelings that told me everything was all right, but my conscious grief, my society-programmed ego, told me that couldn't happen, told me that I must go back to my agony and grief. Looking back, it is obvious that I wasn't ready to receive this most precious of gifts—the gift of peace and acceptance.

That night, the night following the light, I lay awake far, far into the night. Over and over again I went over my near-death experience, my out-of-body experience, and the experience of the night before. I tried every which way to negate them, to trash them. I couldn't. They were real occurrences. If they had been but experiences of the mind, they were real to that which I call my *self.*

Everything you experience, whether you are awake or asleep, is real only within the context of your mind. You know the last two minutes of your life happened. Prove it. Truly, and factually, prove it. Or prove that they occurred exactly as you perceived them to have happened. If you are sitting in the New York Public Library with 300 people around you, you still can't prove that you, or any of the others around you, experienced the last two minutes—or the time it took you to read this paragraph— for each moment is but a conceptualization of your mind. You think you know the last two minutes happened, don't you? The people around you might agree, but then they might be nothing more than part of your life's dream. No, you know the last two minutes happened, don't you? I understand, and I believe you, but through my studies, I have learned that each of us perceives life and our immediate surroundings in a unique fashion, singular to ourselves. Most of all, I have come to understand that there is much we cannot explain, measure, prove or understand at this point in time.

I told everyone in the house about my experience. They were fascinated, but I could read flashes of "flipped out" running through their brains. Only Chris took me seriously. "I wish she had come to me," he said, his intense love for his sister showing in his grief-filled eyes.

Several months later, I sat across from Dr. James Kirsch, a Jungian psychoanalyst. Dr. Kirsch had been a student and colleague of Jung's, maintaining residence in Jung's home for half a decade. When I met Dr. Kirsch, he was an ancient man with a huge brain sitting between two headphones, resting on a withered body. His experience and knowledge concerning the workings of the mind and the unconscious self were incredible. He had his doctorate and was delving into the depths of the human psyche several decades before I was born. I spoke into a microphone so that he could hear my every word, but few words were needed for him to understand the totality of my thoughts and knowledge.

It was my third session with him. My primary motive for seeing him had been to investigate Kim's dream, my precognitive thoughts and the phenomena surrounding the many deaths that had touched my life over the last three and a half years. I had saved my light-rod experience for last. I was quite sure the good doctor was going to put me in a straitjacket upon hearing my tale but instead, he sat slowly nodding his head with an expression of bored recognition on his face.

Picking up on his expression, I asked incredulously, "Are you telling me that you've heard of such things before?"

"Oh yes, they have been seen for thousands of years."

"Well, I've never heard of them and can't find anything in the literature."

"My dear woman, you haven't read enough. Strange phenomena have always surrounded death. Do you mind if I tell you a story?"

"Please, I would love to hear anything you can tell me."

"Several years ago, my friend came to me and asked that I interpret a dream for him. He was himself a fine psychoanalyst but was stumped by his dream. In it he had seen a wolf with 11 legs, which then turned into 11 wolves. To this day, I don't know the meaning of the dream, but on Sunday, May 11th, at 12 noon exactly, he dropped dead of a heart attack in his rose garden.

"The following day, there was a seminar for psychoanalysts. We all met in a large room with many doors that opened to smaller rooms that looked out to gardens. If our colleague had been alive, he would have attended. After our general meeting, we broke up into groups. Four of the doctors went into one of the adjoining rooms. Three of the four doctors experienced and saw exactly what you have just described. A light rod appeared to them just outside of the large window of the room in which they sat. They were quite astounded. Each of them felt it had to be our friend. Being the old man of the group, they came to me. I told them that of course it was our friend who had died the day before."

"And how did they feel while watching the light rod?"

"Void, just as you did."

"But why?"

"I feel that at such times we are nothing but observers."

"What about the fourth man in the room? He didn't see it."

"Who knows, perhaps he was facing the wrong way. Then again, researchers have been unable to determine why some people are receptive while others aren't. I was his closest friend. Why didn't he appear to me?"

"Then you actually think the light I saw in my room was Kim?"

"Of course. Who else do you think it was? The dog from down the street? It was Kim in an illuminated state. It's important for you to know she's not suffering. She's really redeemed. That's what life is all about."

His comments hit me as being more religious than I would have expected, but I was fascinated and relieved to find that light rods in connection with death were known and recorded entities. Maybe my elevator did go to the top floor.

Dr. Kirsch continued, telling me about his years with Carl Jung. "When Jung died on Tuesday, the 6th of June, I flew to Zurich. The memorial was on Friday. It began at 10:00 in the morning with beautiful, clear blue skies. As the service began, it grew dark and a horrid storm came on with tremendous lightning. As the service ended, the sun shown once more and as we exited the church there wasn't a cloud in the sky. Back at Jung's house, we noticed that one of the four magnificent trees he had planted in the back garden decades before had been struck by lightning and totally destroyed. Jung had a genuine fascination with the number four. He had planted that copse of trees for that reason." Then Dr. Kirsch looked at me and said that it might be wise if I didn't speak of my experience.

"Because people will doubt my sanity?" I asked.

"No, because they simply won't understand."

Perhaps, but I know of many who can accept the ineffable with open minds. Through my travels and search for answers, I have come upon people from all walks of life who possess a marvelous mental attitude unknown to many (but not all) in the fields of science. Such people stand comfortably, as Kim had, in two separate worlds, seeing no disparity between the two. They know, trust and love the sciences, yet fly gracefully through the cosmos of the metaphysical. Though they may seek pragmatic solutions, they are nonjudgmental before diverse theories. These people are not easily misled, nor do they shirk the duties of society. Some are scientists who realize that there are many things we have yet to comprehend and are not frightened by the unexplainable. I see them as forerunners living in, or reaching towards, the times of tomorrow.

By the time I had found Dr. Kirsch, I had become a seeker, an explorer of the unexplainable, a hunter in pursuit of truth. But my search was different from most in that it was a mandatory, life-saving quest brought about by the many exceptional and grievous things that had happened to me. So many anomalous occurrences had presented themselves to me that I could no longer push them aside or stuff them into a mental shoebox of oddities to sit at the back of some cranial shelf.

Surrounded by my grief, I found others who were grieving, many who had known grief, and others who had never known it but had experienced an anomalous occurrence and had been changed by the event. And over and over and over again, I heard similar stories that boggled the mind. Was it all of the mind? What was going on? What perceptions had I been allowed to experience? Had I lost my marbles? Were there forces and dimensions yet to be found? How can someone perceive the future? Can those who have died manifest themselves to those still living?

I wanted answers. I needed to understand. I had to gain enough knowledge to carry on with my life. My very sanity depended on finding answers I could live with.

I began with the tools I have always worked with: books and more books and still more books. I delved into prodigious scientific theories, scrambling the networks of my brain in an all-out effort to comprehend. I lost my sense of time in the world of quantum mechanics. I read scores of books on the paranormal, the metaphysical, mind/brain, dreams, telepathy, anomalous occurrences, anthropology, psychology, mythology, cosmology and histories of science. I read new-age books and rattled about in ancient writings. I traveled. I met many people, asked many questions and heard many answers. As I turned the pages of my life, I found things we know conclusively, a great deal we know little or nothing about, and things we accept as fact but are yet to be proven. The wonder of it all was coming to the realization that there is so much more to learn, so much left for future generations to explore and find.

In time, I read the apocryphal books of the Bible, which are ancient texts written by early Christians that were removed from accumulated writings that were picked over in order to compile the Bible we know today. Though excised from the now extant Bible, many of the apocryphal texts were read from pulpits until the late 1400s. The *Gospel of the Infant Jesus Christ* was written by a Gnostic sect of Christians from the second century (around AD 150). Though read in churches for centuries, it wasn't translated and published for the general public until 1697.

In this early Christian writing, the infant Jesus is born in a cave that Mary and Joseph entered when she went into labor as they traveled to pay their taxes. From 1:10: "And behold, it was all filled with lights, greater than the light of lamps and candles, and greater than the light of the sun itself."

And from 2:6: "At that time old Simeon [a priest] saw him [the infant Jesus] shining as a pillar of light, when St. Mary the Virgin, his mother, carried him in her arms."

In this scene, Joseph and Mary were fulfilling Jewish law, which called for infants to be brought into the temple on the tenth day of life. Simeon was extremely old, having proclaimed that he would not die until he saw the Messiah. Upon seeing the infant Jesus as a pillar of light, he is reported to have put his palms together and said, "I have seen the Messiah," then collapsed and died on the spot.

My readings also explained Jung's fascination with the number four, which is considered an unlucky number to the Chinese, Korean, Vietnamese and Japanese cultures, as the spoken number sounds like the word for "death." Therefore, many numbered product lines skip the number four. For example, Nokia cell phones offer no series beginning with four, while the Canon PowerShot G series goes from G3 to G5. And in many parts of Asia, buildings have no fourth floor, similar to American buildings that have no thirteenth floor, as the number 13 is considered unlucky by many in the Western world. In Hong Kong, some high-rise residential buildings do not list any floors containing the number four, so that a building listing a fiftieth floor as the highest, has but 36 floors. On the other hand, the number six, and more important, the number 666 (representing the devil to many Christians), is seen as the luckiest of all numbers.

Looking back, I see myself pushing open every door I could find in order to enlarge my window of perception so as to deal with death and its attendant occurrences, some of which had changed my life. It was a difficult, fulfilling and rewarding journey—a trip to remember.

RADIANT ENERGY

Why do we experience near-death events? How could Kim dream her death in exact detail? What was going on when total knowledge of death due to a blood clot filled my mind—twice? How did I end up on the other side of a room while my body remained standing before my husband? And what—what!?—was the rod of light I saw in my bedroom?

". . . and God said, Let there be light." Genesis: 1: 3

"Then came an intolerable light blazing out, and in it was one whose grace and whose beauty were greater than the beauty of this world." *The Epic of Gilgamesh*, 2500 BC

They say the universe began with a blinding flash of light. If you read up on your cosmology, you will find that the flash didn't occur until a bit later, but it was close enough to the beginning to give us license for poetry. We also find light figuring predominantly in religions where the soul, or spirit, is most commonly referenced in connection with light.

Many years ago, a Yanomamo native from the deepest parts of the Amazonian jungle was the first of his tribe to leave his natural home and visit a large city. Many things stunned, excited or shocked this wonderful man of the jungle, but only one thing reduced him to a quivering mass: if he and his friend, anthropologist Napoleon A. Chagnon, took a cab after sundown, the tribesman would panic whenever he saw oncoming headlights. He claimed them to be malevolent *bores* (spirits) of the dead. So frightened was the man of oncoming headlights that he would curl into a ball on the taxi's floor, cover his head with his arms and lie shivering until their destination was reached.

What had the Yanomamo and his people, who had never known or seen artificial light other than a flashlight or lantern, experienced in the darkness of the jungle night? And what caused them to label what they had seen as malevolent spirits?

The complex workings of the 100 billion neurons that compose the average human brain are generated by electricity. We, along with all life on planet Earth, are the body electro-chemical. Measurements of human brain waves show a complex wave that is infinite in range, though normal readings range from one half cycle per second to one hundred cycles per second, with the average range tracing at one to forty cycles per second. At the time of death, the "power" shuts down.

Ancient Egyptians and alchemists claimed that one resurrected from the body through the transformation of matter. They told of seeing sparks emanating from the body of the dead—"the seed plot"—and spoke of the corpse as "the secret." They firmly believed in an afterlife lived by one's spirit.

Do freed electrons represent the backdrop for a good ghost story? Science tells us that we are still in the dark, still roaming the underworld. In other words, we simply don't know, nor can we prove our thoughts for or against at this point in time.

St. Jerome listed Origen as the greatest teacher of the early church after the Apostles. Origen visited and preached throughout the early Christian lands, but his main place of teaching was in Alexandria, Egypt, where he was born circa AD 185.

Origen believed, as most others of his day, that the vision of Christ after death was a visual sighting of the energy-spirit of the Christ, and that Jesus allowed it to appear as though he was of full body in order to strengthen the faith of his disciples.

In Origen's writings regarding the resurrection, he speaks of *spintherismos* (emission of sparks) emanating from the *seminarium* (seed plot) of the old (dead) body. In Origen's view, the emission of sparks from the seed plot were visible seed, or substance, or source, from which the body was resurrected, not in the form of matter, but converted from matter into spiritual energy seen as visible light. Within the universe we live in, matter can become energy and energy can turn into matter.

Centuries after Origen's time, St. Augustine, bishop of Hippo in Roman Africa from 396 to 430—often referred to as the father of the Christian church—decided against Origen (and all other ancient writers) and for the concrete interpretation of the resurrection extant today. He feared for the faith of followers if mere sparks of light and perception remained the basis of the story. Thus were past observations twisted to form a more palpable story.

As I dug into volumes searching for answers, I followed in the wake of Joseph Campbell and found the same stories and luminous bodies in every Logos I read. No matter how far back I went, I found light and energy in connection with death. And with the light came a belief in the continuation of life on another level.

In the 1930s, Harold Saxton Burr of Yale hooked a voltmeter to a tree and recorded fluctuations of current in response to light, moisture, weather, sunspots and moon phases. At the time of his investigations people thought Burr was off his rocker. Few paid any attention to his work; in fact, they didn't even bother to test his findings. Decades later, others would prove him to be correct. It is now known that all living bodies, both plant and animal, are electrochemical in nature, each giving off detectable signals of electromagnetism; all entities consist of energy and light.

Continuing to dig I found *Man and Time: Papers from the Eranos Yearbooks*, edited by Joseph Campbell. The book proved to be illuminating in respect to light and time. I sat in my reading chair with *Man and Time* in my lap. I sat and read translations of ancient metaphysical writings that had been written on papyrus and parchment in times long past. The title of one paper was "Cyclical Time in Mazdaism and Ismailism," by Mary Boyce. It centered on the age of the world in Zoroastrian Mazdaism.

Zoroastrianism is an ancient Persian religion put to

parchment in the sixth century BC. Older writings had existed but had been torched through times of war and religious upheaval. The Zoroastrians (the Parsis of modern times) believed in a supreme God who required that man perform good deeds in order to help in God's struggle against the evil spirit.

The people of this religion claimed that they came from a celestial world and were manifested in the spiritual state. They claimed that their original state was not the terrestrial state. They believed in preexistence and super-existence. They state in their writings that our moment of birth is not our beginning, nor is death our absolute end. They set forth the principle of a fifth dimension in which beings elevate to the light of eternal time after the knowing of earthly darkness. They claim that eternal time is represented by light, while the absence of light takes one into darkness. According to Einstein, at the speed of light, time stops, whereas in the realm of quantum mechanics, time doesn't even exist.

Had early Zoroastrians observed sparks and/or rods of light following death? Where did their faith and beliefs come from? From what occurrences did they emanate?

The Zoroastrian god, Ohrmazd, is represented by his ubiquitous light. The religion goes on to say that light grounds itself in all living things and acts as another self, an angel protector, an alter ego, a guiding or companionable spirit that eternally keeps ahead of each embodied soul.

Zoroastrians do not refer to the body, or of it being of matter. Life on earth is where darkness is found (evil), representing the "arena for struggle and also the prize." Death restores each being to the luminous state. If we follow the beliefs of these ancient people we find, housed within each living thing, a temporal body and time, as we perceive it, plus eternal time capable of emanating as visual, immaterial light (remember—photons are massless).

Throughout eons past, did people experience near-death? Was Dr. Kirsch correct? Did Kim appear to me as her celestial self, manifested as light through which eternal time is discernible?

The Hindus say that within us there is a column of light whose shadow is the backbone.

Christ referred to himself as the light in John 8:12: "I am the light of the world."

Again and again, everywhere I looked I found light and/or enlightenment.

As I read and searched for understanding, I uncovered a wealth of ideas and thoughts that coalesced into a mainstream of consciousness. Through my own experiences, books, and the experiences of others I learned to push through doors that had previously been closed to me. But real and substantial growth often followed bouts of great trauma.

Five months after Kim's death, I experienced such paranoia that I came close to collapse. In my state of paranoia, I once again grieved for my mother, understanding at last the depth of her pain and fright. Without the inner core of strength provided to me by my parents, and a psychological understanding of depression and mental fatigue, I feel I would have surely fallen from my path and toppled headlong into a pit of depression. Instead, I clung tenaciously to the ledge of sanity, dangling over the abyss, fearing at once both the fall and the pain of hanging on.

Relatives called. "Come with us to Mexico. It will be a good change for you."

"I'm afraid to fly. I might die." I'm afraid, I'm afraid, I'm afraid.

I sat shivering in terror of my own death. I sat shivering in a tomb of embarrassment. Only weeks before, I had longed for death, now I became as writhing slime, powerless, paralyzed in panic, and all for fear of losing life.

"Carole, I don't care if you upchuck all the way to L.A. Pack your bag and get on the plane. If you don't, you will end up in a corner and we will never get you out. If you don't tackle this now, you're finished. Get up! Get on that plane!"

Where the strength came from I cannot say, but I forced myself onto the plane and my relatives helped me onto the next two that got us down to Oaxaca, Mexico, for a walk through another dimension. By the time we arrived back in Los Angeles, I was all right, still a bit squeamish, but back on track.

Before my flight back to Jackson, a friend timidly approached me and recommended a psychologist she knew. She said he dealt with rebirthing and that she knew it sounded hokey but she felt strongly that I would gain a great deal from the experience, adding that she and her husband had gone through the experience numerous times.

Hokey? I thought it sounded bizarre, to say the least. I was polite, but put the suggestion aside. Months later, my friend again mentioned her psychologist. Again, I was polite as I allowed the suggestion to slip by.

Time, linear time, flowed its normal course. My mind slowed it with grappling hooks of pain and sorrow. Then I began to write, to exorcise all that had occurred. I wrote and read and wrote some more. I sat at my electronic screen and laughed in wondrous recall. I sat and cried, and wrote and died. In the end, I was proud that such beautiful people had walked along my life's path, holding my hand, touching my spirit, lifting my spirit, shattering my spirit, so that it might regroup into a better form than before.

After finishing the first draft of this book, I flew to Los Angeles on business. This time a different me boarded the plane. Prior to my departure, I called my friend and asked her to arrange an appointment for me with her rebirthing psychologist, Dr. Stephen Johnson, graduate of the University of Southern California, instructor in the Counseling Psychology Department and director of the Center for Holistic Psychology and Education.

"Carole, this is a hard thing to recommend to anyone, and I have been fearful in urging you into this, but I get such strong feelings from you that I can't help but feel that the experience will be worth the effort." Two weeks later, I sat in Dr. Johnson's office and laughed, "I have no idea why I'm here."

The good doctor laughed with me, saying he could tell that was the case.

We spoke. I told him of the many deaths that had occurred in rapid succession, of my experiences and this book. When I told him of the rod of light I had seen following Kim's death, he replied, "Oh, I have seen one of those."

Startled, I asked him to please tell me in detail what he could of his experience.

"Well, it was right here in this office. I had been working with a patient for some weeks when I got a call from her husband. He said his wife's father had died the day before and he was worried about her condition. I told him to bring her right in. We immediately went into a rebirthing session. The woman was really into it when her face began to change. This is not unusual, the faces of many appear to change during the process, but this was quite strong and dramatic, reaching a point of being rather eerie. Her husband looked at me wide-eyed and mouthed, 'That's her father.' Right after that a tremendous rod of crackling light appeared in that corner, and just as you said, it was a thin rod of intense white light that crackled, shimmered and was gone. "

I interrupted, "What did you feel or think at the time?"

"I felt strongly that it was her father. No, I knew it was her father. The husband was totally bowled over. He was a head electrician at one of the studios and was awestruck with the power of the light. I don't recall what he guessed the power of the light to be, but it was of incredible voltage. He doubted man could duplicate that much power in such a slender rod."

Serendipity = Synchronicity. The friend who had recommended the man sitting across from me hadn't known of my seeing the light, nor did she know (I later inquired) that Dr. Johnson had ever had such an experience.

An excited calm came over me. It is always nice to find

out that you are not crazy. This was the second person to tell me of witnessing a spectacular light following a death. It hadn't been a hallucination but a manifestation of energy, a very powerful energy contained within what appeared to be a slender rod. And both Dr. Johnson and his patient's husband had seen the rod of light on the first day after the death of the patient's father. Dr. Kirsch said they were usually seen on the first or third day following a death. Kim's had appeared during the night of the third day.

The doctor looked at me and said, "Let's get on with what I do. Do you know what rebirthing is?"

"I haven't the faintest."

"Well, it's a form of relaxation and breathing. We call it conscious breathing, a process that integrates body, mind and spirit. You do it yourself. I only work as a guide and comforter in case fear is part of your experience. Mostly, I'm simply with you, helping you along whatever path you choose to travel down."

It sounded too simple. I wanted to query the doctor or balk. I did neither. I smiled and asked what I was supposed to do.

The doctor came to me, asked that I remove my shoes and place my feet and lower legs on the footstool that was equal in height to the chair in which I sat. Then, working a lever, he dropped the back of my chair so that I lay in a reclining position with my body completely supported head to toe.

I said I was cold. He covered me with a thin blanket, reassuring me that he would cover me further if I got colder through the experience. Then he gave me instructions.

"I want you to relax completely. I want you to clear your mind. Try not to think of anything. Allow whatever comes into your mind to come in, but don't work it over or cling to it. Keep the doors of your mind open."

I relaxed to the best of my ability and told myself to let go, to allow whatever was or was not going to happen to happen. The doctor continued.

"Now I want you to take in a deep breath. Good. Now let it out. As soon as you are through exhaling, draw in another breath. Don't wait; take in another breath. Good, good. Breath. Out. Breath. Out. Get the rhythm. Don't wait between breaths; keep the breath of life rolling in and out, in and out. Good. Good."

As I regulated my breathing, I started to feel lightheaded and then my limbs began to tingle, almost throb. My first concrete thought was, "This is nothing but an exercise in hyperventilation. Somebody get me a brown paper bag." My next thought was, "You are here to experience, so experience. Shut up and let it happen regardless of what it is. You can play judge and jury later."

I let go. The lightheadedness dissolved. My body became numb and tingly, both at the same time. I felt lighter, as if in another atmosphere. Then my sorrow hit. They came in, all of them, all of those who had gone on before me and I felt cold and I was crying. Dr. Johnson covered me with another blanket and placed his right hand just under my diaphragm. I shivered and felt tremendous energy coursing through my body that was racked with grief over my loved ones. I found my mind calling to them,

"I love you, I love you, I love you." My tears ran in rivulets. "I love you."

"Breathe," prompted the doctor.

I could feel my face contort into a mask of anguish. I felt I might die of it.

"You are all right," soothed the doctor. "You are here, in your body, and you are all right. Keep breathing and let it happen. You are safe, totally safe."

I went through what felt like real physical trauma. Certainly the emotional trauma was real, and then I seemed to arrive at another level and things were somewhat better. I became aware of all parts of my body, of each tingle, each glow of warmth, of muscle flowing as ribbon, of swirling atoms binding together to form the whole, which seemed to be without boundaries.

Then again my mind raced outward, searching for those who had died, calling to them, asking, "Why? Why? Why?" Suddenly, a powerful force took hold and my mind wasn't asking anything. Both my mind and brain seemed not to exist, whereas my body was all and everything. It was then that I knew that my mind and my body were one, each cell capable of thinking in like kind. There was my body. It housed my mind. There was nothing else. Throughout this period of time, my body hummed, glowed and tingled, and I noted that my arms were rising of their own accord to a height of about six inches over my abdomen, and then my legs were rising and I was floating in a space of total feeling.

Then my body and my mind, which were still one, were being forced through a seemingly impenetrable, invisible wall. It was not a pleasurable feeling, but a painful and wrenching experience. I chafed under the strain of lost composure. As the experience became excruciating, I found my knees drawn up closer to my body, though I still had no sensation of causing them to rise. It seemed they had risen on their own accord and I was powerless to position them in any other way. After a while, my knees curled almost to my head as the doctor righted the chair so as to accommodate the tightly bound, fetal position my body had assumed.

The anguish grew. I think I was crying. I was hanging on for dear life, but to what or for what reason I cannot say. During this particular time of mental and physical anguish, my eyes blinked open for a split second and I saw Dr. Johnson with his face turned away from my pain, my anguish mirrored onto his face as he held me through my flight. Many minutes later, the anguish began to subside and once again I was lying flat in an alert mental state.

I recall saying, "They are all right," over and over again, but can't remember why I said it. The memory of the knowledge imparted to me left as I became totally aware of my new condition, aware that I couldn't move my body. With great effort, I forced my lips to part enough to allow me to speak. I wanted to speak that which I was aware of, and what I was aware of was that I was dead.

With my eyes still closed (though it seemed that I could see), I said through barely opened lips, "I'm a corpse. I'm dead. This is what it feels like to be dead. This is what they all felt like. This is what it's like to be a living spirit in a dead body."

The minute I finished speaking, all of the tingling sensations, from every part of my body, became supercharged and started racing towards my abdomen. My energy, my life force coursed through me to the swirling generator that was growing in my gut, and then my life force spun in such velocity that it formed a vortex and broke free, flying into the cosmos in an ever-expanding vortex that funneled down to me where my inner self was exiting at great speed.

I began to laugh and cry. "I'm a corpse. This is what the dead feel like. My spirit is leaving me from my stomach. It's whirling around in a vortex and whirling off into space. This is what it's like to die. They are all right. They are all right. They are all all right." And I laughed and cried some more.

It was over. As my mind drifted back to what we perceive to be reality, I felt as though I was bound in satin plaster. I knew I wasn't paralyzed, yet I also knew that for the moment I couldn't have moved regardless of will, and so I lay peacefully at rest, savoring the sensations of my body.

I opened my eyes and looked up at the doctor. It had been a rough, but expanding experience for us both. This time I actually spoke to him.

"I have always known that we carry heaven and hell within us. It appears we also carry life and death."

Now I knew why I hadn't accepted my friend's invitation to visit Dr. Johnson the year before. A year ago, I had neither the skepticism nor the searching need for answers, and, in retrospect, a year ago I may not have been capable of having such an experience.

"We must never lose sight of our skepticism," said the doctor.

How true. But my dip into the pool of my unconscious mind was a worthwhile journey that offered much to ponder.

I had cried more than I had been aware of. It took three tissues to get all of the tears out of my ears. The doctor and I spoke. I asked him how rebirthing actually works, citing my initial thought of it being nothing more than hyperventilation. He laughed and told me that every doctor he had ever worked with had thought the same thing, but that every one of them had changed their mind after the experience. "So how does it work?" I asked.

"I really don't know. All I know is that it works."

We analyzed and stated what could be perceived by the experience and what had to be left until we understood ourselves more fully. The session was over.

Ever so slowly, I drove back home. My heart was light. My body felt smooth throughout. I felt that I had allowed myself to receive a grain of knowledge. Most of all, I felt joy in receiving another report of a rod of light observed following a death, a light described perfectly to match the one that had inhabited my bedroom. My experience had been a real event. Repeatable? No. But did it happen? Yes.

I went back through the rebirthing experience, back through my memory of it. Through recollection, I realized that towards the end, just prior to becoming a corpse, I had experienced a feeling of relief and thought myself to be back out of the experience. Now, afterwards, I realized that at that moment, I wasn't out of the experience, but fully into it. At that moment, I had finally broken through a seemingly impenetrable wall to the other side, to my unconscious self where I had managed to glimpse a grain of truth. A personal truth held to be so by my mind.

My mind went into overdrive. If my loved ones were

all right, I had to be all right. My mind drifted back to a year before, several months after Kim's death when comments from friends shifted from pure condolence to "You must let go, Carole." "Kim wouldn't want you to be this way." "Don't hold her on the mortal plane. Let her go, allow her to be free."

I heard the words, but listened not. Then, one morning I awoke with the remnants of a vivid dream that explained my emotional limbo. A friend called. I tried to explain. I related my dream.

"Use your imagination. You are walking through the woods with your child. The path leads you to a steep cliff that looks forever down into a never-ending gorge thousands of feet deep. There is a rope bridge crossing the gorge to the other side. You and your child start across. The child is in front of you. When you are halfway across the child stumbles and falls. You rush to help and as you near your child her body starts to slip over the center ropes. You throw yourself prostrate and catch your child's arm just as her body slips over the edge. Your legs are splayed trying to hook into the ropes. Your left hand is grasping the bridge while your right hand holds onto the arm of your child. You look down into your child's face as you scream her name, over and over again. The child doesn't answer. Your child is dead. There's nothing you can do for your child. The abyss waits. You cannot stay forever on the bridge and it's impossible for you to haul the body up, impossible to get the body to safety, impossible to bring your child back. Now, let go."

Now, a year later, as I recalled the utter joy that had filled parts of my rebirthing, the sense of being, the sense of being more, of whirling off into the ether, of everything being all right, I asked myself what I had asked before. Could I now learn to let go? Dr. Johnson, an objective observer, had seen the light, his patient's husband had seen the light, I had seen the light. Could I now "see" the light?

The following day, I drove to Berkeley to stay and visit with friends who are professors of various sciences. It was difficult driving through Berkeley, remembering the last time I had been there with Kim, remembering the fun she'd had and the joy she had brought to so many. Passing the hotel where we had stayed, I developed heart palpitations.

I arranged to have lunch with a friend and professor on Sunday. Over Thai food and Chinese beer, we discussed my book and the paranormal. He thought that sooner or later science would find a superluminal speed level, even though Einstein and most of the physicists of today thought it impossible for anything to travel faster than the speed of light.

I delighted in the openness of his mind. After lunch, we went back to his laboratory to look over parts of my manuscript. Since his mind was obviously open to all possibilities, I took a chance and had him read the part where I explain my experience of seeing a rod of light in my bedroom.

"Why Carole, I could have told you about these years ago. My mother saw one when she was a young woman. I heard her story a hundred times. She was staying in the country with a girlfriend. They were sitting in the living room with her friend's parents after supper when suddenly a crackling rod of light appeared in the middle of the room. It scared the devil out of my mother; she never, ever forgot it. When it was gone, the mother said, 'Oh dear, someone must have died. Whenever someone in our family dies we see one of those incredible lights.' Sure enough, two days later, a buggy pulled up and they got word that the father's brother had been killed in an accident."

I sat staring at the professor. I told him of my meetings with Kirsch and Johnson. He smiled and said, "Carole, if you'd had that experience and never been able to talk about it you would think you had lost your mind. If I had known you'd had such an experience, I could have put your mind at ease months ago."

So Dr. Kirsch knew of the light, Dr. Johnson and another man had seen the light and now a professor was sitting across from me reassuring me as he retold his mother's experience.

The professor's mother having seen a rod of light in the company of three others is key testimony for the defense as no one in the house was aware that anyone had died, proving that observations of light rods following a death are not brought on by grieving or distraught minds. Emotional and mental anguish must be ruled out as a creating factor. It should also be noted that the three psychoanalysts who observed a rod of light on the day following their colleague's death might have been dismayed over the death of their friend, but they certainly would not have been in a state of deep mourning.

DREAMING OUR DREAMS

The human brain is an awesome thing. And though we may dissect it, probe it, CAT-scan it, PET-scan it, MRI it, study it, and map its hundred billion neurons, a complete understanding evades us. It is a wondrous thing.

Brilliant ideas, realizations, and discoveries have come forth through the portals of dreamtime when the creative connectivity of the unconscious flows into the confines of the conscious mind. $E=mc^2$ came to Einstein as he dozed on a grassy hill on a summer's afternoon. Mozart often slept at his piano only to awaken with a new composition running through his mind and flowing out the tips of his fingers. In 1863, Bismarck dreamt of being victorious in his plan to unite the German states. The deed done, he became Germany's first chancellor. And in 1940, D. B. Parkinson saw his all-electric gun director in a dream. From that dream came the M-9 electrical analog computer.

Countless scientists, and others in various fields, have searched for an understanding to a principle, formula or method of proof, only to find the complex answer made simple through the power of dreamtime. Have you not slept on a problem only to know the answer by morning?

While few people of today look at or listen to their dreams, in times past the majority of the world's people held dreams in high regard and acted upon them.

The long-accepted power of dreams began to wane some 500 years ago with the advent of the Age of Science. This golden age led to the machine age and a huge expansion in the number of proven theories in the field of physics and other hard sciences. Such advancements in knowledge led to man strolling on the moon and the instant communication skills of today. From science came new innovations, better medical treatments and advanced technologies. As life became safer (yet more deadly in the wake of more powerful armaments), realism began to replace, or modify, the way we think. Anything that could not be scientifically explained and/or replicated was labeled "paranormal," "superstitious," "false," "irrational," or just plain baloney. And, in a majority of instances, the catcalling was warranted. The earth is not flat, man has walked on the moon, germs and viruses do exist and laying a newborn on another woman's bed will not cause the bed's owner to become pregnant. Nevertheless, the golden age often threw the baby out with the bath water.

Goethe said, "Man must cling to his faith that the incomprehensible is comprehensible, else he would cease to investigate."

The eighteenth century Age of Enlightenment, also known as the Age of Reason, emerged from fertile minds of feudal Europe. Born in France, Britain and Germany, it spread across the entirety of Europe and America, influencing the Bill of Rights and the setting up of the United States of America. The Age of Enlightenment led to humanism, which followed in the wake of emerging sciences. Together, these new egalitarian systems of thought and laws begat the age of pragmatism and reason that demanded that all things believable had to be repeatable and testable in a laboratory. Reductionism came forth as instinctual traits and things that go bump in the night were pushed to the back of the closet. Modern man couldn't be concerned about, or connected with, anything unprovable or unscientific. And as the Enlightenment modified thought, Goethe's profound words were forgotten.

While dreams were heady stuff from our very beginnings, in the current age of sound bites, the Web, and constant, mind-bending information—full of as much fallacy as fact—we seldom give credence to the power of our dreams.

But even today, as the pragmatic, "civilized" world works on farms, in factories and laboratories, those living closer to nature continue to give a great deal of credence to their dreams. The Australian Aborigines speak of the "Dreamtime," a term that speaks to and explains all that is, including how the earth came to be and how it will end, much as the Maya of Central America wrote more than a thousand years ago. Meanwhile, the diminutive !Kung of the African Kalahari Desert tell us there is a dream dreaming us—but who is, or was, the original dreamer?

And long before any European met the !Kung of the Kalahari, Edgar Allan Poe chimed in with "All that we see or seem is but a dream within a dream."

In the 1950s, dream researchers discovered REM (rapid eye movement) and proved, once and for all, that we all dream whether or not we retain a conscious memory of doing so upon waking. Dreams take up approximately 20 percent of adult sleep time, while children and infants spend 60 to 80 percent of their sleep time in the dream state. This makes perfect sense when we remember that from birth through the first seven or eight years of life, the human brain absorbs enormous amounts of data on a daily basis as it configures itself. Additionally, research has shown that dreams rework and ingrain things we learn during hours of wakefulness.

Not only do we all dream, we possess both mental and physical needs for dreams, as without REM time we become mentally disoriented. The ancient Eastern torture of keeping a person awake for days or weeks at a time is based on this fact. It's not the lack of sleep that unravels a person's mind, but the lack of REM time that scrambles the brain and loosens the tongue. A person will say anything for the promise of sleep and the opportunity to dream and travel through other realms of the mind to the other side of oneself.

I enjoy the sleep-aid ad where Lincoln, a beaver, and a silent individual in a spacesuit visit the guy whose dreams they usually inhabit. "We miss you," they tell the man—and they really do. It's a salient advertisement but for the fact that sleep aids often suppress REM time, leaving you with a less than complete feeling in the morning.

I find it fascinating that though our eyes are closed and we lie in darkness, our eyes—as seen through the lids of our eyes—move rapidly whenever the mind is dreaming. The rapidity of the eye's movements testifies to the fact that dreams that seem to last for hours usually occur within a matter of minutes or mere seconds.

During sleep, and especially during dreamtime, the old reptilian brain—the brainstem—shuts down several of the body's reactions that are automatic during wakefulness. This closing down produces what researchers call sleep paralysis. Sleep paralysis is no doubt an extremely ancient protective device that evolved for obvious reasons. If we physically acted out our dreams, we could do real harm to ourselves or a sleeping partner. Sleep paralysis has been observed in all animals that dream. And all animals have been observed dreaming except for snakes . . . no limbs, no dreams? And consider this: without sleep paralysis, chimpanzees would fall out of their nightly made tree nests.

When you dream, only your fingers, toes and eyes are capable of movement (though, at times, the entire body, or parts thereof, may jerk or convulse). At the same time, incoming stimuli are shut out by way of your own personal "cloaking device." While your brain operates within the confines of your cranium, your mind wanders the labyrinth of your unconscious self or plucks thoughts, facts and ideas from the universe or the habitable, oxygen-rich atmosphere that surrounds our planet. We know from humankind's earliest writings that many have received provable information during REM time. Kim's dream is a strong example while my "knowledge" of death by blood clot shows that such forms of information can come also to a wakeful mind.

As a person enters dreamtime, the business-decision-making areas of the left hemisphere of the brain go quiet while the primary visual cortex and the artistic, memory-grabbing frontal lobes and right hemisphere go into full gear. During dreamtime the amygdala and the hippocampus, a multipurpose lump that stores memories, show activity. In combination, these fascinating areas of the brain supply the dreamer with the ability to feel and sense everything from raging, wild fear to lust in the land of illusions. But the question remains, on what screen are our dreams projected, or do we dreamers enter a holographic realm that allows us entrance into our dreams? Where were you in that dream last night? Wasn't that you making love to a stranger who turned out to be someone you saw at the bank? Were you not the one running from that pack of wolves, or mowing the lawn over and over and over again until the alarm went off? When we dream, we rarely view ourselves as on a screen, but exist as characters within a play, acting out our dreams on some mystical stage. It is as if we are the dream, and the dream is us, which, of course, we are and it is.

As ever more modern man races about using ever more technical inventions, more remote societies continue to give credence to their dreams, often molding their lives around them in ways that mirror writings of the past.

From Genesis 3:5–7: "And Joseph dreamed a dream, and he told it his brethren: and they hated him yet the more. 'For behold, we were binding the sheaves in the field, and, lo, my sheaf arose, and also stood upright; and, behold, your sheaves stood round about, and made obeisance to my sheaf.'"

By the age of 17, Joseph had a thorough understanding of dreams. Later, in Genesis 40, he correctly deciphers the dreams experienced by the butler and the baker to the pharaoh, both of which came to pass. When we get to Genesis 41, we find one of the most famous of all dreams dreamt by the pharaoh himself, a dream that foretold of seven good years followed by seven lean. Without Joseph's interpretation, without credence being given to the pharaoh's dream, starvation and death would have surely overcome the people of Egypt.

Of the billions of dreams dreamt nightly, few are prophetic, the majority working as a reviewing and dumping process that cleans our mental cupboards of everyday annoyances and occurrences, or deal with worries and emotional or physical desires. Some researchers view dreams as nothing more than clearinghouses for the brain. Like cleaning up your computer by trashing unnecessary files. However, a majority of dream researchers find every dream to be intricately related to the life of the dreamer. But while all dreams may have meaning, accurate deciphering remains difficult.

More important to this volume is the fact that there are unique dreams; dreams that are stark and clear, "more real than life itself," dreams that don't speak to you via metaphor or with confusion, but with total and complete clarity. These singular dreams are never forgotten and often warn of danger or tell of coming events. History and legend tell us that singular dreams have always been a part of the human story, often affecting lives and guiding belief systems. In both legend and religion, such dreams are referenced as prophecy.

As I read through one book after another and talked to people from various professions from many parts of the world, I came across remarkable data, such as findings that show that dreams experienced by critically ill people, in which they fight death, never fail to recognize death, regardless of how it presents itself. In these dreams, death may be personified as a male or female of human form, animal form or some unknown thing or species. Statistics show that if a person dreams of fighting with death and loses, he or she will die, usually within a few days, but those who dream of fighting death and winning, recover quickly, despite professional prognosis. Dream gatherers also offer evidence that if a critically ill person dreams of a deceased member of his or her family—as Kim dreamt of her great-grandmother—and in the dream interacts with the departed person as in normal life, death usually ensues.

Dr. Kirsch explained to me, "I'm afraid her boyfriend was right. The great-grandmother came to get her, to help her along, but you must understand that Kim sent for her. She asked her to come." (Please keep in mind that the people in these studies were critically ill and that their dreams were singular in nature. If you simply dream of a monster trying to get you, or of your deceased aunt, it doesn't mean you are on your way out.)

Though research has come up with some startling information, and collected data seem to prove the point concerning precognitive dreams, we are still standing on the outside looking in, still wondering who's on first.

Most people find it difficult to have faith in dreams since all things are possible within the confines of dreamtime, such as flying or being able to breathe underwater. During dreamtime, the underlying layers of the mind appear to ignore the limiting dimensions we experience during wakefulness. Singular dreams, on the other hand, stand out starkly against the average, as they feel and seem to be totally and consciously real. "The dream was more real than life itself," said Kim, not once, but three times during the telling of her death dream.

On the night of Kim's death, the family in Los Angeles was notified by phone. Staggered by the news, grief gripped the crowd that had gathered for the traditional Thanksgiving feast. Diane was the only one not present when the phone rang. She had left the gathering early as she had to arise at 5:00 AM the following morning. It was decided best not to call her; she was living alone at the time and she and Kim had been extremely close. As cousins, they had grown up together and become fast friends.

Early the next morning, Diane was taking a pre-dawn shower when the phone rang. She reached out and answered it. Cries shattered the darkness as agonized sounds reverberated through the apartment building. Through her first tears, Diane told her mother it wasn't possible. That Kim had come to her door the night before. She told of sitting on her couch watching television, of hearing a knock at the door and going to answer it. There stood Kim looking happier than Diane had ever seen her. She said that Kim seemed consumed with joy.

Later, Diane would say it was a dream, but when her mother first notified her of Kim's passing, Diane spoke as though the experience had actually happened.

It is one of philosophy's oldest questions. Where does reality end and dream begin? Or are they one and the same?

Dr. Kirsch, the dream analyst, student of Jung, experiencer of life, said of Diane's dream, "Believe it. It's probably true. She may have had an actual vision but was unable to consciously accept it, so she tucked it into the safety of a dream."

Five or six days after Kim's death, Gerry, Kim's boyfriend, was taking an afternoon nap. In his sleep, he heard Kim whisper his name. He felt her bending over him trying to awaken him. Slowly, he was drawn out of his sleep into consciousness. Still Kim whispered his name as the feeling of her presence over him became acutely sharp, almost tangible. When all of his senses were convinced that she was actually there, he opened his eyes to an empty room.

A few weeks later, during the night, Kim came to him in a dream. She said that everything was all right now and that he could come home. He wanted to join her, wanted to go to her then realized the danger. At the very last possible moment, his conscious mind pulled him back.

End of dream.

Did Kim visit Diane or Gerry? Did she try to lure Gerry to the other side? Gerry felt he had come very close to death. "It really shook me up," he exclaimed after relating his dreams. One would think so, but can the *spirit* of one who has passed on actually visit this earthly plane? Or is it memory, coupled with desire? Diane had no knowledge of Kim's death. Why the dream or experience? What possible desire could she have had? And what prompted her unconscious self to dream such a dream on the very night of Kim's death?

It is said that to dream of whales is a sign of great danger or great change. Sometimes what is commonly believed turns out to be correct. A week and a half prior to Kim's death, her brother Brett had a startling dream.

In Los Angeles, there is a large blue-glass building, which has been called everything from the Blue Whale building to the Milk-o-Magnesia building. I happen to like the building; it is most distinctive. In Brett's dream, he was inside the blue building. As he looked up and out through five stories of glass, he saw nothing but blue sky and clouds; no earth or other buildings could be seen. Los Angeles had disappeared. It was as if the building was suspended in air. It was very quiet. The inside of the huge blue building was hollow. No five floors, no rooms or dividing walls, just the immensity of the blue glass shell. Hanging from the steel metal wires was a gigantic dark-blue whale, so large as to barely fit inside the building. There were about half a dozen other people in the building and along with Brett they were wandering over the black glossy floor, looking up at the whale, whose underbelly had been slit from jaw to tail. The incision was perfectly clean, cleaving up in pie wedge fashion. The flesh that showed was a deep, glistening, reddish salmon color. No blood was seen, and the black glossy floor was spotless. Brett felt a sense of awe coupled with an overwhelming, all-consuming fear.

End of dream.

Brett had dictated his dream to me following his sister's death in 1986. In 2007, as I began again to rewrite this volume, I called and asked him if he remembered his dream of the whale. Over the phone, quietly and full of wonder, came his words, everything in exact detail but for two perceptions he didn't mention. Brett didn't recall looking through the blue glass and realizing that Los Angeles had disappeared, and he didn't mention the glossy blackness of the floor. I said, "Listen to this," then read what is written above. Afterward, he claimed no recollection of looking out through the glass, but said that as I read his words about the glossy black floor he had a re-experiencing, as if he were back in the dream, commenting that the floor was incredibly frightening, sinister and threatening. "Mom, I've got goosebumps so bad the hair on my legs is standing straight out."

I, too, had goosebumps as my son's retelling gave credibility to the staying power of singular dreams. Dream and brain researchers speak of cellular tracks laid down between the prefrontals and the hippocampus that form permanent "memory paths," thus creating memories that are never lost.

Isn't it fascinating that Brett's brain subconsciously picked the Blue Whale building in which to house his dream; a building he had only seen once from the confines of a car. He was 15 when we moved from Los Angeles to Jackson.

Four months after Kim's death, I dreamt I was looking up into the faces of an immense group of people. Suddenly, my mother was there, close, her face well lit, as if spotlighted on a stage. Then the other people faded from sight and my full attention went to my mother, who said, "You know, it wasn't the horse's fault."

End of dream.

At a dinner party in Los Angeles, I told psychoanalyst Arthur Ourieff about Kim's dream. He stared at me with wide eyes, "I have nothing to say to you." Then he said with troubled eyes, "I know of no concrete explanation." He looked down at his dinner plate for a moment, then looked up and proceeded to tell me of two cases he had encountered that seemed to border on the subject of my quest.

"There was this man who had been coming to see me for some time. One day, he came into the office and said he had had a dream in which he was walking the high wire in a circus tent. He was terribly frightened and kept feeling that he was going to fall at any moment and meet his death. Following some discussion, I advised him to have a complete physical, just to be on the safe side. He did and it was found the he was in the preliminary stages of a cancer that is fatal unless caught in its earliest stages. If the doctors hadn't caught the disease in time, he would have surely died."

The other case told of a female patient: "She said she had dreamt that her bedroom window was open. As she lay in bed a raven hopped onto the windowsill and then onto her left breast where it set about pecking at a spot in the upper left-hand quadrant of her breast. Then she awoke. I asked her when she had had her last mammogram and suggested that she have another, just in case. She did and two weeks later they removed a small lump of cancerous cells from the upper left-hand quadrant of her left breast which, if left unchecked, may have led to her death."

In both of the above cases, it is possible that the body, through chemical messages, signaled the brain that cancerous cells were multiplying. The brain then transferred the message to the individual through dreamtime. . . . Score one for reductionism. However, both dreams gave life and death information in allegorical form and were only understood with the help of a third party, i.e., the psychoanalyst. Nevertheless, the future was swayed and death was set aside for the time being. If the future were pure fate, both patients would have failed to get medical help and would have died. Or were their dreams, and their interpretations, part of their fate? If so, what is the message of the warning? Why not allow people to live in health until their time to pass on? Or were the dreams and the detection of disease all a part of their life's learning? Are all experiences of life entered into for a reason applicable only to the individual? Was the process of discovering a life-threatening disease, surviving treatment, and suffering through the multiple emotions involved, a cycle of learning for the dreamers mentioned above? Surely such physical and mental traumas affect all individuals deeply. Few go through such processes without change and growth. And it should be remembered that such traumas affect others, who, in turn, must process through tough learning curves.

Could our dreams and deaths be windows into a more comprehensive plane of consciousness where a profusion of knowledge flows? When people have near-death experiences and feel to be a part of all knowledge, are they simply tapping into their own underground library or something more universal? Did Galileo, Einstein and all other thinkers open up to that which was already in existence? Of course! Humans don't create knowledge. Science didn't invent the principles of physics. The principles of physics have always been extant since, and quite possibly prior to, the beginning of our known universe. Humans find and discover what is and always has been possible within the realm of our existence. Hopefully, we will never be so blind as to close the doors that open to yet-to-be-discovered truths as surely there is more . . . much more.

Death often brings people together who normally don't come into contact with one another. In the case of Patty and myself, I was Kim's mother and she was my daughter's friend. We had been acquaintances, nothing more. Now, through our mutual love of Kim, we found ourselves able to communicate on a full and compassionate level.

At lunch one day, I discovered Patty to be precognitive through dreams. She seems to follow a common precognitive pattern. People who manifest their precognitive powers through dreams, go through on and off cycles. For instance, they will have a series of precognitive dreams over a six-month period, and then the well seems to run dry for six months up to two years. Most of these people, while in an off state, put their precognitive powers into a mental wastebasket, since their powers seem to have deserted them.

Patty has come to realize that there has to be some principle at work. Whether it's telepathy, psychic intuition or precognition, she doesn't know. What she does know is that her psychic, singular dreams have always proven out conclusively.

Over lunch, Patty told me three precognitive dreams. I will begin with two, one of which is rather ordinary, the other more spectacular. What is interesting about these two dreams is that the events corresponding to the dreams usually took place six months after the dreams. This phenomenon has happened with most of Patty's vivid, singular dreams. Please recall that singular dreams are remembered—often for a lifetime.

DREAM ONE: Patty is watching two men. She has never seen them before and doesn't recognize them. They are in the basement of a house she doesn't recognize and they are having a discussion about her, the house and people she's never met. Patty doesn't interact with them as they talk; she is simply an observer. One of them says, "You mean she's going to live upstairs?" This question, in particular, stays in her mind, as do the faces of the men in the dream.

End of dream.

Six months later, Patty moves into *the house*. She lives upstairs and meets the two men she had seen in the dream, becoming good friends with one of them. After moving into the house, she meets the people the two men had spoken of in the dream. One day, her new friend tells her of a discussion he and the other man had in the basement of the house she is now living in. Patty recognizes the entire discussion as the man relates it and is struck speechless when he says, "And then Tom said, 'You mean she's going to live upstairs?'"

I must add that the house in question is tucked back off the road. Patty had never seen the house or known of its existence, yet the first time she entered it she knew the entire floor plan.

DREAM TWO: Patty is flying through space. She gets to a door and goes through it into a room full of people. She is communicating with them, not through speech but through what she later recognizes as a form of telepathy. As the dream progresses, Patty realizes that the people in the room are mostly older people, and then it dawns on her that they are all dead. Suddenly, she becomes aware of another door at the other end of the room. The door is slightly ajar and through the opening streams a bright, marvelous light. The light from the door glistens in the eyes of the dead people and their eyes come alive, though their bodies still appear to be dead.

Patty tries to go towards the light coming from the partially opened door but all of the dead people tell her no, it isn't her time and that she mustn't go near the door.

End of dream.

Six months later, Patty attends a family reunion at the home of a distant aunt. Patty's father is there. In the past, they had never been close or able to communicate with one another. Now, at the reunion, they sit and talk. Finally, after so many years, they find common ground. Patty's father tells of finding some old photo albums in the old aunt's attic and goes to get them. As the withered pages are turned, Patty feels numb as all of the people from her dream look out at her.

Patty had never seen any photos of the people in the pictures prior to that day. In fact, she had not even known of their existence, yet she recognized them all, especially the two sisters whom she vividly remembered from the dream, sitting on a couch in the exact manner and dress as they sat in one of the photographs in the old album.

Could Patty have visited her ancestors? What about the

six months? That's a long time, and memories fade, but Patty said her dreams are singular and uncanny in their ability to sit solid in her memory bank, just like Brett's dream, retold 20 years after the fact, a dream he hadn't thought of in decades.

Patty also stressed the fact that she recognized the people in the photos with a total sense of knowing; there was no, "That sort of looks like . . ." about it. And the light, with the standard words, "You can't go there. It's not your time."? Was the dream actually a near-death experience? Patty was in excellent health at the time of her dream.

Now we get to Patty's dream of Kim, experienced three months after Kim's death. To my way of thinking, it's a winner. As to its meaning? Your thoughts are as good as mine. Of importance is the clarity of Patty's memory.

DREAM THREE, as told by Patty: "As the dream starts, I'm in among familiar buildings, then in the countryside, which I take to be California, a place I've never been. [Kim was born in Santa Monica, California.] As I ascend a beautiful hill, Kim appears. It is SO good to see her, to hear her laugh, to hug her. She is completely real and the dream is so singular that in my dream state it is as real, or more real, then when I am awake. [At the time of this telling, Patty didn't know the wording Kim used when relating her dream of death.]

"A wonderful rush of emotions embrace me as Kim and I hug one another, and then I become aware that we are tumbling through space, then flying effortlessly as Kim and I talk. Kim says she's fine, that she's sorry she had to go. As we talk, Kim changes composition and yet I still see her and recognize her as Kim even while at the same time I recognize the fact that she is changing. Eventually, Kim exists as what I perceive to be a prism, but she is still Kim and we are communicating, but now there are two problems. One is that as we are flying and traveling through space. I am having to struggle along as there are very strong currents and forces working against me and I have to use all of my strength in order to continue my flight.

Kim, on the other hand, is oblivious to the currents and travels with ease. The second problem comes when I ask Kim where she is in space and time and in what form. Kim doesn't hesitate to tell me, but I can't understand her. Kim is talking to me, and describing exactly what she is and where she is in her present existence, but I can't understand the words. Perhaps the best simile would be to say that it was like I was living 200 years ago and you were trying to tell me about nuclear fission using the most modern and technical terminology. Emotionally, I would be nodding in recognition of your efforts to communicate the knowledge to me, but I wouldn't understand what you were saying. So, although Kim explains to me what and where she is, I can't grasp any of what she's telling me. All I can get out of her explanation is that everything is wonderful and that I want to be with her. I tell Kim I want to join her and that is when you appear and both you and Kim say, 'No, it's not your turn. You can't come here, you have to go back.'

"At that moment, my conscious mind took hold and I realized where I was and that I was dreaming and that Kim was dead. The instant I recognized Kim's death as a conscious reality, Kim's form began racing away from me at an extremely high velocity. I tried to follow her but could feel myself falling back onto my bed, back to life on Earth. I called to Kim and tried to push my conscious self aside, but it was of no use whatsoever.

"As I floated back down into my body, time seemed to pass very slowly, or perhaps I had a long ways to travel, but as soon as I was back and in a normal dream state, I awoke. It took some time getting my mind back onto a rational, earthbound plane. 'Wow!' finally escaped my lips, but my emotional feelings were of serenity, joy and peace. Though I recognized myself, I felt unconnected to my earthly body and the earth per se. Most of all, I was overjoyed that Kim was all those wonderful things I couldn't understand.

"The dream, just as you recall your near-death experience, didn't leave me, but has stayed with me, comforting me with a warm glow of remembrance of my dear friend, who is not only okay, but better than I could have ever imagined. The dream has helped me a great deal in my sorrow and still sits solid in my mind."

NOTE: The night of Patty's dream followed a day of hiking up and out of the Grand Canyon, an all-day trek. She had consumed no alcohol or drugs. Though she should have been exhausted, she felt marvelous the following day.

I read the above three dreams to Dr. Kirsch. As I finished reading the last dream, I looked up to find him staring at me. His face was ashen and his eyes showed great agitation and concern.

"Can you get hold of this young lady?"

"Why yes, I think so."

"You must get hold of her. She is in great danger. She is capable of the true transcendental experience. [I finally understood the word in its metaphysical sense.] She is going too far. She could die."

My eyes became as big as his. He was serious, and having listened to Patty tell her dreams firsthand, I instinctually felt that he might be right. Her dream telling had carried the weight of truth. Surely the experiences had been totally real for her—real within the space-time of her mind. Patty had always been ethereal, a bit outside the norm, and now I understood what others had sensed.

"What must I tell her to do."

"I know she has control. Tell her to leave the other side alone, tell her to ground herself to the earth. Does she have children?"

"No. Why? Do children ground us to this plane of existence?"

"Yes. And tell her to get involved with all she can here on Earth. Tell her when she is an old woman she can travel to the other side, but she mustn't go there now. She is too young. She could die."

I called Patty. I felt silly, yet the reality of the doctor's fear held me up. By a fluke, I managed to get her by calling the store next to her shop. When she got on the line, she was surprised to hear from me, but glad, adding that something must be going on, because when she had entered her neighbor's store to answer the phone, all of the people in the store had stopped what they were doing and left.

I recounted my conversation with Dr. Kirsch. Patty began to cry.

"Oh Patty, I didn't mean to frighten you."

"Don't be silly. I'm crying from joy. I have been so dark in spirit lately, and many things have been happening. I understand the doctor's words."

At the end of our conversation, Patty's last words were, "Oh thank you, thank you, thank you."

A month later, back in Jackson, Patty seemed very happy and gave me an extraordinary hug. She still looks at me with tears in her eyes and says, "I miss Kim so much. She was the only person I could really talk to. But I know she's all right. Really."

I told an old friend about my writings. He blew. He said I had no right asking *those* questions as I had no right to know the answers. That if I went around talking about all "this crap" I was going to be hauled off to the loony bin in a straitjacket.

"Who do you think you are? God?" he asked. I replied that so far my investigations seemed to indicate that we are all a part of God, since we are all made up of atoms as old as time itself that work within the entirety of the whole. I explained that I was more skeptical than most, but that too many things had happened to me, as well as to millions of others from around the globe, for there to be nothing, and that if there was something, then I had every right to ask every question that came to mind, as only through searching can we ever find the truth. "And," I emphasized, "only in truth can we come to understand the force that prevails; call it what you will."

As I spoke my religion, my friend calmed down as his legalistic/religious mind wrapped around the propositions I was throwing at him. I asked if he had ever had a paranormal experience. He thought. Finally, he said, "No, I don't think so. Of course, in the war [World War II] with death all around you, there are a lot of feelings and experiences that are hard to describe, but in the realm you are talking about I don't think I have had anything significant happen to me, but . . . I did have a dream about a woman whom I had loved very deeply and who had died. To be honest, it wasn't really a dream; at least it didn't seem so at the time. I had gone to bed and was sleeping soundly when I felt a familiar touch of hands trying to gently shake me awake. As I came into consciousness, I reached out and sensed, rather than felt, the body of this woman. At the same time, I felt a tremendous emotional surge of being loved and cared for, then she slipped out of bed and was gone."

My friend became pensive as he mentally relived his dream. Then he looked up somewhat misty-eyed and said, "You know, it was the damnedest dream I've ever had. I could actually smell her marvelous body fragrance and feel her slipping out of my bed. I knew it to be real at the time but later I said to myself, 'Hell, it was just a dream.' The funny thing is that I never remember my dreams—ever."

Another pragmatic skeptic told me that what I was looking into was crazy and a misinterpretation of the facts. I had asked him for his opinion as his IQ is known to be in the genius category and his entire life has been wedded to the sciences. I laughed at his put-down and said that I was doing research that included asking people from all walks of life questions pertaining to death, dreams and what is often referred to as the paranormal. As we spoke, he got an "I'm thinking" look on his face and then admitted to one experience that might touch on the type of accounts I was collecting. It seems he had a longtime friend named Sam. For years, he and Sam would go to Sam's mom's house for dinner. Sam's mother had watched my friend grow up and succeed in the scientific community. My friend continued, "I hadn't seen Sam in some time and I hadn't seen his mother for an even longer period of time. Then one night I had this dream. Actually, it didn't seem like a dream, it seemed as though Sam's mom was actually standing in the corner of my bedroom. She was talking to me, but after all this time I can't recall what she told me. Anyway, it was pretty weird and I remembered the date of the dream because of things that happened the next day. A few weeks later, I ran into Sam. He told me his mom had died on the night of my dream. I didn't tell Sam about my dream . . . but hell, you know what Scrooge said in regard to Marley's ghost: 'Must have been a bit of bad beef.'"

Aha . . . bet he had chicken that night.

Eight months from the date of Kim's death, I had a dream about my pregnant daughter-in-law, Mary. I was in a hospital corridor with a couple that I took to be Mary's parents—though they didn't look anything like Mary's real parents. The three of us were trying to find Mary's room when a tall, thin, gray-haired nurse came up and told us we had to go to the office. The nurse was quite old and as she spoke I detected that something was wrong. When we got to the office, there was a pair of large leather sandals resting on top of a tiny pair of sandals. There was nothing else in the room, just the sandals and an office window, through which we could see another nurse. As I stared at the sandals, I heard the nurse behind the desk say that Mary had died. The old skinny nurse said it happened often, that when you have a troubled pregnancy, it often happens. "Now that you know, you can go in to see her," said the old nurse. She was still telling us this as we walked down a very sterile hallway towards Mary's room. I began to lag behind

as I moaned, "Oh no, oh no, not another death. I can't take it."
At this point, I felt I was going to faint, as I couldn't control
my body, which was starting to slump to the floor. Then I consciously recognized that I was dreaming and lying on the couch.
At the same time, I felt an entity approach me that was of such
blackness that mentally I could only equate it with a black hole.
This entity seemed to have a cumulus cloud body in the shape of
a human and I could *feel* it pushing an arm under my shoulder
in order to pick me up. I also felt its right arm going under my
right leg. As this pitch-black entity tried to pick me up, I lay on
the couch, now fully conscious, yet unable to move, open my
eyes or dispel the black entity from my mind. The black entity
was all pervasive, and although it gave off no threatening vibes
and seemed desirous of helping me in my grief, its magnetic
blackness filled me with a tremendous amount of fear. By this
time, its left arm was under my shoulders (I could feel it) and
its right arm was under both of my legs. In the process of trying
to pick me up, it bent over me, its shadow passing over my eyes,
first covering my right eye then on over the left, plunging my
closed eyesight into a darkness I cannot describe. In total panic,
I forced my eyes to open to the bright sunlight of the afternoon.
There were no clouds in the sky. My shoulders still tingled from
the touch of the black cloud spirit and I could still sense where
it had touched my legs. My heart was pounding in my head. It
took me many minutes to recover.

  When I told him of my dream, Dr. Kirsch said, "I don't
think your daughter-in-law is in any danger. The actual meaning of the dream has little to do with the scene in the hospital. If
that part means anything, I see it as your concern for the human
race; your caring for the millions who suffer. The important
part of the dream is the black entity that is indeed representative
of death, but not the death of the body. Women often see this
Black death; rarely do men see it. It represents the death of the
ego and is the finest of all deaths. It means for you an elevation
of spirit and a lessening of your ego."

I thought of my readings concerning karma and the ego, and about the faults I still felt bound to; the faults listed in the young psychology student's paper that Mother had left on her desk. I looked inward and hoped the good doctor was right as opposed to placating me in my time of grief.

Twenty years later, I cannot recall the part of the dream concerning Mary and the hospital, knowing it only from my writings, but the sensory and emotional reality of the Black death has never left me. As to Mary, she had a very troubled pregnancy and the worst week of trying to deliver I have ever heard of. The baby? Rebecca Elizabeth, beautiful, healthy and a giggler who is now an extremely healthy adult.

We no longer look upon dreams as illusions of the imagination, and though most dreams may be frivolous, or a form of mental house cleaning, many dreams carry a wealth of information, import or warning. Research in the field of dreams continues and many theories and ideas are coming forth. Researchers, such as Rosalind Cartwright, psychologist, author and major dream researcher, have shown that if a problem is bothering you, your mind, through successive periods of REM time experienced during a single night's sleep, will deal with the problem, with the night's first dream being troublesome, followed by ever more gentle dreams as morning approaches. Interestingly, such dreams rarely appear to have anything to do with the problem, but through examination the dilemma can be found standing in the wings as the progressive dreams work to ameliorate the problem.

Psychologists and dream gatherers such as Rosalind are putting forth their fascinating findings through books and articles. Their dedication to understanding the ways and whys of dreams, including those that are prophetic, is prying open doors into the workings and underpinnings of our dreams.

In my search to understand Kim's dream, I came to believe the following: first of all, I give no credence to dream books that tell you such things as, "a dream of diamonds means a growth in spirit," etc. Each and every dream is intimately connected to the dreamer. If two men dream of new clothes, they mustn't run to Robert D. Bruce's fine book, *Lacandon Dream Symbolism*, and believe their dreams foretell of a death. In Lacandon (Mayan) society, dreams are as much a part of life as is the wakeful state. Remote bands of Lacandon are few in number, closely related and fully integrated mind to mind. Hence, in their case, dreaming of new clothes may indeed (for various reasons I will not address here) foretell of death, but to the mechanic in Los Angeles and the clothing store owner in Boston, a dream of new clothes is going to have two separate and diverse meanings.

Your dreams are your own, most being difficult to interpret but for those singular in nature. With a singular dream, you have a clear, realistic picture, coupled with a detailed memory that lasts. What you do with it is up to you. Many should be looked at carefully, especially those that seem to give warning. Others should be analyzed within the context of your life. Where does the dream fit? What is it trying to tell you? If you have a totally perplexing dream, or dreams that gnaw at you, I would consider going to a psychologist who specializes in dreams. Your dream, or dreams, may very well be your unconscious self scratching at the door for attention.

I believe in precognitive dreams. I believe as my entire life was changed by Kim's dream. What did my society do to my thought processes that allowed me to listen to Kim's dream of dying, and other precognitive dreams she had experienced in the past, and simply brush them aside as I would a fly? Are we all so very frightened? If we are to proceed in growth, rather than sit stymied in societal ruts, then we must find the courage to look at the other sides of ourselves.

GRIEVING

Around the globe, and into our darkest past, people have exorcised their grief through observances that stretch from celebrations to the eating of the corpse. Each and every one of these observances served to heal and exorcise the grief of those left behind.

Burials and memorials in the United States range from grand and elaborate to small and quiet, each one honoring the dead and helping those who mourn to accept the death of their loved one. But accepting death is one thing. Grieving to a place of true acceptance is quite another.

Several times during the first months following Kim's death, there were days when I lost my innate will to live. I wasn't suicidal, but it seemed to take all I had to stay alive, to keep breathing. Those were the days I crawled into my shower and stood beneath its rain in an effort to drown my tears. And those were the days when my years of study in the field of paleoanthropology saved me. You see, I know that for millions of years our forbears lived without medicine, surrounded by predatory beasts and nasty neighbors. I know that the vast majority of my "sisters" suffered the death of a child or children. And during disastrous times, many lost all of their children, be it to weather, war, natural disaster, disease, snake, tiger or hunger. Few of my sisters journeyed through life unscathed. Nevertheless, they traveled on. Somehow they found the courage to go forward. I know, or I wouldn't be here. My ancient relatives gave me strength. I couldn't fail my species. I had to stand up. I couldn't disgrace myself or let Kim down. She, above all others, would have never forgiven me. There is, within each one of us, something we cling to. Whatever its form, grab it and hang on.

Within my initial agony lay guilt. Innumerable times I

thought I might die from it. Guilt over every word said and not said, things done and not done, everything that had occurred during those fateful months, from the time of Kim's dream to the time of her death. Mentally, I would put a mattress into the back of the Suburban, lay Kim upon it, cover her and drive her to Los Angeles and the doctors I knew. Over and over again, I ran my make-believe movie in order to reverse that which had already happened. The pain of thinking that I might have been able to save my child, or thinking it was my fault that she had died, created ineffable suffering.

So it wasn't grief but guilt that buried me when I thought of Kim's dream and my precognitive thoughts of blood clots. How, in all those weeks could I have never once remembered them consciously? Even when she mentioned her dream on the day of her death, though I instantly recalled it word for word, I pushed it away, slipping it under a cloak of self-protection. It seemed incredible, unforgivable and inconceivable. Countless times I crawled on hands and knees to the shower—my scream-ing cell—to stand in its rain, screeching out the words, "I killed her! I killed her!" It is difficult to write the words; the memory of my nightmare haunts me still.

Then, in March of '87, I met an old friend on a street in Los Angeles. He was a clinical psychologist who had been a customer of my family's restaurant for decades. I had seen him on the same street after Mom's death. He had adored Mom and had been grief-stricken by her passing. When I told him about Kim, he wept openly. We talked. I told him of not remembering her dream or my thoughts of blood clots until it was too late. I spoke of my guilt, of my failure to comprehend my mind's abil-ity to forget such important, indelible information, information that might have saved my daughter's life. "How could I not re-member?" I cried.

"Your mind couldn't let you remember at the time as it would have killed you. Your conscious mind wouldn't have been able to cope with that kind of knowledge. If you knew the future, you couldn't have handled it, you couldn't have lived the moment. The mind has to protect itself so that it can live each day. Answer me this, if I had come to you two years ago and said, 'Next year your mother is going to commit suicide and your daughter is going to die,' could you have lived a single day?"

"Not a single moment!"

"Don't you see, the lower levels of your consciousness know that. It's a built-in mental protective device. Appreciate it."

Back in Jackson I repeated the doctor's remarks to my old friend Herb. We discussed my feelings of guilt along with the guilt that seems to attach itself to all deaths. Herb summed it up, "Hell, I even feel guilty when some bastard I didn't like dies. I feel guilty because I didn't like the son of a bitch."

Well said, and I knew the truth of his statement and the wisdom of the doctor's explanation. However, guilt, as gold leaf on an antique frame, wears off bit by bit. Through the coming months, I found there to be no quick cure for my self-flagellation, but now I battled my guilt with a blade of wisdom and understanding, and gradually put my nemesis in its place.

Then something happened that illuminated a part of me, a part of grieving I never knew to exist. Some seven months after Kim's demise, I was in the Salt Lake airport on my way back to Jackson. As usual, I had my head in a book.

A voice said, "Hello, Carole."

I looked up from the pages of my book into the eyes of the doctor who had diagnosed Kim as suffering from lupus. Instantaneously, my body primed itself to spring upon the man and tear the jugular vein from the left side of his neck. Fortunately, the brain works in nanoseconds, and my higher plane of consciousness overrode my instinctual response. As my body began to lunge out of my seat, my hands grabbed the arms of my chair in a vice-like grip. I tried to nod. I don't remember if I said anything as my brain was still in the act of killing the man. The adrenaline was there, providing the strength I would have needed, and I recognized that on some instinctual plane I knew how to complete the grisly deed. Deep within, I knew that in another time and place I would have killed him; that hidden within me were ancient instincts to prompt and guide my actions. I would know how to kill him, how to leap upon him and get to my target. My weapon? The oldest evolutionary tool known to all species that ever sported teeth.

I shook for what felt like hours.

While the adrenaline rush left me weak and fatigued, my mind was a whirlwind of thoughts and questions. How could a female experience impulses and feelings of such a bloodthirsty nature? I am a small person. What made me think I could attack and kill a man almost twice my size? But there had been no thoughts, no time to think, only instinctual reaction. As horrifying as they may appear in this day and age, such instincts allowed our species to continue towards the present. Though I would have doubted it before that dismal day, I have known ever since that we are all capable of extreme violence.

Once again, I returned to my books. The sight of the doctor had triggered an age-old instinct inherent within us all: DANGER! A THREAT TO LIFE! Response: FLEE OR FIGHT! I fled. Back into my chair, back into the pages of my book as I tried to forget the adrenaline and knowledge of the fight still coursing through my veins, but they—the adrenaline and the knowledge—were still there. They have always been there. Only my societal training had kept me in check, forced me to be civilized, reasonable and curb my natural desire for vengeance.

All species, including humans, follow the four Fs: flee, fight, feed and fornicate. In order to survive, one must, first and foremost, avoid threats to life by either fleeing or fighting. Fleeing, being the most prudent course of action, usually comes first. But when trapped and threatened with the possibility of death, fighting will become, or be deemed, necessary.

Next comes feeding; food must be found and consumed. But, while feeding, the first two Fs are still on alert; they are always on alert.

Though vitally important to the survival of the species, fornication comes in last. Though impromptu coitus has occurred during times of eminent peril, as in wartime when lives are threatened and the subconscious urge to have one's genes continue into the future is flowing, sex among most living organisms is usually performed when there are sustainable foodstuffs coupled with relative safety.

When life first evolved on this fair planet of ours, the first multicellular organisms had no more than a tiny ring of 15 to 25 neurons. Your brain has 100 billion neurons! The first and oldest complex neural system was the old reptilian brain (the brainstem) that sits deep within all complex brains of today. It prompts responses to physical needs and incoming stimuli, keeping a sharp eye out for danger. It also keeps your heart pumping and your lungs working. The reptilian brain works 24/7 as a composite tool for keeping your body alive and running. Other than autonomic functions, the brainstem's primary focus is self-preservation, a part of which is aggression expressed in any way that will ensure the survival of the organism in question.

Nestled in the nooks and crannies of the old reptilian brain are add-ons that comprise the old mammalian brain known as the limbic system.

The limbic system is the center of emotions and sensory systems that allow for more complex life forms. The system is made up of several small parts that accomplish many tasks, from main-event memory storage and sense of smell to gastronomical and sexual appetites. Through chemical releases, it motivates you emotionally, filling pregnant women with feelings of motherly love and, at the other end of the spectrum, promoting fear so that you will act to defend yourself (in such cases, it teams up with the brainstem for acts of aggression).

Encapsulating the brainstem and the limbic system is the neocortex (cerebral cortex), the crinkled up sheet of gray and white matter that makes for a smarter, more cunning animal.

In humans, the neocortex is made up of six layers of neurons, which houses consciousness, language, comprehension, abstract thought, problem solving and the capacity for brilliance. In *Homo sapiens*, the neocortex is large in relationship to body mass and surpasses (as far as we know) all other living organisms in the realm of mental capabilities.

But deep inside every human brain sits the ancient reptilian brain, and it was that old reptile, deep within me, that wanted to avenge the death of my daughter.

Months after the airport incident, I met with a psychiatrist in Berkeley in regard to threads of grief I couldn't seem to shake loose. I told him of the many deaths and then started to ramble. One of the things I told him was of two men, a stock broker and an insurance man, both of whom had tried to take me to the financial cleaners, and how I had wised up in time and faced each of them in turn with their greedy ways. I wasn't aware of the anger I was expressing, but the shrink saw right through it. "Weren't you fortunate to have people on whom to vent your anger?"

My eyes snapped open as a mental floodgate released a wall of anger, unimaginable anger. Anger over being left alone, for years of my life confined in the prison of death, for moments lost never to be replaced, for the pain, the tears and the fears.

From some dark place, I vented my anger at each of those whom I had loved and lost. I blasted them with loud and horrid words as one memory prompted another. Then, suddenly, my anger spent, I began to wail and cry as I had never cried before. And I cried, sobbing to no one, "I loved them so."

And so the good doctor had worked a small miracle and once again I had learned a truth I had never known to exist—death elicits many emotions and we hide from many of them.

As I healed, I studied my sciences, along with myths, the unknown and history in a constant search for answers to all that had occurred. Invariably, I came up with more questions.

I knew that my mind had chosen to block out certain

occurrences that I believed might have helped my daughter survive. The question was, why? Could the answer be that I could not have helped, no matter what I had done? Was there nothing I, or anyone else, could have done to sway the outcome?

It is well known that the mind is capable of suppressing anything it deems too traumatic for the conscious mind to handle, but how did my mind know that Kim's dream and my insights were real and dangerous enough to hide from? What distinguished them as portents of valid events to come, and hence too traumatic for my conscious mind to handle? Did my mind know the truth—"the future"—on an unconscious level and consciously push the knowledge aside in an effort to shield me from information too painful and disastrous for me to handle?

Years ago, a beautiful young friend had risen within her father's corporation. One night, she and her boyfriend left a party in the Brentwood Hills. The boyfriend begged to drive her home in her new Porsche. She acquiesced. There is a bad curve on Sunset Boulevard that is faced with a huge retaining wall of large cement blocks that holds the toe of a small mountain in place. The boyfriend was speeding. He didn't know the danger of the curve so he didn't slow down, and the Porsche crashed into the wall at full speed. The boyfriend was decapitated and our friend was pinned in the wreckage with a broken femur and the steering column lodged in her liver. It took the firemen 20 minutes to cut her out of the twisted metal. She was taken to UCLA medical center—a 10-minute drive of blaring sirens. Our friend doesn't remember the accident. She doesn't remember sitting next to a decapitated body gushing blood, nor does she remember speaking coherently with the firemen. Throughout the ordeal she never lost consciousness. Due to shock, she felt no memorable pain, and the entire scene was so horrific that her brain scotomized the event. Scotomizing is a fairly new psychiatric term for not laying down a memory. It has been learned that the brain can shut down memory circuits when it recognizes or perceives a situation too dire for it to handle. It is a protective device. The bad part is that some personalities begin scotomizing during their youth when they witness a beating or something that frightens them, and then, as they grow older, they scotomize anything their mind deems unpleasant, including harmful things they themselves do to others. This brain trick works so well that psychiatrists have taped transgressors who have repeatedly said, "I wouldn't do what you are accusing me of! I never talk to anyone like that!" When they hear themselves on tape, they are completely bewildered, as they have no memory of what they said or what they did since there is no extant memory to recall.

Obviously, our friend went into shock at the time of the accident, a classic time for scotomizing. When she awoke from surgery, she asked what had happened. For her, the accident never happened. As years became decades, no memory of the crash ever surfaced.

But my forgetfulness was completely different. I didn't scotomize Kim's dream. She and I discussed it at length the morning she awoke from it and the two of us discussed her dream in detail with a mutual friend two nights later. Still, my mind chose to tuck the memory away until Kim asked me on the day of her death if I remembered her dream, at which time I experienced instantaneous and total recall. I remember reliving her telling me of her dream—her every word. As the memory flooded my brain, I looked down at my daughter lying in her hospital bed connected via IV to a bag full of prescribed medications that slowly dripped down a slender tube into her veins. I remember going numb, the words of her dream-telling lowering in volume. Kim said something and the volume clicked off.

One of the imponderables blocking the answers I seek is that I don't know if Kim remembered or, like me, suppressed the memory of her dream. Did she remember it on the day of her death, or had it been rattling around in her brain all along? Up to the very end of her journey, she tried to persuade us that she was fine, while we stood before her mute and blind. Were

Kim and I forewarned, mentally eased into a tragic reality? If so, by what prescient or mental force? Why didn't either of us take our experiences seriously at the time and then consciously work against them? Certainly they were powerful enough, singular enough, to be remembered and repeated in great detail days, weeks, months and years later. What processes and powers were at work, and to what purpose?

President Abraham Lincoln dreamt of being killed in a theater by an assassin's bullet, yet he insisted on going to the theater. People tell the story in a half-hearted, half-joking manner. Why? Fear of fate? Fear of the unknown? They say, "It's just a story." But it isn't just a story, it is an historic event that tells of a famous person who, through a dream, was told his destiny and went to meet it. Just as amazing is the fact that Lincoln had another dream in which he saw his body lying in state in the Capitol rotunda. The fact that he had such a dream is extremely impressive, as no other president, or any other person, had ever lain in state in the rotunda—Lincoln was the first.

Kim and Lincoln, along with a long list of rulers, writers and scientists, are in good company. Throughout the ages, we find thousands who dreamt their own demise, the deaths of others, and future disasters with incredible accuracy.

Dr. Kirsch, the Jungian psychoanalyst, said, "Of course, at the time of her [Kim's] dream it was already written, but one can do something about it if one is conscious of it and analyzes these things. You must understand that in these particular experiences there is a psychological meaning. However, there are always people in whose case there is no possibility of changing the outcome."

Did Kim's death fall into the latter category? Did Kim understand her fate on some unconscious level and go to meet it?

Psychology, the science of mind and behavior, states that if we believe in a precognitive thought, dream or vision, our sub- and unconscious selves will work to fulfill the prophecy.

They support this belief with documented evidence of cases in which a voodoo doctor tells a believer that he is going to die on a certain day at 3:00 PM, and the man does just that, his death purportedly brought about via his faith in the powers of voodoo. Or is there more to it? Mind control? I think so. Hypnotism? Perhaps. Whatever the case, the explanations are mind-bending as they give an individual complete power to control the mind and life of another. In the case of voodoo, we see powerful evidence of the mental capitulation of a man, brought on by the mental persuasion of another. But then whole populations have fallen under the spell of charismatic leaders who led them into war, genocide and self-destruction, and even to committing suicide en masse.

But in Kim's situation, there was no "other," simply a singular dream that brought forth prescient facts about the future. At the time, neither of us appreciated the reality of the dream enough to work against it consciously. Or was she, as with a victim of voodoo, caught in the entanglement of her own mental web? Or, did we both recognize, on some unknown level of the mind, that there was nothing to fight against?

Reductionists, who believe we possess nothing but a brain that produces everything we experience, would say that Kim's brain created her dream and then worked to fulfill its own prophecy. Reductionists, and their good friends the materialists and determinists, find their mechanistic view to be rational and pragmatic.

My "mind" rejects the idea that Kim's "brain" created her prescient dream of death and then set up and created each and all of the events that led to her death. I view the brain's non-autonomic neural activity, its myriad synapses, thoughts, ideas and "Eurekas!" etc., as responses to incoming stimuli, as opposed to being the creators of everything an individual experiences.

If you spend hours, months or years, researching the concepts of mind and consciousness, you will come away with the knowledge that the hard sciences, for the most part, leave these heavy subjects alone. Science cannot prove, disprove or replicate experiences such as those detailed in this book any more than it can solve the mind/brain argument, so it prudently and realistically offers these experiences over to the soft sciences, metaphysics and religion.

Still, the argument remains, which prompts the other? Does the brain produce reality, or do responses to reality produce neural activity?

So we are back at square one. How do our minds (or brains) know of things to come? Many children who lay dying in our hospitals know when they are going to die, though they rarely tell anyone about their dreams, thoughts or knowledge. I asked a director of a pediatric ward, "How can you tell when a child knows he's going to die?" "Two ways," she replied. "First, you walk in one morning and they are all business and their eyes are different, and right off, if you have walked this floor before, you know. Then, very quickly, usually that very day, your feelings are confirmed when they start giving their toys, their plants and other things away. The most uncanny part is that they must know the day and time as they give away the last thing or things on the day of their death—or by the night before if they go during the night or very early in the morning. When we remove the body the room is empty."

The overriding, primary instinct in all life forms is to live, to defend the corporeal bodies to the very end. Within the scope of Kim's death, we would have to say that Kim, an ardent lover of life, gave up her strongest instinct in order to fulfill a dream. Or was her singular dream intact prior to her birth? Was there a death notch on some strand of her DNA? Can DNA reveal our future? Can a brain read its own DNA? Silly questions often have amazing answers. A hundred years ago, people would have laughed you off the street if you went around predicting that humans would walk on the moon.

In Kim's case, we are left with several alternatives: either Kim had a precognitive dream that proved to be accurate, or she had a dream and made it happen, or she had a dream that was accurate in its prophesy but whose outcome could have been changed if she herself had worked to modify it, or she had a prophetic dream whose truth could not be altered. But what about my intense premonitions of death due to a blood clot that I received not once, but twice, at an altitude of 31,000 feet?! Who, or what, was knocking on my door, and why didn't I answer it?

SEMANTICS

I dislike the word "paranormal," though I still use it at times. First of all, it has a rotten reputation. Secondly, the word discriminates, as its definition tells us that a paranormal experience is outside the realm of normality. But near-death experiences are not abnormal. Singular dreams are not abnormal. Telepathy is not abnormal. And, apparently, rods of light can be seen as normal when all historical writings and anecdotal materials are taken into account. This being so, such occurrences are simply experiences that stump researchers and are inexplicable at this point in time. More important, statistically speaking, "normal" is but a mathematical averaging of all possibilities. As brain researcher, Daniel Buxhoeveden said to me the other day, "Another way to understand the meaning of a statistical average, i.e., normal, is having your head in a fire and your feet in a block of ice so that your mean-average temperature is "normal" somewhere in the middle of your body.

　　　Another brilliant man illuminated the subject. Years ago, a marvelous and learned doctor lay dying in a hospital. My physician husband went to visit him for the last time prior to flying off to a medical conference where he was to present a paper. The dying man asked my husband what his paper was about. My husband told him and showed him the statistical charts he was going to use to prove his point. The dying doctor looked deep into the eyes of my husband and repeated the words first penned by Aaron Levenstein, "My dear boy," he said, "statistics are like a woman's bikini. What they reveal is intriguing, but what they conceal is essential."

PART FIVE

REMARKABLE MINDS AND FRAGILE WRAPPINGS

Neither life nor death reside in the fixed world of Flatland, where things exist on a single plane in one dimension, in a place where it is impossible to perceive anything of height or depth. The Man in the Long White Nightgown comes to us in various garbs, being as varied as those who pass from our lives. It is also true that both life and death are often accompanied by events we are investigating but are a long ways from understanding.

MIND STUFF

With new knowledge coming forth on a daily basis, we have become absorbed in the physical and demonstrable. Through science, we are unraveling the inner workings of DNA and investigating the 100 trillion cells that work together to form the human body. Many are mapping and dissecting the brain with its hundred billion neurons, giving credence only to what can be viewed through an electron microscope or studied in the proverbial test tube. And while the physical researchers explore within, astrophysicists are looking ever further out into the vastness of space, putting forth and proving theories while struggling to understand the components of our seemingly uneven universe.

One afternoon, I wiped my weary eyes and realized that I was sitting spread-eagle on the floor of my library with dozens of books in disarray about me, some with paper strips dangling from their tops, others opened to poignant passages. Volumes on sciences and séances, the evolution of the human brain and emotional response systems mingled with Yung and Freud as I tried to bring meaning to my life.

Herb Jillson, friend, mental antagonist, critic and prompter, sent me the following in the midst of my search for understanding.

"5 Feb. '88—Carole, re mind stuff, this is from a book you should at least scan. *The Media Lab—Inventing the Future at MIT*, by Stewart Brand. It's 302.2 at the Teton County Library. See page 259."

I did. Brand thought the importance of structure in the brain explained its workings. Then he interviewed MIT neurophysiologist Jerome Lettvin. Lettvin was not supportive. "Let me tell you how bad it gets," he said quietly. "There was a case at one of the hospitals here just a few months ago that has scared the hell out of everyone. It was a leader of a motorcycle gang, a good talker. You don't become head of a gang without having some talents. Wild guy. He died in an accident. His brain came to autopsy. The cortex was completely unorganized. It was roughly the kind of un-corrugated cortex you find in a whale or a dolphin. It was not a human cortex in any sense. All of the laminations that we have carefully documented—none of it was there!" Lettvin went on citing other anomalies. "It is not that these are exceptions that demonstrate that there's a rule," he concluded. "These are exceptions that destroy anything that you care to say."

Back to Herb, re the quote above: "The biker's brain: think about it; thought can be shattering—just think about it. What the hell's going on here? Tell me, wild-eyed biker, are there any more at home like you? A few, you say? Or you don't know? Ten fathoms deep, you say? Listen here, Caliban [the ugly, beast-like slave of Prospero in Shakespeare's *The Tempest*], you scare the hell out of me and you're shooting some lovely theories full of rabbit hair."

Herb's letter, with its fascinating information and cryptic comments, intrigued me. As I typed up quotes from *The Media Lab*, my mind went flying and I began saying to myself, "I want to talk to this Dr. Lettvin." I repeated the thought over and over again until I finally said, right out loud to no one, "I have to speak with this Dr. Lettvin." Within minutes, I managed to contact him when his secretary accidentally put me through.

Dr. Lettvin agreed that we know very little about most everything, especially the brain. He claimed the brain to be just so much jelly and that he didn't find it all that amazing that the biker could function normally with a brain that appeared abnormal and non-human. My own brain rattled on that one.

It's known that all brains differ in size and corrugation, and that size alone does not gage for intelligence. Einstein's brain was on the small size with normal corrugation but for one area that codes for autism (he had a lot of trouble in school). However, the number of axons and dendrites sprouting from his average number of 100 *billion* neurons exceeded the norm, and the more branching of axons and dendrites the more neural connections and mental processing. So, large or small, highly corrugated or dolphin smooth, the mind/brain appears to be capable of functioning within any reasonable assemblage of *jelly* nature puts forth.

Interestingly, it has recently been discovered that compulsive liars have more axons and dendrites in their prefrontal lobes than average because they need them in order to remember their lies so as not to step on their tongues.

As for mapping and categorizing the brain, Dr. Lettvin stated that only adult brains could be mapped with any accuracy. Children's brains are too busy organizing themselves in relationship to their environment.

Since my talk with Dr. Lettvin, science has learned that full-term infants come into the world with a full complement of neurons, many of which die off as others form. From birth, a child's intellect, behavior and personality are molded in accordance to its genetics, environment and incoming stimuli. So it is that the brains of infants and small children are molded not only by their genetics, but also by their surroundings and emotional input. A child can be programmed to love or hate, learn or stagnate. By the age of eight, much of the human brain is set by its environment in ways that cannot be reversed, though some areas of the brain continue to mature into the twenties. For instance, the prefrontal lobes of the brain do not fully mature until the age of 24. Your prefrontals allow for wise and salient decisions, help lay down memories and are active during dreamtime. What's important to know is that from infancy on through childhood, a child's brain is a malleable organ that can easily be destroyed without harming the exterior of its container.

I told Dr. Lettvin the premise of my book, to which he replied the usual, "Oh, I don't believe in any of that," then went on to agree with many of my comments. A gleeful moment came when he agreed with me that the mind and brain are two separate entities. "How could they possibly be one?" he asked. "Look at the definitions. They are two completely different things."

Neuropsychologist Warren S. Brown, in a lecture entitled "Numinous or Carnal Persons," addressed the composition of an individual: "Am I a body; a body and a soul; a body and a mind; a body, a mind and a soul; or what about a mind, a soul and a spirit?"

Your personal answer is relevant to what you believe, the ways in which you think about yourself and the world around you and how you perceive life and death.

To be "numinous" is to be a non-material spirit. Carnal persons see themselves as simply a physical body with a brain that produces their every thought as well as their behavior and experience. A statistical majority of people think of themselves as being both; a physical person that possesses an inner, non-material "part," i.e., soul, spirit, mind, inner self or any combination thereof. Those with strong religious beliefs will speak of their soul or spirit, while those of the secular world will speak of the mind or self. I have been known to use all of these monikers according to experience, mental situation, emotional state, or the nature of the topic being discussed. Whatever the truth may be concerning who and what we are, many things happen to the plural we for which there are no explanations.

DIMENSIONS

I t is said that life is an illusion, that what we think we see as reality is not. Quantum mechanics says that whenever (a particle) is observed or measured, the act of observation and/or measurement alters that which is observed. So where does reality begin or end?

RC crossed the Golden Gate Bridge as she headed for home. Exiting the Waldo Tunnel, her mind filled with a horrifying mental image of her car glancing off the guardrail. Her flash of instant knowledge showed the car spinning out from the railing and entwining itself with other cars, causing a horrendous accident. On full alert, RC clutched the steering wheel and safely maneuvered the area in question. Shaken by the experience, she spent the rest of her ride home wondering what on earth had possessed her mind to be flooded with such a frightening thought.

Upon entering her home, RC asked her husband if their friend Frank had arrived from San Francisco. She said Frank might have arrived first as they had both left San Francisco at about the same time. Frank had not yet arrived. RC then told her family about the strange mental vision she had experienced on her drive home, then started making dinner. An hour later, Frank turned into the driveway. He entered the house apologizing for being so late. He said he couldn't help it. On the downgrade, just past the Waldo Tunnel, a car had careened off the guardrail, spun out and collided with two other cars. Four people had been killed.

In Ryback's book, *Dreams That Come True*, he tells of a 14-year-old boy who dreamt of a terrible accident. Upon awakening from his dream, the boy rushed to rouse his family, as he believed the accident had occurred a few blocks from their home. The boy was agitated and crying. He said a car had hit a power pole that had snapped and hot power lines had fallen on the car and killed the man who was driving the car. Then he told of a female passenger who was injured, but not dead. He said that she was on the front floor of the car and the firemen didn't know she was there. He said the man's body had been laid by the side of the road and left uncovered and that there were ambulances and firemen everywhere. He said the injured woman's name was Cleo—a name he had never heard before.

The boy was so distraught by the vividness of his dream that the family couldn't calm him down. Finally, the entire family drove to the intersection where the boy said the accident had occurred. Nothing. Everything was in its place. The family returned home to their awaiting beds. An hour later, all were reawakened by the sound of numerous sirens. Again they piled into the car and drove to the intersection in question. The accident the boy had seen in a dream two hours before had taken place. Every detail proved out and the injured woman's name was Cleo.

In the two precognitive occurrences related above, the receivers were totally unknown to, and unconnected with, the subject matter presented to them. Neither was emotionally upset, and both were in good health. In both cases, it is inconceivable that the receivers could have *made* their prescient thought or dream come true, either psychologically or in any other perceivable way, yet the information they received proved to be accurate down to the details. RC's prescient thought and the boy's dream demonstrate that prescient knowledge can enter the human brain in various forms, i.e., dream or wakeful thought. That simple fact opens a thousand doors, behind which sit questions as to the workings of the particulate matter and energies that bind together to form our universe as well as the human brain.

We don't yet understand how a mind can receive such information, why it receives such information, or the true strength of the mind. In such instances, could there have been a packet of energy that existed as a blueprint for disaster? Did the minds of RC and the young boy happen to pick up on, or somehow enter, that energy field, thus reading (seeing) the future? In the case of the boy's dream, the victims were accurately identified prior to the incident. Did similar occurrences act as ancient stimulants for belief systems that see fate as inevitable? Karma? These strange, spine-tingling events can be found in writings, myths and tales from around the globe, from the most ancient writings to events concurrent with the present.

Somehow, I received a correct thought concerning death due to a blood clot twice, at an elevation of 31,000 feet. I took those thoughts of death to be for me and forcefully pushed them away, believing them to be the workings of a grieving mind. I was wrong. The messages—those packets of future occurrences—were valid, but I was not to be the victim.

The famous artist and illustrator, N.C. Wyeth, had five children: two boys and three girls. Two of the girls and son Andrew became artists. Ann Wyeth McCoy became a composer, but it was N.C.'s inventor son, Nathaniel, that father Wyeth singled out in a cautionary way. Over and over, he would tell Nathaniel, "You must be careful when taking your son in the car, and watch out for all railroad crossings." Through a period of several years, father Wyeth repeatedly admonished his son to watch out while driving with his son, especially when crossing railroad tracks. But in October of 1945, it was old man Wyeth himself who was driving his grandson home in his big old station wagon when they got stuck on a railroad crossing. It is said that Mr. Wyeth stretched his hand out towards the train as if to stop it by will. . . . Again, right message, wrong person.

Some researchers would propose that the messages I received of death due to blood clot were caused by my grieving state of mind. Not that my grieving over the deaths of so many loved ones caused my prescient thoughts, but that my grief placed me in an unusual mindset that opened mental doors that, during most of our lives, remain tightly closed. Researchers find that sensory channels are more open during times of heightened emotions. I have come to believe that many anomalous and curious things occur in proximity to death because those surrounding a dying person are emotionally awake and focused on the patient and the processes of death rather than a daily routine, a tough meeting with the boss, or what to have for dinner. During highly charged, poignant times, our minds do appear to open to multiple experiences and lay down lasting memories.

Our ancient ancestors of 20,000 to 30,000 years ago understood the power of highly charged experiences on memory. In a French cave, there is a narrow passage that you can crawl through until you reach a naturally occurring "room" with a low ceiling. On its earthen floor, laying up against a natural outcrop, are two clay bison, a male situated behind a female. When first discovered, the floor of the room was imprinted with the footprints of young boys. No adult size prints were found.

Ages ago, a shaman lit an oil lamp and commanded young initiates to follow as he entered the pitch-black passage. When he reached the room, he placed the lamp just inside the entrance to the room and ushered in the boys. Imagine yourself crawling through pitch-blackness behind a small light barely seen from in front of the shaman. If you are one of the last boys in line you are following by feel in total darkness. Your adrenal glands are setting your brain and body on full alert, so the words and teachings of the shaman will never be forgotten.

So, I can accept that my grieving, pent-up mind may have been open to receive a prescient thought, but where did the information come from? And by what process did I receive it? And how long before an event can a mind know the inevitable? *Is* the past, present and future all one?

From ancient fables told by our earliest forebears around nightly fires and throughout our collected writings, come stories of people experiencing the unfathomable. Not only prescient thoughts but also various unexplained experiences that muddle the mind. For many, such events are too alarming to be accepted as reality, so they are conveniently remembered as a dream or negated altogether. Others recognize that something real and strange has occurred but choose to relegate the incident to a personal file marked "classified." But while "modern" man scoffs and hides, other societies accept anomalous occurrences as a part of life. Of these societies, many lack any kind of formal education and are often without a written language of their own. These societies have been labeled "primitive," and while a lack of basic scientific, engineering and medical knowledge puts a society at a disadvantage, the negating of their seeming connection (openness?) to the anomalous has also been used as proof of their lack of sophistication. So it is that anomalous occurrences that are experienced in Los Angeles, New York, Paris and Madrid are thrown into a back closet for fear of being looked down upon.

After Kim died, I felt I had nothing more to lose, which led to my not caring what other people thought, even if they thought I was crazy. I began to study, read, travel and speak with anyone willing to give me the time of day. I told the heads of foreign museums, professors, doctors, psychiatrists and people I chanced to meet of my multiple experiences. To my surprise, no one thought I was crazy and approximately seven out of ten told me *their* stories, most prefacing their words with statements such as, "I have never told anyone what I am about to tell you, but I know you will understand." (Translation—I know you won't think I'm crazy.) And I did understand and I knew they weren't crazy. They were simply people who, like others from every corner of the planet, had experienced something science has yet to explain or replicate.

Through intriguing conversations, I learned over and over again that life is full of imponderables. People of all faiths, ages and walks of life experience prescient dreams, mentally receive precognitive information, experience telepathy, see or sense "ghosts," and have near-death experiences or out-of-body experiences.

While most of the hard sciences work to negate such

events, many individual scientists realize that something must be going on for all generations of mankind to have known like experiences. I personally know scientists and well-positioned individuals who are amenable to, or have actually experienced, an anomalous occurrence, but speak of such things only in arenas of utmost privacy as to speak of such things publicly could bring ridicule or, in some cases, loss of tenure. It can be safely said, that professionally speaking, such items are taboo. For this reason, I have changed most of the names connected with the following stories so as to keep safe people who have been kind enough to share with me their memories of singular events. In good faith, I cannot break their trust, but I can relate their experiences in the hope that future generations might look for, and eventually find, some answers.

Pete and Beth were having marital problems. Beth ordered Pete out of the house. Pete went to stay with one of his colleagues and two nights later had a vivid dream—a singular dream. In his dream, Pete saw a van, a white van with two doors that opened at the rear of the vehicle. The van was parked along the hillside street in front of Pete's house, the one Beth was now sleeping in . . . alone. As the dream progressed, the back doors of the van swung open and flopped back and forth. Inside the van, Pete could see a large white coffin and somehow he knew that Beth was in it. The dream ended. Upon waking, Pete considered the dream a nightmare, though he had not felt frightened during the dream. The dream remained solid in his mind so he entered it in his daily journal.

Some weeks later, Pete was back home trying to reconcile things with Beth. It was morning and Beth was still in bed while Pete rummaged about getting ready for work. Both were throwing words at one another when Pete suddenly walked over to Beth and said, "Beth, no matter what happens between us, I will be by your side when you die."

Taking mental note of his words, Pete was stunned. What had made him say such a thing? He knew that statistically, being a man, and older than his wife, *he* should be the first to die, but regardless of the odds on which one of them might die first, there was the oddity of the statement itself. It seemed to have come out of nowhere and was certainly not a common thing to say during a marital spat.

Twenty-six years later, after years of marriage punctuated by periodic separations, Beth contracted cancer. Pete, who was once more out of the house, came home, took loving care of his wife, and was indeed by Beth's side at the time of her death.

When the men from the mortuary came for the body, they placed Beth on a gurney and draped her with a large white sheet. Pete watched their every move then followed the gurney out of the house to see an awaiting white van, its rear doors flopping and swinging back and forth due to being parked on the steep road that borders Pete's property.

On a Saturday afternoon, a 12-year-old child prodigy, a lover of baseball, finished his usual four hours of practice at the keyboard, grabbed his catcher's mitt and ran out the door to meet his death via the wheels of a car that screeched in terror at having caught him in the act of darting out into the street on his way to baseball practice.

Weeks later, the young pianist's school papers were gone through, and there, among his English class papers were light-blue lined pages detailing a story of a youngster, much like himself, who was a genius at the keyboard and loved baseball with all his heart, and who, at the end of the story, lay down his head on the keyboard of his piano and died.

A week after writing his story, the young pianist's story became a reality.

J im shared ownership of a small plane with a friend. On a
certain morning he awoke to tell his wife of a most peculiar
and vivid dream. In his dream, he saw the trees that grew
in front of their house swaying and rustling in the wind. Then
his plane partner flew into view above the trees, spiraled around
and around and then dove straight into the ground between the
trees. In the dream, Jim knew his partner was dead, but casually
watched as his partner appeared through the wreckage of the
plane and cartwheeled out of sight.

Four hours later, both Jim and his wife were at work
miles from their home when Jim's phone rang. A shaky voice
said, "I'm sorry to call you at work, but a terrible accident has
just happened at your place." To the amazement of the caller,
Jim said, "I know, Larry's gone down in our plane."

T om had enjoyed the party thoroughly, too much in fact,
and as the alcohol worked to deaden his perceptions, his
car careened off the Pasadena Freeway, flew through the
air and fell crashing onto the Hollywood Freeway. Tom was pro-
nounced dead upon arrival at the hospital. Tom's parents could
not accept their son's death and believed that Tom could have
been saved. They thought Tom's death was due to misdeeds performed by the ambulance drivers rather than injuries caused by
the flying crash. In grief, anger and sorrow, they locked themselves inside their home and called their lawyers.

Three months later, Bill and Barbara Baines were on
their honeymoon in England. Bill and Barbara had attended the
same party as Tom and were in attendance at his funeral.

Ten days into their journey, the couple was taking an
after-dinner walk through the streets of London when they noticed a basement walk-down with its door wide open and its
room full of people. There seemed to be some sort of meeting,
and for reasons they later couldn't explain, they descended the

short flight of stairs to look in on the gathering. "Come in, come in," said a nice-looking gentlemen, and again for reasons still to be explained, they entered and joined the crowd which was in the process of seating themselves in neat rows of chairs.

When everyone was seated, a man walked onto a podium and began speaking. Bill and Barbara looked at each other with amusement and dread as they realized that they had walked into a meeting of psychics. Bill wanted to leave, but they were trapped in the middle of a row and Barbara whispered that it might be a crazy fun thing to tell their friends about back home so they stayed.

The man on the podium was calling out messages that he claimed were from the other side and taking questions from the audience when he suddenly said, "Wait, wait, I am getting a very strong message from a man who died recently in an automobile accident. Is there anyone here who understands what I'm talking about?" Bill and Barbara gave each other an "Oh brother" look and said nothing. "Please," continued the psychic, "this person is very determined to get through. I am sure his friend is here." Bill and Barbara sat silently, now holding hands.

Five minutes later, the psychic again said, "Please, I have never received this strong a message in my life. This young man seems to have been from America. He says he died in a car crash. I think his name is Tom. He has a message. Please, someone come forth, he is pounding in my head. *Is* there someone here who knew a Tom?"

Feeling that he might as well play the game, Bill raised his hand. The psychic came close to weeping. "Thank God," he said. Then he began to question Bill. "Did your friend die in a car crash recently?"

"Yes"

"Is his family taking this very hard? Have they closed themselves off from everyone and everything?"

"Yes."

"Good, you're the right person. Tom's message is this,

'Tell my parents I am all right and that I was already dead when the ambulance got to me."

Bill and Barbara, lifetime skeptics, sat in their hotel room going over everything that had happened. They were positive that they knew no one else who had attended the meeting and they ransacked their brains to assure themselves that they had not spoken of Tom since weeks before their wedding. There was simply no way that anyone in London could connect them with Tom's death. Bill and Tom had not even been the best of friends, just casual old college friends who ran within the same social circle.

After much discussion, Bill called his good friend Mark in Pasadena. Mark had been a close friend of Tom's and knew his parents well. Bill asked Mark to forgive the crazy call but to please listen to the whole story and then do with it what he would. Mark listened. As the final words of the psychic were repeated, Mark developed gooseflesh and promised to do what he could.

Feeling that it couldn't hurt, Mark went to the home of Tom's parents, persuaded them to open the door and as delicately as possible told them about the amazing experience Bill and Barbara had had the night before in a basement hall in London. Later that day, Tom's parents opened their curtains, called off the lawyers and rejoined their church.

An eleven-year-old girl and her eight-year-old brother were visited one evening by their recently deceased grandfather, who appeared as a wisp of smoke but then attained enough form for the children to recognize it as being their grandfather. Of interest is that the woman who told me about this event could describe in detail the way the mist entered the room, how frightened they were at first, how the mist took shape and went to the side of her brother's bed and finally sat down beside him, but she couldn't remember what he told them. She thought it was just about how much he loved them.

Many like occurrences have happened to a great many people only to have those involved retain the memory of their feelings and sensory sensations while forgetting the actual words spoken. They get the message, but the words are forgotten, something akin to my childhood garden experience when my great-grandfather "visited" me.

AFTERSHOCK

On April 7, 1993, as I sat at my computer, the phone rang. It was my son Christopher calling from Houston to tell me that his wife, Kiera, had experienced seven extraordinary occurrences during the two previous months. She had asked him not to discuss them with anyone but Chris was worried and, considering my line of research, he felt it important that he relate Kiera's night travels for documentation.

Kiera's experiences as told to me two days after the final episode: "In the middle of the night, she [Kiera] experiences herself getting up, walking into the hallway of our home and ascending 'in a rush' up into 'heaven.' She is very aware of her surroundings and of being fully awake, out of her body and away from home. What she takes to be heaven is very lovely and there is the proverbial 'light' off on the horizon. In the first and second of these experiences, she said she tried to get to the light, but there were so many people crowding towards it that she backed off. In each of these night excursions there was a woman who seemed to be Kiera's communicator. She and others repeatedly told Kiera that it wasn't her time. During the sixth experience, Kiera asked the woman why she was being brought up to this place if it wasn't her time, but received no reply. In the last experience, there was a higher-up next to the woman with whom Kiera usually communicated. Kiera again asked why she was being brought up there so many times, "Why?" she demanded, "Why?" The woman looked to the higher-up, then responded by saying that all she could tell Kiera was that she [Kiera] would die before her husband Christopher."

Christopher went on to explain that upon waking from these experiences, Kiera would relate everything she could remember in detail. Of psychological significance is the fact that after each occurrence, Kiera felt homesick. Her feelings of missing the other place were so extreme that she showed signs of great emotional distress, coupled with bouts of melancholy. Christopher said her melancholy persisted for one to three days following each episode.

I listened to my son's words in a state of amazement, disbelief and internal dread.

Something within me sensed that seeds of illness were coursing through Kiera's electrochemical self. The mind had read the signals and allowed for a warning through some form of out-of-body, dreamtime experience or taken her on some form of unexplainable mental excursion through a flight of memorable dreams. I found it hard to believe that this type of indeterminable prescience was occurring again within the framework of our family and resolved that day to fight it. As soon as I hung up the phone, I made a call to my friend Rosalind Cartwright, psychologist and dream researcher. Like my son before me, I related every detail of Kiera's nighttime experiences, adding that Kiera was a young mother in good health. Rosalind and I took notes and discussed what mental course of action Chris and Kiera should take in regard to her night travels. I called Chris back and urged him to encourage Kiera to meditate on not leaving her bed once she was asleep, on living a long and healthy life and living in and for the present. It was also advised that she keep her mind on doing things for herself and her family, that she practice life and live it fully.

That same day, I recounted Kiera's experiences to several others, many of whom work in the fields of science and medicine.

Over the ensuing months, Kiera had no more experiences and seemed of good cheer, but then paranoia began to rear its ugly head. Freeways frightened her, causing her to shop locally. By choice, she became more and more housebound. On the positive side, she began taking better care of herself through diet and long walks.

Six months later, on October 25, 1993, Kiera went to the doctors for a checkup. Chris said she had begun showing signs of spontaneous bruising and had become extremely weak and tired of late. Blood tests showed a low platelet count. Thoughts of leukemia plagued us. Through testing at MD Anderson Hospital in Houston, Kiera was diagnosed with ITP, idiopathic thrombocytopenia purpura. Over the next month, her platelets slowly rose of their own accord, during which time it was discovered that Kiera was pregnant! The pregnancy was a complete surprise as their first child was conceived only after an onslaught of fertility pills. Following the birth of Allyson, they had been told they would have to go through the same process should they ever desire another child so the pregnancy was a total surprise.

During the ITP crisis, Chris's employer changed medical plans and Kiera was forced to go to a new doctor whom she disliked at first meeting. She said he didn't seem to care about her and more or less ran her through the exam as if she were in a car wash. She explained her episode with ITP and told the new doctor that blood tests should be taken regularly in order to keep tabs on her condition. In February, he ran a check: 204,000 platelets. As the months went by, Kiera asked for more blood tests. The doctor said she didn't need them but finally complied. In early April, Kiera's platelets fell to 94,000, a number that should have sounded an alarm, yet the doctor never called in a hematologist or alerted Kiera to the possibility of a life-threatening situation. A normal platelet count runs around 250,000. Kiera didn't mention her low platelet counts until later. Her only complaint was of her total dislike and disregard for the new doctor.

On June 19, 1994 (Father's Day), Kiera went into labor and entered her local hospital. A pinprick blood test was performed. Kiera's finger bled for 18 minutes. They checked her blood: 4,000 platelets. The small local hospital quickly shipped her to St. Luke's Episcopal Hospital at Texas Medical Center where Drs. Moiese (OB-GYN) and Moake (a specialist in blood diseases, specializing in TTP) held off labor with magnesium sulfate. After much testing, they diagnosed Kiera as suffering from TTP (thrombotic thrombocytopenic purpura), a blood disease of unknown origin that killed all sufferers as late as the mid-eighties, but currently shows a cure rate of 80 percent if plasmapheresis (a blood exchange process that removes and replaces a patient's plasma) is administered in time.

Kiera was plasmapheresed daily for eight days until her platelet count read 108,000, at which point, on June 27, 1994, baby Lauren was born via natural childbirth, surviving her mother's trauma in perfect and beautiful condition.

Following the birth of Lauren, Kiera's platelets fell like a stone, even though she was plasmapheresed daily. When my husband and I arrived at the hospital on July 5th to help care for baby Lauren, Kiera's platelets were down to 5,000. Amazingly, Kiera showed little bruising and no signs of end organ problems commonly caused by blood clots, which are an inherent part of TTP. Her only problem was blurred vision in the left eye.

July 7—5,000 platelets . . . again. From the beginning

I had been working with Kiera in visualization. We were both trying to counter her night visions. She was very good at it. After learning more about TTP, I told Kiera she needed to change her visualizations. She could stop working on making platelets as I now knew that her body was making platelets on a regular basis. The problem was an arterial condition that was destroying and clumping her platelets and threatening her life. With the first suggestion, Kiera started running imaginary trains through her system, loading up the awful, unknown stuff and hauling it out of her system.

July 9—A rise to 16,000 platelets. Kiera awoke wide-eyed and smiling to tell of a wonderful dream. In her dream, she was inside her circulatory system where there were thousands of snow-white angels in space suits. They had large filigreed wings of extreme beauty—Kiera went on and on about their wings—the awesomeness of her dream still shining in her eyes. She said the angels were neither male nor female, but amorphous and universal in beauty. She said she could see their porcelain-like faces through the visors of their space helmets. She said again and again how lovely and full of grace her space-suited angels had been. Then, with a giggle, she told us the best part of her dream. Each one of her beautiful angels had a bright red Hoover vacuum cleaner and was vacuuming up the horrid agent that was agglutinating and destroying her platelets!

I was overwhelmed by the fact that Kiera's angels wore space suits. This showed that her unconscious self understood the hazardous nature of the disease. Not only did the dream foretell a better count (16,000 in the morning, 21,000 by the end of the day), but her blood smear showed fewer schistocytes and many fat new platelets. The dream brought smiles and hope to us all.

The following day, my husband and I left for home and Kiera's mother arrived.

July 12—Some improvement, with 23,000 platelets and a great-looking smear. Kiera's left eye began to improve and she continued to show little bruising. Best of all, she looked great, very unlike most patients in her condition. Attitude: magnificent. She constantly said, "I'm going to get better." Then disaster. Kiera's mother called Chris in a panic. She said she didn't know what was happening, that the doctors were on their way and that he had to talk to Kiera right now, then she put the phone to Kiera's ear. "M-m-ma-m-m-mmm," then more of the same was all that came out of her. Chris knew she was trying desperately to tell him something but clumps of platelets were reaching the speech centers of her brain and eventually she went silent.

Years later, Chris would confide that the recollection of Kiera's last efforts to speak were the hardest moments to remember.

On that fateful day, at 3:00 PM, some of the micro-clots of agglutinated platelets piled up in Kiera's brain, causing major infarctions. Kiera lost the ability to eat, speak or make facial expressions. She suffered 95% paralysis. All that remained was movement of her head and left arm. With effort, she could squeeze people's hands as a form of communication. Her blood pressure was sky high. Kiera was moved to intensive care and hooked up to oxygen and an IV.

July 14—With a count of 26,000, the respirator was removed as Kiera was able to breathe on her own. On many occasions, Kiera was encouraged to write on a marker board. The results were slim and not very reassuring. Then, one day, she brought tears to the eyes of all when she wrote, "I want to be Mommy to Lauren," and "I'm a non-exist mother." It was by far the most she ever wrote . . . and certainly the most poignant.

Days passed with no real progress towards a remission. On July 18, Monday, at 3:00 PM, the doctors performed a splenectomy as a last ditch effort. Removal of the spleen works well in ITP, but the effect on TTP is poorly documented.

Following the operation, Kiera's platelets continued to hover in the 16,000 to 30,000 range. Enough to sustain life, but not enough to effect a cure or remission.

On and on and on it went with more infarctions to the brain. All the while my son Chris continued to hope for a remission of the disease and a mental and physical recovery for his beautiful Kiera. Kiera's mother stayed in the hospital, in Kiera's room with baby Lauren as weeks ebbed into months.

On August 30th, I returned to Houston to find that sometime during the night Kiera had experienced another major infarction or bleed in the brain. She failed to recognize me, the baby, her mother, or even her husband, Chris. I stood in the gaze of her wide-eyed stare only to see that she was looking through me, or past me, and then her gaze drifted off to the side where it remained transfixed.

Chris and I took baby Lauren home to her sister, Allyson, who would soon be three years of age. The hospital had allowed the baby to remain with Kiera in the hospital as they believed the infant's presence was helping Kiera survive. I cooked and cleaned and got busy with the business at hand, finding a nanny for the two girls. After three days an angel arrived at Chris's door. No, I wasn't dreaming; a real, live angel by the name of Edith Josephine Handy came to interview for the job of nanny. She was everything I had hoped to find.

On September 1st, Chris agreed to stop treatment. The doctors had plasmapheresed Kiera daily for 72 days, a longer period of time than any other known TTP patient. Still, the disease persisted, with Kiera degenerating mentally to a point where she lacked any signs of conscious recognition. Miraculously, her body continued to function despite a low platelet count and poor blood smear. Then on the third of September, peristalsis (the movement of the stomach and gut muscles that allows for digestion) stopped. Nasogastric feeding was discontinued. Now, only the administering of saline with morphine was continued. Kiera would open her eyes but couldn't focus. We all believed it couldn't be long before her night travels proved their prophecy.

On the twelfth of September, the doctors suggested pulling the saline. To quote my weeping son, "Mom, I have to accept the fact that my wife died many weeks ago."

"I'm afraid you're right, Christopher. I hope she's dancing on the ceiling. If she is, she must be wondering why she can't move on."

"Yeah, I know, Mom. I wouldn't keep an animal alive in her condition. She told me when her dad died to never plug her in or allow her to be in the condition he ended up in, and here she is, lying in a state far worse than that of her dad."

On September 14, 1994, Kiera was moved to a hospice care center across from the hospital where only her pain and comfort were attended to. For two days prior to the final decision, Christopher and Dr. Belford, the doctor Kiera loved best, had tried over and over again to get Kiera to respond to some form of stimulus. Kiera gave no response and the attitude of her eyes, when open, showed further progression of cognitive decay.

No one in the literature on TTP had ever survived so long in such an acute phase of the disease. To date, no one understands how Kiera managed to hang on so long, though, perhaps, prior to the infarctions to the brain, she continued to work with her angels, keeping her thoughts positive and trying with all her might to remain here on this earthly realm of existence.

Then, on September 16, 1994, Chris got a call at work from Kiera's mother saying that he needed to get to the hospital as soon as possible and that he "wouldn't believe it." And indeed a seeming miracle had occurred.

When Chris entered Kiera's room, his eyes met hers. She was looking straight at him. Kiera's eyes were focused and full of cognition. The old Kiera was saying hello with eyes Chris knew and loved. Beaming, Chris went to her side. Kiera showed him that she could move her left arm with some agility and intent, but that was just for openers. Peristalsis had started up again and she opened her mouth! For two weeks, they couldn't get so much as a small syringe through her clinched teeth. Now she was accepting ice chips with relish, then, to the amazement of all, as much food as they offered. They asked her to hold up one finger—she did. They handed her an upside-down picture—she turned it right side up. She grabbed the coat of her doctor and gave people hugs. She gently stroked the face of her husband. She wiggled the toes of one foot and moved the fingers of her right hand. The tragedy was that she was still unable to speak or stay focused on a subject for any length of time. But her bodily health appeared to be improving on all fronts but for her blood count.

On the medical side, it is very possible that when the saline drip was removed and dehydration began, the edema (swelling) in the brain diminished and whatever neurons were left unscathed by the infarctions did the best they could to make her functional. Patients in need of a saline drip are usually given more than they may need, as should too little be given, disaster can strike. The general rule is to over-hydrate rather than under-hydrate.

On the psychological side, the shock of Kiera's comeback was tremendous. For a period of months, the entire family, plus hundreds of friends, had wept and prayed and anguished over Kiera. As her condition grew to be irreversible, our hearts had sunk further and further as we struggled to accept her approaching, inevitable death. We, with the concurrence of her many physicians, had placed her in a hospice so that she might go in peace. Then wham! Voilà! I'm back! Just fooling! Gotcha! But it was much worse than that. Kiera's story made me understand more fully how the human brain works to maintain life. We naturally cling to life, so when we are forced to give up on a loved one, the pain is excruciating and debilitating. Accepting death is very difficult. Therefore, when a dying person "comes back" after so much mental and emotional work has been done in an effort to accept their impending death, the mind is outraged over what it considers to be spent emotions—the days of agony, tears shed in grief and the days and weeks that were reshuffled in order to accommodate the dire situation that had dragged us all into a state of sorrow. It took each individual time to handle the shock and then rejoice in Kiera's partial comeback. But our rejoicing was coupled with a new and tragic fear: Kiera might live in a semi-vegetative state, eating and drinking and eliminating while still paralyzed and incapable of speaking or having any kind of functional life. We became terrified that she might get stuck in a limbotic hell, hooked up to machines and medical processes that would crucify her and those who loved her.

Our fears and concerns were misspent. On September 19th, Kiera went into withdrawal from the morphine that had been administered for so long, but removed with the advent of her comeback. Then her kidneys began to fail. There was infection. Chris had tests performed. If the infection was causing the numbers that suggested renal failure, he would allow them to treat the infection. If small blood clots from the TTP were blocking up the kidneys, he would allow nature to take its course. He knew from sitting through his grandfather's demise that death to kidney failure is not painful and should Kiera show signs of discomfort they could administer more morphine to minimize any discomfort. Then deterioration showed its ugly face once more, with a vengeance. After watching Kiera's spastic form and unseeing eyes, Chris ordered the re-administering of morphine for his angel and came to realize that infection or clotted kidneys, the time had come to release her from her agonies.

We waited in the wings with jumbled neurons and mangled emotions. What could be sadder than to watch a loved one manage to refocus on her world only to return to a state of wide staring eyes, now completely devoid of cognition. Kiera wounded the hearts of all who loved her. She remained in limbo as a loving husband tried to maintain the courage to help her complete the journey she had started so long ago. She lay in a relentless gray area created by modern medicine—a place gotten to through tremendous efforts, incredible equipment and failed miracles. Kiera was in the 20% who still die of TTP. Her doctors had tried everything known to them. To a man, they wept over nature's victory despite Kiera's valiant efforts to survive against all odds.

Of historical and medical significance is the fact that a comeback prior to death is very common. Dick's ability to speak clearly, just hours before his death, after 36 hours of being completely incapable of speech, is a classic example. Anyone who works with hospice or intensive care can tell you story after story after story, as can those who have sat with dying loved ones. But Kiera deserves special credit. Her comeback was exceptional. Few come back so far, in so many ways, for so long a time. Her miraculous comeback mirrored her tenacity for surviving as long as she did in such critical condition.

As with most deaths, the final fall was swift. Kiera had not returned to lie motionless and speechless in some dull green room of beds and machines. She had returned for two days of hugs and lots of last suppers. At one point they had asked her to write the letter *A*, she did. Then she wrote a capital *D*, some scribbles, then a capital *I*, more scribbles and what looked like a little *e*. Were the scribbles between the letters produced by uncontrollable hand movements, or were they part of a larger message never read?

Christopher, Kiera's brother, had arrived in town and was staying with my son Chris. The two men had visited Kiera in the early evening while her mother took her daily walk. Despite her inability to focus or communicate, they held her hands and told her how much they loved her. Finally, they nodded to one another and left, informing the nurse in attendance that they were leaving. Shortly after they left, Kiera's mother returned. She sat down by Kiera's side, resuming the vigil she had kept for months. Suddenly, she was overwhelmed by the presence of death. It permeated the room. With multiple emotions and feelings of being driven from the room, Kiera's mother almost ran from the hospice care center, got in her car and drove out of the parking lot. Forty minutes later, she found herself on a strange freeway heading out of town. To this day, she has no recollection of how she got there.

After leaving the hospice, the two men decided to go

down the street to the Holiday Inn, where they sat in the bar and discussed Kiera's life and tragic condition. An hour later, they exited the building into a strange and tumultuous wind that seemed to whip them from every direction. Chris slipped in behind the steering wheel, put the key into the ignition and turned it. "Click" is all the men heard, as if the battery was dead. Chris tried several times to start the car; it was a no go. The men returned to the inn and as they were walking through the lobby Chris' pager buzzed. He looked at the number, went to a phone and called the doctor. Kiera was gone.

More than an hour later, the two men returned to Chris' car. It started with the first turn of the key. The air was still. The two men looked at each other then drove home to Allyson and Lauren and their nanny.

A hospice nurse was with Kiera when she passed; someone Kiera didn't know, someone she wasn't emotionally attached to. Her long ordeal was finally over. She was 27 years old, a mother of two. She had hated hospitals. She had dreamed of angels. She had experienced seven episodes of "going up to heaven." During her last night excursion, she had been told she would die before her husband . . . and she did. The best of doctors had tried to save her after the first had failed her. We had all worked with her psychologically, mentally and emotionally while Kiera worked diligently through meditation, visualization and attitude. Still, her excursions held sway.

We laid Kiera to rest next to her sister-in-law, Kim, on a hillside above Jackson, two young women who were forewarned of their impending deaths through processes yet to be under-stood. Their dreams were documented—their deaths are evident. Side by side, they share a view of the mountains they loved.

Remember Dr. Kirsch, the Jungian psychoanalyst, the person to whom I took my experiences and Kim's dream? What he said was this, "Of course, at the time of her dream it was already written, but one can do something about it if one is conscious of it and analyzes these things, for you must understand that in these particular experiences there is a psychological meaning. However, there are always people who just don't have the possibility to change it."

Did both Kim's and Kiera's demise fall into the latter category? Surely, Kiera had worked against the fate proposed to her in her night travels. Or did she? They must have stayed with her as two things happened in relationship to her night journeys prior to her fatal illness. First, as the lung cancer that plagued Kiera's father began to exact its toll, Kiera, frightened by what she saw, coupled with her growing paranoia, began to change her story, telling Chris that her night travels, her memories of heaven and death and light, were probably nothing more than warnings in regard to her father's approaching death. And, secondly, some six months after her father's demise, Kiera and Chris were going through an old photo album that had been found among her father's things. As they turned the pages, they came across pictures of a long-deceased grandmother Kiera had never met or seen pictures of. Her name was printed beneath the photo followed by the word "Mom." The moment Kiera saw the first picture of her deceased grandmother, she exclaimed, "That's the woman who was my communicator." Kiera recognized the woman immediately, though she had known little of her existence.

Kiera's changing her story to fit her father's approaching death is a typical form of mental protectionism that needs no further explanation, but it is sad to think that the knowledge given to Kiera must have plagued her to the point that she did what Kim did on the last day of her life. Remember? Kim, on the morning of the day she died, said that perhaps she had misread her dream, that her rapid heartbeat and the ice on the windows might constitute her mental prophecy. Obviously, the annihilation of the material body is incomprehensible to the conscious mind . . . and hope does spring eternal. It is such occasions that cause me to side with Jung and the multiple layers of the mind, each with its own abilities and shortcomings. Like ion gates, opening and closing to information via chemical messages, the layers of our mind communicate, one with the other. Some messages (knowledge) are prophetic while others are consciously unacceptable.

Taking a more pragmatic view of all these phantasmagorical occurrences I would like to hypothesize that all diseases and/or weaknesses within a system are present long before they manifest themselves overtly. If this be so, then the electrochemical nature of our bodies would allow for the information of impending doom to reach the brain where the mortal message might be processed into dreamtime, thus warning the dreamer of the future.

The foregoing hypothesis works well in Kiera's case, very well as a matter of fact. But what of Kim's dream? Kim died because of a horse fall and misdiagnosis, not from a disease. But the hypothesis can work for Kim if we put this fact into the equation: Kim had taken birth control pills for many years. Estrogen is known to promote the clotting of blood in a small percentage of takers. Kim may have been among the fractional pool and the potential for excessive clotting may have lain in wait within her bloodstream, waiting for the fall. But how did her system, her mind/brain, know that such an occurrence would indeed happen and how did she get to a doctor who stood by a misdiagnosis that others had questioned? Why didn't he ask what medications she was taking? The questions are endless, but what on earth does one say about her foreknowledge of dying under ice water . . . like ice water in a glass, but lots of it?

Pragmatism often falls short when things are laid out on the table in plain view. If Kiera had been with a better doctor, she would have received much earlier treatment and probably would have survived.

Moving away from the arena of Kiera's and Kim's deaths, a biochemical hypothesis fails completely in explaining Abraham Lincoln's dream of being shot in a theater, and yet again, how did my mind receive knowledge of death from a blood clot—twice? Those powerful mind bytes of information were clear as to how death would occur. There was no person attached to the messages, but I, being a normal, egotistical bipedal ape, thought the message was for me.

DEATH'S PARAMETERS

Many primitive peoples of the past, as well as some today, believed that people got sick and died because someone had cursed them or wished them dead. In some societies, the "killer" was sought out, identified and put to death.

Three law firms in Houston came to Christopher and asked for permission to look into the possibility of filing a suit against the doctor who had failed to take medical action when Kiera's blood counts showed gross signs of trouble. If nothing else, they wanted his license revoked. The doctor's negligence warranted a case, so Christopher agreed. The lawyers discovered two things: according to their investigations, six other young mothers had died under the watch of the doctor who failed to monitor Keira's blood count, the one she seemingly disliked on an instinctual level, and, unfortunately, there was no way to prove that Kiera would have survived had she received proper treatment at an earlier date since approximately 20 percent of people (mostly women) still die of TTP, even under the best of care.

As to Kim's death, there were a great many in Jackson who were incredulous I wasn't suing her doctor. It was true that he had held firm in his diagnosis of lupus while we screamed in the background that the culprit was the fall. But Kim had insisted on returning to Jackson, stating that she had to go home.

I believe that people are (or should be) responsible for themselves. I believe that every grown individual must accept responsibility for his or her own life and, most of all, his or her own actions. The doctor didn't want Kim to die. No doctor would want a young, healthy patient to die and no sum of money could repay me for the loss of my daughter or bring her back. You can't pay for or buy a life. I didn't want blood money—I wanted my daughter. Mere money or wealth couldn't replace Kim. We don't own other people, not even our children. An individual cannot be valued in dollars, and money for money's sake has never made anyone happy (exceptions: sociopaths). Only if Kim had children who needed to be cared for and educated would recompense have been warranted.

As my wise grandma Faunce said, "Our loved ones and friends are only loaned to us and we to them."

On a philosophical plane, I concur with Dr. Kirsch in that death belongs to the individual and those connected with a death (including doctors) have less power over the life and death of an individual than one might think.

Of all the doctors I have interviewed, whether pragmatic or open to the possibility of unexplainable phenomena, every one of them admitted that he (or she) had known patients who should have died and didn't, and patients who died though there was no deducible physical evidence as to the cause of death.

Is our demise encoded on our DNA? Is DNA our dance card? Or is it all back to the mind, once more? When a person is in great pain, the mind reaches a point of panic and capitulation at which time the person becomes a patient willing to give in to anything or anyone who can alleviate his or her agony. (The torturer counts on this psychophysical characteristic.) Kim was in horrid pain prior to her departure from Berkeley. I, her mother, friend and confidante, stood with open arms offering all assistance, begging her to go down to Los Angeles with me, yet she declined with eyes I will never forget, eyes I read more fully now then I did at the time; eyes that spoke of what she already knew: "Mom, I have to go back to Jackson. I need to go home."

I offered to go with her.

"No."

For months after her demise, my mind would race back to bodily force Kim into my car and take her to a big medical center where she could be *saved*.

A doctor: "You don't know that, Carole. You might have gotten her to a big hospital and the outcome would have been the same. The only difference would have been that you would have known the cause of death when it came."

Another doctor: "She could have been saved. Hell, they should have started her on heparin weeks before her death. She could have been saved, no doubt about it."

A friend and lawyer: "It was her decision. When was the last time any child over the age of puberty agreed with or followed his or her parent's advice? Did you?"

Another friend, another lawyer: "Malpractice, pure and simple. But you couldn't take the trial, Carole. You have no idea what malpractice suits are like. In your emotional state, you couldn't handle it."

The mortician: "I've never seen so many clots in a chest cavity."

Dr. Kirsch: "If I could put you back three days before you ever got on the horses—if you could reverse everything—you still couldn't change your daughter's death. The only person who could have changed your daughter's death was your daughter. Each person's death is his own. Those surrounding it have far less power than you might think."

And from one of Kim's favorite books, *The Tao of Health*, by Michael Blate, a book she read many times during her last weeks, come words that helped keep me on track through my grieving:

Though I may share a karmic experience with another,
his karma is his—not mine, not ours—
and my karma is mine;
I—my own karmic jury and executioner—
determine the impact of each thought and deed.

It took a long time to forgive myself for deeds undone.
Time to know that as a mother, I didn't have the right to over-
rule my daughter's wishes. Time to remember that we had been
notified and more time to accept that, for reasons known and
unknown, we had failed to act. Time to accept that we don't
all live long lives and come to the realization that no person
has control over the life of another. We are individuals working
within the whole, like an atom that is bound up within itself yet
binding and interacting via free electrons with those around it.
Though all alike, we are all separate unto ourselves. To chastise
oneself for deeds undone is folly. Most of us do the best we can
at any given time in our life. As we go through life and gain new
knowledge, we are not allowed to go back and do what we now
think we should have done. Bruising your brain with, "If only
I had . . ." will do nothing but plague you with worthless guilt
you never earned.

Time, as always, passed, and when the time was right,
when my heart and mind were ready to accept that which is and
that which was, a healing of the mind occurred. My friend and
distant relative, Kim Fadiman, a man of great depth and knowledge, went with me to the ranch for some cross-country skiing.
But a refreshing snow-gliding tour was not in the cards. After a
lunch set before a warming fire, we settled down to an amazing
seven-hour discussion about Kim, her dream, my precognitive
thoughts of blood clots and the many occurrences that ensued.
We spoke of things my daughter had done and said during those
last six weeks, things that now made sense. Piece by piece, everything came together.

We know the mind often protects itself from pain, hiding offensive knowledge in the basement of the unconscious. When one accepts this, many things take on new meaning.

Those of us closest to Kim had sat for a full week following her death recounting, over and over again, each act she had performed and every word she had spoken from the time of the accident to the moment of death. There could only be one conclusion: Kim knew she was going to die. Outwardly, consciously, she had fought the good fight, but underneath, in her sub- and/or unconscious minds, she must have known what was taking place. Statement after statement and deed after deed spoke of her inner knowledge.

And me? My friend recalled seeing me in the market just prior to Kim's and my departure for Berkeley.

"Your words were telling me that Kim had water on the lung but that she would be fine in a few weeks; however, your emotions and speech pattern gave off great and serious alarm. It confused me at the time. I went home and thought about it as you had intimated through your words that things would be fine, yet I received a strong message from you that the news was disastrous. When I heard about Kim's death, I understood, and now that you have told me about her dream and your precognitive thoughts of blood clots it all fits together."

So both Kim and I knew. It was a hard nut to swallow. This new understanding was alarming, yet it produced within me a degree of calm I hadn't known previously. I went back to my books.

Some months later, through a chance meeting, I became friends with the late Jesse Greenstein, renowned astronomer and the first to say and write the now famous words, "We are nothing but star stuff." These words came out of his discoveries and understanding of the fact that all of the base elements in your body, along with everything else on planet Earth, were manufactured in the furious furnaces of exploding stars. Hence, we are nothing but "star stuff." I like that.

I had read books written by Jesse's astronomer son,

George, and in turn, Jesse read an early version of this book, one that was filled with particle physics and cosmology, realms I had explored in an effort to gain some understanding of my experiences. During Jesse's reading, and for many months afterward, we would engage in one- to two-hour phone discussions on what we know and what we don't know. One night, he said something about being incapable of accepting what my writings intimated.

"Jesse! Don't you believe what I've told you?"

"Of course I believe you. I've heard of experiences more profound than yours."

"Then why can't you accept them?"

"Because they smack of fate?"

"So? If there is such a thing, what are you going to do about it? If fate exists, nothing is changed, it's just what it is."

"I don't like it," he said, deep in thought.

"Why?" I asked."

"Because it frightens me. I'm a man and I wish to be in control of my destiny."

Few people are capable of such honesty. Jesse was an exceptional person in many ways. In his later years, he became irate as one "scientist" after another, used, or stole, his famous words about us being nothing but star dust, without giving him credit. Jesse was the first to realize the fact and speak/write the words. The wars within science are much the same as in all other realms of human endeavor.

I went on, explaining what I have come to believe. First, I believe we have a great deal of control in regard to our lives and, perhaps, our deaths. I see us entering life as a malleable, continuous-line cartoon that equates to our DNA, which, in many ways, sets a partial fate. Our looks, heritage, physicality, propensity towards certain diseases and some of our personality traits are set in proverbial stone via tangles of DNA that reside in every cell of our bodies, individual blueprints coiled up in every pocket lest you lose them. But an outline alone does not a person make. The environment into which we are born molds and configures our developing minds, thus coloring and animating our cartoon. So, while genetics may fatalistically dictate our form and many of our individual traits, they do not constitute our destiny. . . or do they? There is much to learn. At this point in time, we can't explain or replicate anomalous occurrences scientifically but I'm not going to stick my head in the sand because concrete explanations are currently beyond our grasp. Where would we be—where would humankind be—if we stopped asking questions?

PART SIX

LIFE'S MOSAIC

Life is an opportunity—do not waste it. Though we be little more than grains of sand within a vast universe, we possess remarkable capabilities.

How we use those capabilities creates the world in which we live.

MEMORIES

Death is a part of life. That which is born eventually dies. We are no different than any other form of life. Denying reality puts a person in a place from which the beauty of a spectacular sunset is never seen and sand between shoeless toes is never felt. Each moment we are given is a gift.

Your visual cortex picks up everything within your field of sight while your brain ignores most of the incoming stimuli except for that on which you have chosen to focus. That is why when you go to the museum or an art gallery, or are trying to figure out which chair to buy, you should use an old movie director's trick. Pick out, let's say, a painting that you particularly like and wish to view in its entirety, then curl your fingers into your palm so as to produce a little telescope. Put your telescope to an eye, close the other and focus on your picture of choice, making sure that nothing but the painting meets your visual cortex. Voilà! No extraneous input, so now you can truly see the artist's work. Memories that hold fast are like looking through a telescope at selected moments of our lives.

Years ago, using a lead rope, I quickly rigged a cinch halter on my horse, Ebo, and tied him to a buck and rail fence. He wasn't the kind to spook or shy when tethered and I usually did a good hitch knot that would come undone if pulled with any force.

What frightened him I'll never know, but just as I was

about to exit the tack house with his saddle, he bolted up and away from the fence with such force that he tore the top rail from its bucks. The knot held. The 14-foot rail whipped around, one of its six-inch nails hitting him in the chest. No real harm done to him, but it scared the devil out of him and he tore off down towards the hay barn, rounded it, and raced back towards me at full speed until he stepped on the rope, thus cinching down the halter around his nostrils, cutting off his air supply. The rope pulled his head down to within a foot of the ground. He stood with legs splayed, his eyes bulging as suffocation took hold of his form.

By this time, my neighbor, Tina, was there. I went to loosen the rope.

"Don't, Carole! As soon as he gets some wind, he'll explode."

"I know, but I can't watch him die."

With adrenaline pumping, I stooped down onto my toes to loosen the rope. With one tiny whiff of air, he exploded, his head hitting my chest, throwing me back onto the ground as if I'd been shot from a catapult. Then he was rearing up high above me. Tina grabbed my right arm and in one incredible movement flung my entire body against the tack house as Ebo's hoofs crashed down where I had sprawled on my back a bare second before.

Ebo raced back to the hay barn, the rail bouncing along beside him and amidst his feet. When he reached his destination, he stood frightened and spent.

Two lives saved. Terrifying input to three brains produced incredible fear, but with the release of adrenaline and other brain chemicals, our fear was replaced with strength and daring and we all survived. Our brains didn't create the situation, but they did their jobs to save us.

The horse wreck proves the built-in power and speed of our brains as the first two Fs, flee or fight, went into action. But it was my mind that made a compassionate, knowingly dangerous decision to save that which I had put in harm's way. When I saw Kim's doctor in the airport, my conscious mind overrode the impulse to kill, while on the day of the horse wreck, my mind overrode my natural instincts for survival in order to save another.

Such decisions have been made millions of times, especially during times of war or disastrous situations.

Years later, the deaths detailed in this volume changed my life dramatically. I rode less as life consumed me with its many passings. Following Kim's demise, I couldn't get on a horse. My sons had negated the thought of putting Cocoa down. "Mom! You know Kim would never forgive you! Sell him or give him away." My thought left me before their admonishments had ended. Cocoa loved people more than any other horse I had ever owned. I found him a good home.

A friend called. She is as close to a true shaman as I have ever met. Her ability to track is only surpassed by her healing ways; the Park Service hires her to find people lost in the park. "You must get back in the saddle," she said. So the next day, she and her husband drove over to the ranch. First she worked with my four remaining horses, who had been alone for months on end, then her husband eased me up into a saddle, mounted another horse and we set out on a slow hour's walk. I cried the entire time, but the shaman was right, I had to get back on a horse, I had to forgive.

After that, I tried to ride but Ebo read my inner thoughts and let me know that he didn't want me on his back. Another year passed. One day, I became determined to ride. I looked at my two remaining horses, Ebo and Half-Ass (long story, but a proper name). With the other horses gone to their graves, the two had become inseparable, which was amusing, as previously they had hated one another—it was a class thing. "Okay," I thought "I'll ride Ebo and lead Half-Ass so he can be with his new best friend."

When all was ready, I went to mount Ebo. Ebo would

have none of it. I was alone at the ranch so there was no one to help me. I felt frustrated and furious. Taking Ebo's reins and Half-Ass' lead rope, I said out loud, "Fine! Then we'll just take a walk!"

The horses walked as far away from me as they could without pulling their leads out of my hands. Their body language said it all—we don't want to be with you. I persisted. We had walked around past the old red hay barn and were nearing the inner road when everything in me fell apart. I stopped. The aloneness of the moment, the replaying of Kim's fall, the agony of her absence and all who had left my life, filled my entire being. In wailing tones, I screeched, "I'm so afraid!"

Immediately, both lines went slack and then two huge heads were gently, warmly pressing into my chest, hugging and holding me the only way a horse knows how. I stood with bowed head resting on hairy foreheads and wept. They stood holding me, comforting me, loving me, understanding me.

The three of us remained thus for many minutes, then we took a walk. This time, two compassionate creatures walked beside me with slack lines, their heads almost touching my shoulders.

It has long been observed that horses sense the inner emotions of their riders. They often buck neophytes sensing their fear and/or their total lack of riding skills, which, in the mind of a horse, presents a danger, and horses don't like dangerous situations. Ebo and Half-Ass sensed both my fear and my cry for release and responded with compassion, an emotion seldom equated with *Equus caballus*.

Biggest hugs I have ever received.

Many mammals exhibit a keen sense of death. When Kim died, I had the family's black-and-tan hound, Captain, who was still recovering from the loss of his brother, brought over from the ranch. Captain had grown up in the old Jackson house. It was usual for him to enter the house and then run around to see if anything had changed and check things out, but this time was completely different. As he entered the door, he went on full alert. Taking a somewhat wide-legged stance, he stood stock still, his eyes unfocused, his marvelous nose roaming the house. Then slowly, he looked up at me, stepped over to me and leaned his body against my leg. For the next month, we all knew who was having the hardest time at any given moment as Captain was by his side, leaning, comforting, absorbing his pain.

A group of common chimpanzees (*Pan troglodytes*) was out foraging, going from tree to tree, gathering and eating ripened fruit. A male of the group accidentally fell out of a tree and died from the fall. A nearby male ran to the body, screamed, bent down over the body of his friend, looked, listened, sniffed, then bolted upright and raced around screaming. Soon the entire group was congregated around the body, each individual crying, hooting, screaming and/or thrashing his arms about in the air. Many went to the body, bent close, listened, sniffed, then returned to the torments of grieving. Time passed, females, babies and the young began to gather and sit in clutches while the adult males formed a rough circle around the body and sat down. Now there was silence, which lasted until the males began to moan and "oooooo" in unison.

When a wild chimpanzee infant dies, the mother will (in most cases) carry its body around for a period of three days. At first, she will hold the infant's body to her chest, but as the days pass she will end up dragging the body along by one of its arms. At some seemingly meaningless moment, as she ambles through the forest, she will simply let go without looking back. Gorillas have been observed to do the same.

Grieving has been observed within many higher species of animals other than humans. Such observations speak to the antiquity of sensing and emotionally reacting to loss. Elephants will "bury" their dead, collecting the bones of a relative from the death scene and carrying them into the woods or jungle to place them in a scattered grouping. Before leaving the bones, they run their trunks over them, over and over again, often swaying through the process. In some cases, the herd returns periodically to the site of the remains and again runs their trunks over the bones or picks them up and carries them around before replacing them among the group of bones.

LIFE

L ife is a classroom. As soon as you learn one lesson, life presents another. As soon as you solve a problem, another falls in your lap. Many lessons are joyous: learning to ride a bike, building houses out of blocks and cities out of sand, learning to read, playing a musical instrument, playing Juliet in the school play, learning to drive. Some lessons work to save your life: learning to be careful, to watch your step and look both ways when crossing streets; learning about fire, lightning, and riptides; learning how to climb mountains, which animals and insects offer death as well as beauty, what not to eat, and how to drive a car safely. Some lessons expand your inner self and increase your knowledge. Such lessons are often learned through pain and loss. The biggest teacher of all is death.

A man died and found himself standing next to God.

Looking down, God said, "Let's look over your life." The man looked down and saw a long stretch of shoreline. God continued, "Those footprints are a record of your journey." The man looked closer. "There's another set of prints next to mine but they're not continuous." And God said, "I was walking beside you." Once again, the man studied the footprints. "God, I don't understand. During the worst, most difficult times of my life you left me. There are no prints next to mine during any of my times of suffering. How could you leave me like that?" Quietly, God said, "I was carrying you. The continuous line of footprints is mine."

In the third grade, I met my best friend, Katherine, who was (is) a very smart individual with a keen sense of humor. During our grammar school days, I spent many of my summer nights at her house. Whenever I stayed over, we would laugh ourselves silly into the wee hours of the night. But it wasn't all laughter; Katherine and I seriously planned to be doctors in a time when only boys aspired to the medical profession. (Abdominal surgeries were performed on helpless rubber dolls.)

Katherine became a doctor. I fell in love, married and had children.

A few years back, Katherine suffered a cardiac arrest, called out, then collapsed, with most of her body ending up under the dining room table. Her doctor husband, Dan, raced in and crawled under the table, shouting her name over and over. Katherine came around. As her eyes focused, she looked into Dan's eyes and said, "Dan, we've got to stop meeting like this." The ambulance arrived and she's still cracking us up.

Life is what you make of it. One day, early on in Dick's cancer, I got weepy. Dick would have none of it. "Look! When you came out of the womb was there a little man standing there in a bowler hat with a bouquet of roses? Life isn't a joy ride. Things don't always happen the way you want them to. Grow up."

Months later, fear took hold of his brilliant mind and wreaked havoc with our lives, but through it all Dick did some things I believe helped him to survive far past the doctors' predictions. On a day when he had it all together, I asked him if he knew anything about meditating.

"No."

"Would you care to learn?"

"Yes."

I was amazed and took him immediately into the bedroom, had him lie down and began to teach via explanation and then into a trial effort. Within three minutes, he had his feet and hands tingling. I was impressed.

We never spoke of meditation again until a short time before his demise when he admitted that he had meditated twice daily since the day I taught him the little I know.

But there was another thing that I know helped him, something oncologists now know to improve the condition and longevity of cancer patients.

Chemotherapy for cancer can be very rough on the patient, including on one's appetite, which flies out the window with the first pill. With Dick's first round of chemotherapy, and all that followed, he could hardly stand to walk by the kitchen as the smell of food made him sick to his stomach. After three days, I put on my food-knowledge hat and my fake, never-earned medical coat and looked at the situation. I knew from reading and looking at Dick that chemotherapy is a blessing that fights the disease but wounds the body in many ways, particularly in that the patient won't eat and thereby loses weight—something he can't afford to do if his body is going to fight for survival.

Dick was a chocoholic (me, too), so I went down to his office and said, "I know you can't stand the smell of food and eating is close to impossible for you, but what if I made you a best-ever chocolate malt twice a day? You can hold your nose if you must and just drink it down. Boom, boom, you're done for the day and we can maintain your weight. I then explained my thought processes around the fact that he couldn't afford to lose weight.

"Okay. Your thinking is sound. I'll do it."

Every time Dick went out of remission and onto chemotherapy, it was malt time, which provided him with the calories his body needed. As a result, throughout his three-and-a-half-year ordeal, Dick never lost a pound until the last days of his life.

Here's the recipe:

A Malt to Live By

In the Morning:
Stir 1½ tablespoons Café Vienna coffee mix into ¼ cup boiling water and set aside. Or use a strong, cooled shot of coffee instead of the Café Vienna.

Add in Sequence to Blender Container:
½ cup half and half
2 tablespoons canola oil
1 raw egg
2 heaping tablespoons malt
3 squeezes Hershey's chocolate syrup (don't squeeze the bottle until you've collapsed it, just three big squeezes)
Café Vienna (or shot of coffee)
1 more cup half and half
(Ice cream: optional—not too much)

- Blend at high speed for a minimum of 20 seconds.
- Pour into glass, paper cup or mug and serve with a straw.
- The straw (get the big fat kind) is important. When you are weak, don't want food in your mouth or are suffering from pain of the esophagus, drinking through a straw is far more effective in getting the most down in the shortest amount of time. Dick downed his as quickly as he could.

For the afternoon/evening malt, repeat exactly, but delete the Café Vienna or coffee.

If you wish to add a powdered protein, do so.

Make the recipe your own by tailoring it to the patient's needs and desires. Strawberry? Use jam (and omit the Café or coffee)! Grand Marnier?? Ummm. Yes.

Ten days prior to his death, when all false pride, prejudices and emotional hideouts had fled before him, I told Dick that the one thing that made me mad and sad was that I'd never been able to convince him that he was a handsome man. Looking deep into my eyes, he finally accepted my words. With a wide grin spreading across his face, he quipped, "So put a mirror in the lid of my coffin."

SEARCHING

Over the last three and a half centuries, the hard sciences have burgeoned forth with forces and equations that have allowed for everything from the computer I'm working on right now to telescopes cruising the Milky Way. One of the primary discoveries of recent history was that of the second force, electromagnetism, i.e., the "light" and the "energy" that courses through our bodies, minds and brains making them functional.

We may be the newcomers on the block, but we're the only creatures that live pole to pole and around the middle on our third planet out from the sun. And while sharks have been around in pretty much the same shape for 455 million years, our earliest, small-brained kin stood up a scant seven million years ago. Humans of today possess the most highly developed brains in existence on planet Earth, and some have used theirs to the maximum.

In 1687, English mathematician Sir Isaac Newton put forth his theory of gravity, which explained the planetary movements of our solar system, thus discovering the first of the four known forces that help to explain our universe.

In 1864, James Clerk Maxwell wrote *A Dynamical Theory of the Electromagnetic Field*, in which he first proposed that light was in fact undulations (waves) that function within the same medium as electric and magnetic phenomena. Maxwell stands alongside of Newton and Einstein in the field of physics.

Now there were two fundamental forces to help us understand the universe in which we live.

During the twentieth century, the strong nuclear force, which holds atomic nuclei together, and the weak nuclear force, which allows for nuclear decay, were discovered when the fields of particle physics an quantum theory were electrifying the minds of many (pun intended). The accepted thought of today is that all possible forces ultimately derive from these four known forces. However, using all four known forces, scientists have failed to prove or find a grand unified theory (GUT) or a theory of everything (TOE) without fudging on their block-long equations. Right answers in science are always short and simple—for instance, $E=mc^2$.

Are there more forces within our universe waiting to be discovered?

George Verity was a strapping young lawyer fresh out of law school when he entered the army during WWII. He ended up surviving the Bataan death March and was then thrown into a Japanese prison camp. Little food was offered. A year later, George became deathly ill. The US medic did all he could for George. It was winter; the cold was intense. The doctor lay George on a bench and covered him with the heaviest blanket he could find, tucking it in everywhere he could in an effort to keep George warm through the bitterness of the night.

"George, I'm going to cover your face. Your breath will provide a bit of warmth. I'm right here. I won't leave you."

George sensed how sick he was. It was very black under the blanket. George felt his life force slipping away. Suddenly, he was bathed in an incredible white light. When he told me about the experience, his description of the light that surrounded him equaled the quality and strength of the light I saw in my bedroom. In the morning, George was better, much better. When he got home to Oklahoma, George joined a church of his liking but admitted that he often sat in meditation on the power of the light as opposed to listening to what the minister was saying. He lived to a good age. As an individual, he was an example to all who knew him.

What wavelength of electromagnetic radiation produced the rod of light I saw in my bedroom, or bathed George with a healing light? I have looked under every rug without finding the switch. I remain open to all thoughts and evidence—I know nothing. I remember the incident with great clarity, as did George remember his up to the time of his passing.

Looking at another type of phenomenon, what can be said about Kim and me both receiving telepathic messages on the morning of my mother's death? Neither incident was of a warning nature, simply a sense of her—her love, her person—pounding in our brains.

To cover telepathy would take another book, and it's been done, but it's interesting to know that evidence of telepathy, evidence even the skeptics will accept, has been produced with animals other than humans. Possibly the best example was performed many years ago by the Russians, who, along with numerous other peoples, accept telepathy as real, obvious and provable.

The experiment, according to *Psychic Discoveries Behind the Iron Curtain*, by Sheila Ostrander and Lynn Schroeder: Russian scientists took day-old rabbits from their mother and boarded a submarine, outfitted with clocks precisely synchronized with those in the land lab. Scientists who stayed behind attached electrodes to the mother rabbit as the sub submerged and headed out to sea. About an hour out at sea, the scientists aboard the sub killed one of the baby rabbits. Then, over a period of many hours, at random times decided upon after submerging, the other babies were put to death, one at a time. The timing of each death was noted precisely. Then the sub (which was on a training run), returned to port and the two groups of scientists compared notes. The mother rabbit had exhibited extreme stress every time one of her babies was killed. The times of her distress matched exactly with the timing of each infant's death.

The substance of the book is intriguing. The authors make note that as of the late '60s, the Soviet government funded numerous and varied parapsychological studies. To my knowledge, they continue to do so.

The only known force that might be involved in the workings of telepathy would be some wavelength of electromagnetism. Or, since years of research have shown that telepathic communication is instantaneous, the answer might lie in particle physics. Though quantum mechanics is now an accepted theory, it is an incomplete, not fully understood theory. One of its principles holds that when you interact with a particle (such as a photon), its twin particle reacts in the opposite way, instantaneously, even if it's millions of miles away (look up "entanglement"). Though Einstein's theory of relativity led to quantum mechanics and entanglement, he refuted both to the end of his life and referred to particles reacting to one another as "spooky action at a distance."

A man in New Jersey draws a picture of mountains with a red car parked on a road that runs along their base. A man in France tells an investigator what the man in New Jersey is drawing. A five-year-old dog had never been away from his mistress when she suddenly took off for Europe, leaving the dog and servants to guard the house. The dog was incredibly lonely for his owner and wouldn't eat for the first three days following her departure. A few weeks later, the dog awakened the household in the middle of the night with horrendous barking and whining as it raced madly around the house. After a moment or two of this, it ran to the front door and fell dead of a heart attack. At the exact same time in a London hotel his mistress exhibited immense distress then collapsed dead of a heart attack. Most people say, "Just a coincidence."

A young woman in Los Angeles lost three of her relatives, including a brother, within a period of a year and a half. When she and her sister got word that their brother was in the hospital, they boarded the first available plane. As sisters will, they took to talking about everything. Then, for some unknown reason, they stopped talking. A moment later, they looked at one another and said in unison, "Dave just died." And so he had.

The stories are endless but they don't (scientifically) explain how the thoughts of one person can be received by another. The most scientific study into the field of telepathy and other workings of the human mind can be found in *Margins of Reality: The Role of Consciousness in the Physical World,* by Robert G. Jahn and Brenda J. Dunne.

It's an absorbing read. Jahn is a professor of aerospace science and dean emeritus of the Department of Mechanical and Aerospace Engineering at Princeton. Dunne is at Princeton Engineering Anomalies Research.

Many years ago, after putting the core of this book together for the first time, I asked a well-versed friend to read what I had written. Upon returning the manuscript she said, "Wonderful," with less enthusiasm than I'd ever heard in my life.

"You didn't like it."

"No, no, it's really good."

"We are very close, we read one another. Tell me why you are upset?"

In anguish, she said, "Well, I feel so small, so left out, as if I'm incomplete. In my entire life, I have never had an anomalous occurrence."

I couldn't help it. My face broke into a grin. With a chuckle, I asked, "Don't you know why?" She shook her head in the negative. "You've never needed one, you big silly. From what I know of your life, you have never been in a situation where your mind needed to open the door and lower the drawbridge. I may never have one again."

A smile replaced her look of despair and then we were both laughing.

Kim's prescient dream joins a long list of prophetic dreams that go back to times prior to writing. On a more current note, I would like to share the following with you. A marvelous young composer and friend, Kyle Werner, asked to read this book prior to publication. I sent him the first four parts.

One of his remarks was intriguing:

> Interesting about the dreams and foresight. The composer Gustav Mahler ended up prophesying events in his life through his music. He wrote a song cycle called *Kindertotenlieder* ("Songs of the Deaths of Children") during a completely stable, happy period in his life. Then his young daughter died a few years later. During this same stable period, he also composed his Sixth Symphony. This work includes three massive "hammer-blows of fate," in the last movement. These all came true through events in his life: he lost his job at the Vienna State Opera, his daughter died, and he was diagnosed with a severe heart condition. I don't know if he dreamt about any of this, but it all came out in his music. Fascinating.

I have never seen or felt the presence of a "ghost" but for my great-grandfather in the garden, but I can't help but wonder if my grandmother's brother actually visited her. If so, was he welcoming her to the other side or simply preparing her for the inevitable? It's interesting that she didn't see him, but heard him, seemingly through the innards of an old spittoon.

Going through the anthropological literature, ghosts and spirits abound. Every society, clan, tribe or culture talks about ghosts. They are everywhere. Among primitive peoples, their reality is never doubted and most are thought to be malevolent and capable of bringing death or harm to a person, or, at the very least, making trouble. In New Guinea, boys are taught to lie, to shout out to the ghosts of the jungle that they are the fierc-est warriors of their tribe, that they have killed many enemies, that they are a force to be reckoned with. This shouting is done to frighten the ghosts and keep them at bay.

In more sophisticated societies, ghosts seem to be less threatening since no one has died from seeing or sensing a ghost. All of the personal ghost stories I've heard over the decades have been positive and/or healing in nature.

Many dying patients, who have never experienced an anomalous occurrence, speak of visits from dead relatives. Kim's boyfriend thought her dream of her great-grandma was real and foretold her ultimate demise. The Jungian psychotherapist agreed, adding that I had to realize that Kim asked her to come. Kiera's father changed completely in attitude, going from being depressed and fearful to calm and accepting after having a dream he refused to talk about. All he would say was, "I had a dream. It's all right. Don't worry."

Two of Kim's friends claim to have seen her months after her demise, one in the old Jackson house in the bedroom Kim inhabited for several months, the other in the ranch house when he "saw" her walk from the dining area, past the front door and into the living room. Another friend felt her protective, loving presence (in no uncertain terms) whenever he entered the ranch house at night.

One night, Kiera's daughters, Allyson and Lauren, had a long discussion with their father concerning the deaths of their mother and Kim. The girls were eight and eleven years of age. "It's time for bed. Go get ready," said Chris. Leaving their fa-ther's room, they started down the stairs to get a bedtime snack when they both saw Kim, Kiera and their old dog, Barney, seem-ingly walk from the den, then through the wall at the bottom of the stairs. They looked at each other and said in unison, "Did you see that?" They hurriedly compared notes, then ran in to tell their father. Today, both girls hold firm to their story but neither can remember what Kim and Kiera were wearing, although Lauren has a fleeting memory of the dog's leash being either bright red or bright green, but can't state with any confidence the actual color perceived.

There is the physical body; there is the mind/brain, which runs via electrochemical processes; and then there's that thing we call a soul, spirit, psyche, or consciousness. Do we have one? When we die, what happens to the electromagnetic radiation that kept us ticking?

The Law of Conservation of Matter and Energy says that matter cannot be created or destroyed, but can change its form. For instance, matter can become energy, as when you burn wood to warm youself with its radiant heat. More important is that the total amount of matter and energy extant within the universe is a fixed quantity, never more, never less.

Eight hundred years before the Christian era, at a site in southeastern Turkey near the Syrian border, a royal official saw to the completion of an inscribed stone monument, or stele, to be erected at the time of his death. The writing on the stele instructs mourners to honor his life, as well as his afterlife, with feasts "for my soul that is in this stele." It is the oldest written evidence of a belief system in which the "soul" was believed to be different and separate from the material body. The royal official belonged to a society/religion that cremated their dead while surrounding societies buried their dead in the belief that the body and soul were one and inseparable. In their eyes, to cremate the body would have been to annihilate—as opposed to liberating—the soul. But why did the official assign (confine) his soul to live within a stele?

Several decades ago, a young man—I'll call him Henry—went through medical school, did an internship in surgery and then became a pathologist at a major university hospital. For some 20 years, Henry performed autopsies and taught anatomy to young medical students. In the old days, every student got his own cadaver to work on, then it was teams of two or four working together on a single body. Now, it's often a group, which means less hands-on learning. (Promote learning; leave your body to science.)

One day, Henry decided he'd had enough of autopsies and re-entered the surgical ward. He told me, "Carole, there was nothing to working on cadavers. You get used to it right away. It's no different than butchering a steer, but more interesting of course as you are looking for clues and helping medical science. I never thought anything about it, and then I went back to surgery. It was a whole other ball game. Of course, I knew I was working with live, pulsating flesh, but that wasn't it. There was something dramatically different. One day a guy died on the table. We were trying to perform a miracle with the odds set against us. We did everything we could for him, but he passed on. When the monitor went flatline, we looked at one another acknowledging our defeat as well as our efforts. I said I would stay and fix him up for the mortician. The others left and the nurses said they would send someone to care for the body. As I was sewing, I suddenly sensed, felt, knew, that the guy's soul, his essence, his consciousness, his whatever-the-hell-it-is had left. Beneath my hands was nothing but flesh—meat. I sewed him up real nice and cleaned him up as I came to the realization that there's something more. His brain activity and electrical field had shut down long before I began sewing him up. Ever since, I have approached life with a different attitude."

My daughter-in-law, Mary, was working in an end-stage critical care unit in a hospital. It was the first time she had sat with a dying patient. She was holding the woman's hand when the heart monitor went flatline. The woman had signed a DNR; death had been expected for many days. Mary checked her watch, made notations on her chart, got up and left the room. Twelve steps down the hall she got an overwhelming sensation of having left the woman when she needed her most. She rushed back into the room. It felt empty, devoid of life. Death hung in the air. From that day forth, Mary never left "dead" patients until she sensed their passing, which she claims is palpable. Did

Dick's passing wake me from my slumber?

A close friend was raised by a fine and intelligent father who considered the word "atheist" as being too religious in connotation. After his death, she was sleeping when something awakened her. She opened her eyes and saw her father standing at the foot of her bed. "Everything is all right," he said, then disappeared.

During World War II, many parents, mostly fathers, had like experiences of waking in the middle of the night and seeing their son standing at the foot of the bed. One father's son told him that he'd just died, but that everything was all right, adding that he thought his father would want to know. Three days later, the family got a call from the Red Cross.

It has been said for many years that Lincoln's "ghost" visits—or lives—in his old quarters in the White House. Many dogs of many presidents have been found with hackles up, barking at the end of the hall that leads to Lincoln's suite, including dogs that never barked in any other area of the great white house.

TEACHINGS

The loved ones I lost to death would have wanted me to grow through the experience of their death. In fact, many of them would have demanded it. True to their individual natures, they took whole chunks out of my being then gave back in full measure.

As a child I had known the deaths of others and had come close to knowing my own. Then, starting with the year

1981, when we learned of Dick's leukemia, my life experiences concerning death began to multiply and increase in uncommon proportions to the norm.

D uring my early years of culinary training, my father would taste my efforts and say, "My darling, it's wonderful, but you could have . . ." And so I learned.

Daddy's death created a huge void in my life that eventually filled to overflowing with a million marvelous memories. He had been my constant teacher, my accomplice in thought. Even today, as I cook and create in my kitchen, I can hear my father's words, especially if I make a mistake, "Godt damn it!" and then I'm laughing and correcting or simply accepting the fact that I'm not perfect.

A few months prior to his death, my father looked at me and said, "You know, you can never know it all, even on a single subject. There will always be someone who will think of something new, or know things you haven't a clue about. Never stop learning. It is the greatest and most lasting of all pleasures." His words were a gift, an enhanced, end-of-life version of "You got to tink!"

A t Christmas, Dick would play Santa Claus. Getting up long before the dawn of Christmas morning, Dick would silently pile beautifully wrapped presents under the tree with tags reading "For Carole." Then cancer arrived and canceled the party.

Dick's long walk towards death was fraught with confusing emotions. He handled the approach of death admirably in public, dreadfully in private. He left me with admiration mingled with disgust, love mingled with anger. Now, years later, I can only think of Dick with love. He was a hell of a man and he loved me. I have grown to realize that given the same situation I might act as poorly or worse. None of us knows until we get there. The knowledge of approaching death is an incredible burden to bear.

Long before my first husband and I divorced, I sat and cried tears of anguish in the arms of my grandma Faunce. She listened to my travails, cuddling me in her love, then commented that I still loved my husband and so things would continue until my love died. My grandma was full of wisdom. As to her death, what can you do but smile? She had a long life filled to overflowing with love. She had known the loss of a child and the love of family. She gave her life to loving and caring for her children and others. How lucky to have been a part of her experience. Was she perfection? No, no one is, but she was close, real close. I wonder if Charlie was waiting for her.

My mother, Caroline, was an exceptional person whose life crumbled towards its end. My poor mama; my strong and beautiful teacher. I won't lie; it hurts, but not as much as you might think. Mom's death was prompted by a rare form of alcoholism in which a person can consume many drinks and never show signs of inebriation. Mom was always the designated driver, "You drive, Caroline. You're the only one who's sober."

For a time, I transferred my anger to Mother's alcoholism, then the same clinical psychologist who met me on the street and helped me understand why I couldn't remember my precognitive thoughts of death from a blood clot or Kim's dream approached me. He had been extremely upset over Mother's suicide. "Damn it, Carole, I knew Caroline for 30-some years and I know an alcoholic and a suicide when I see one. It doesn't fit. I can't figure Caroline for a suicide and she never exhibited a single trait of an alcoholic. Would you have lunch with me?"

"Of course."

At the end of a three-hour lunch, the doctor looked at me. "You are right, it was the alcohol. Without it, she never would have done it. But Christ, I never would have taken her for an alcoholic. It's hard to believe. You say she never drank until after five? Poor thing. Between your father's death, her bad back and the booze her depression became overwhelming. Grief, alcohol and pain make for a depressing, killing poison."

"You know," I said, "she stopped drinking several weeks before she did it."

"That's the Caroline I remember. Always thinking, always doing things to the best of her ability. What a tragedy."

Another comment from a reformed alcoholic: "Hell, the stats on alcohol? The part they don't tell you is that a great number of alcoholic deaths are suicides. The facts are real ugly, not for broadcasting."

I anguished over the last sad years of my mother's life but eventually I reveled over decades of health and vitality, mentally cheering on the woman who took us all to camp and taught us all to scream-sing "We LOOOOVE you"; the woman who taught me to dance, and make bread, grape jelly and jams. The mother who supported me when I was down and comforted me steadfastly through my childhood illness.

Everything is intertwined. Those close to us unavoidably affect our lives, but each life is also unique to the individual, and more important, our deaths are most assuredly our own. With or without the alcohol, my mother didn't want to live without my father. She had said so from the time I was a child, a time when alcoholic consumption wasn't in the equation. My father was my mother's foundation. When he died, her house fell down and all that was left were blocks of memories.

When Kim was eight years of age, she met her best friend, Megan. Every summer, Megan's family would invite Kim to join them on their annual camping outing on a piece of land they owned in the wilds of Idaho.

At the age of 11, Kim returned from Idaho in an elated mood. I asked her about the trip.

"Mom! You won't believe it! I had the weirdest dream!"

"Oh? Tell me about it."

"Well, yesterday we hiked and everything all day long then, after dinner, Megan and I went to our tent. We always put our tent way away from the others as everybody complains about our talking and laughing into the middle of the night. Anyway, we finally went to sleep and I had a dream. . . . Well, I thought it was really happening, but I know it was a dream because I never left my sleeping bag. Anyway, this morning I couldn't wait to tell Megan about it. As we dressed and rolled up our sleeping bags, I told her how we had gone out to breakfast and how Megan's dad had come to the table with a map. He said he'd been going over the map and that if we were all in agreement we could add an extra hour to the trip and go over a beautiful pass and see some scenery we'd never seen before. Everyone agreed. The pass was really beautiful and near the top we started around a sharp U-turn of a curve and perched on a big rock, sitting on the edge of a cliff, was a huge golden eagle. He was so boss and as the car got closer he spread his gigantic wings and flew off."

"So, you had a wonderful dream."

"Mom, you don't get it. By the time I finished telling Megan my dream, we were through packing up and ran out to breakfast. Mom! Every single thing in my dream, even Mr. Owen's words at breakfast, were exactly as they happened in my dream. I even knew what the pass looked like as we drove up it and when we saw the golden eagle, Megan and I grabbed each other and as he spread his wings and flew off we started screaming and hugging each other. Everyone wanted to know why we were acting so goofy. Megan told them but I'm not sure they believed us."

"It's pretty spooky, but kind of wonderful, too. I believe you."

"Mom, everything in the dream came true."

Kim was an artist through and through. My father taught me about art, my daughter taught me how to see through the eyes of an artist.

I was raised with a strong work ethic and have always been good at letting some of the important little things slip by. "Mom! Turn out the desk lamp and get on your walking shoes. We are going for a hike." So off we'd go to mesh with nature and be at one with all that is. And then we would talk . . . and that's what I miss the most. We could talk by the hour and never tire. We both loved the sciences and animals and philosophy. We loved to share our lives with one another—every juicy tidbit. Kim would dissolve into peals of laughter after telling me about some bizarre occurrence from her frenetic life. She had the ability to take herself mentally out to the sun's fifth planet to look back at the ridiculousness of our earthly existence. "My life is crazy, but it sure isn't dull," she'd say. "No wonder I hate soap operas. Compared to my life they're boring."

Kim's life wasn't all that crazy, but she experienced it to the full, making it appear to be more and bigger than most. She truly lived life. She experienced her karma, in which I think she believed. She brought beauty, joy, learning and laughter to all who knew her . . . then bowed out early.

Dr. Kirsch, after hearing about Kim's biological father, of how she chose the wrong men, how she was one of those "women who love too much," said Kim had died of the heart, to the men in her life. That the physical death always equates with the death of the psyche. He said she had died to the father who had broken her heart.

I thought back to the night of Kim's death when I, too, had said she had died of a broken heart. A statement uttered from knowledge unmasked by shock.

Her friends—they are still her friends—believe that love was Kim's quest. They believe Kim entered life searching for love, for the experience and understanding of it, as surely she knew the rest. Surely, she was wiser and more profound than most, surely a giant giver of the little things that make life worth living.

Do you ever get over the loss of a child? Not really, but you heal, you carry her with you and when your grief wears itself out she rides within, whispering funny things to say, telling you to look again at the sunset, and then, when you finally reach acceptance and understand death for what it is, she takes up residence in your heart and never leaves.

The old saying that it is better to have loved and lost than to have never loved at all still holds true. Life is a precious thing. And speaking of life, it goes on you know—you can't stop it—so live it, make the most of it and learn all you can in order to broaden your horizons; there are so many to explore.

My son, Christopher, walked by the windowed office of the assistant manager and noticed a beautiful blonde with twinkling eyes being interviewed. "Nice," he thought. Kiera got the job and introduced herself on her way out. "Did you get the job?" Chris asked.

"Yes, I'll see you tomorrow."

Beautiful Kiera was cut down in the prime of her years by a blood disease we know little about. No one knows what prompts it or what conditions or genetic inheritance trigger it. We do know that it strikes women more often than men, especially during or after pregnancy.

Kiera's night travels still haunt me. They were so graphically experienced and so draining to her psyche. But why, in each of her mental excursions, did she have to get out of bed and walk into the hallway, where she was suddenly whooshed up to another realm? Why couldn't she have been "taken aloft" from her bed—her slumber? Why was getting *there* always the same? Was there only one way for her to enter her place of prescience? And what about the tragic toll on her husband and children? Kiera's death changed each of their lives on an individual basis. There was a long period of adjustment but they are well. The dents death created are now camouflaged with strong exteriors that permeate to their cores.

We are tough-minded survivors with soft spots. Kiera broke many hearts. Fortunately, hearts mend as minds remember and hold fast to the goodness that was.

UNDERSTANDING

U nexplained phenomena are experienced by people from around the globe regardless of race, religion, schooling, sex, age or physical condition. For me, that simple fact proves that such occurrences must reach back to our earliest times.

When did we first experience unexplained phenomena? Are such occurrences known only to *Homo sapiens*, man the wise? I see primitive thoughts of what could be referred to as religion and mysticism beginning with the first efforts to control fire some one and a half million to two million years ago. Surely the control of fire was early man's most important discovery. With the harnessing of fire, the night was made safe from other animals, and as we slowly learned to take away the darkness there had to have come a heightening of all our mental and emotional powers. With freed upper limbs, stone tools and the control of fire, the inventive areas of the brain most assuredly began to configure themselves allowing for the marvelous ideas and inventions that would come forth in the ensuing millennia.

Think of the first time fire was taken to a hearth and fed by man's inventive genius. It must have been done millions of times then lost to rain, wind or lack of attention. But once glimpsed, fire surely became the most sought after prize ever found. By taking away the night, in the act of illuminating the darkness, fire transformed humankind from a mere animal controlled by the spinning of his planet and its weather into an awesome thing. Could we but imagine the emotional awe of the first people to tend a fire beneath an undercut of a limestone cliff or within the arched cavern of an ancient cave and there see, for the first time, elongated shadows of themselves dancing across the walls as they moved between fire and limestone. Magic—incredible magic. Surely, man's imagination took a gigantic leap in that spellbinding moment played out over and over again more than a million years ago.

Now, thousands of millennia later, we stand, once more, awestruck at the font of discovery as we unravel the mysteries of DNA, peer into the structure of the atom, query the theory of quantum mechanics and explore the cosmos in order to understand our beginnings.

The magic of our shadows is still with us; it has always been with us.

In a large limestone cave known as Shanidar, located in the Zagros Mountains of Kurdistan in Iraq, nine individuals were laid to rest at various times, while a tenth individual lay decapitated and broken beneath a massive rock fall from the cave's ceiling. One body was curled into a fetal position and placed in a shallow grave with an abundance of flowers of known medicinal value. But the most famous remains are of an aged man who was born with deformities and later lived through the loss of an eye and further disfigurement, whether from an attack by another Neanderthal, an animal or falling rock is unknown. What is known is that this man lived for decades after the trauma that left him severely crippled and unable to sustain himself. Important is the fact that the only way he could have survived those many years is if his people cared for him and fed him. It is theorized that the man, referred to as Nandy by his excavators, acted as a shaman for the Neanderthal clan that inhabited Shanidar at the time. Labeled Shanidar I, his burial and remains were the inspiration for "Creb" in Jean Auel's book, *Clan of the Cave Bear.*

The Shanidar cave burials date back between 60,000 and 80,000 years. They represent some of the oldest burials ever found. Neanderthal graves are fairly common, dotting the maps of Europe, Eurasia, and Northern Africa. Many contain grave goods. Stone tools, flint, red ochre, animal bones and teeth along with flower pollens have been found in connection with numerous bodies. Various body positions have been observed, often in relationship to the placement of accompanying artifacts. Such burial practices speak to us of conscious intent coupled with the ability to feel, care, and grieve for others.

Did Neanderthals believe in an afterlife? Some of their burials suggest the possibility. Had some experienced a near-death that prompted a belief system in connection with death? Had dreams or visions brought forth a variety of beliefs? What encouraged those first burials? Were group members simply trying to protect the body from scavengers? If that was their sole intent, then why the red ochre, flowers, artifacts and/or stone tools? Stone tools speak of heightened intelligence, invention and expertise. The bones and teeth of large animals speak to us of fine hunters and providers of meat and people of cunning and courage. Red ochre has been used for millions of years, throughout biblical times and is still in use today, usually ground together with animal fat and used to cover the body as a symbol of healing, power, and divinity. It also works to ward off insects and is still used to make a colorful house paint.

The meagerness of evidence garnered from ancient burials curtails what we can know for sure, but it is obvious that the Neanderthals were complex and capable members of the genus *Homo* (man). *Homo sapiens* still follow many of Neanderthal man's ways. We still bury our dead and we often place "grave goods" within the caskets or burial places of our loved ones. Think of Dick's marvelously outfitted body along with his cousin's blanket and Kim's beautiful flowers and letters speaking to the love she inspired.

We are caring creatures blessed with the ability to love.

TIME

Cultural evidence suggests that man was keeping time as early as 30,000 years ago. Evidence aside, I believe *Homo erectus*, who started walking around the globe close to two million years ago, was innately cognizant of the passing of the seasons as are the plants and animals of today. The movement of the sun, south to north and back again through the sequence of seasons, and the moon's 27-day cycle, regulating tides and bringing menses to women, have always worked together as giant time pieces that allowed (allow) all species to foretell weather changes, the movement of herds, the arrival of birds and the growth of plants. *But what is time?* Science uses time as a measurement. Without rotational time, set by the movement of our planet, equations wouldn't work and you couldn't figure out the velocity of the train passing by. Rotational time was set by man's observations. The sciences couldn't function without it (but for quantum mechanics, which seems not to have any real use for it).

But what is time? There is epic time, which marks time by remembered events, "I was born the year of the fire," or historical events, "She died in the year of the plague." *But what is time?* I once spent a month reading about time. I learned a lot but found that there are no concrete answers other than that time is a tool for measuring. However, I can tell you this: when you're happy and having a marvelous time, time flies; when you are waiting for the man you love to arrive, time creeps by slower than a snail; and when a person is dying, time warps.

Seventy million years ago, there were no Himalaya Mountains; they didn't exist. The highest of Earth's above-sea-level mountains were born when an island, now known as India, slammed into and subducted beneath the Asian continent via the moving forces of plate tectonics. The plate upon which the island had sailed tried to maintain its northeast course, but Asia, being as large as it is, stood its ground, so to speak, and the meeting seam began to bulge and buckle until mighty mountains stood where once a level plain had existed. Though it may seem impossible, in time the Himalayas will weather away, leaving little trace of their existence. Whatever takes form comes into existence only to go out of existence as the constant sum of universal matter and energy reworks itself. We are part of that universe.

We are star stuff made up of particles billions of years old. We are an illusion. We are created in the likeness of God. We are molded from Mother Earth. We are created and sustained by the sun. We are masters of all we survey. We are a part of the universal whole. We have dominion over all but ourselves.

Regardless of our beliefs, we all have a need, a need to know, a need to believe in something, and what we believe is reflected in our perceptions of life and death. As humans, we are, and always have been, searching for what is; it is what makes us different from the other animals on this planet. It is what makes us human.

In the Bible, Genesis, Chapter 1, paragraph 26: "And God said, Let *us* make man in *our* image, after *our* likeness" (emphasis mine).

Were the Gods who created man from outer space? If not, why would an entity or agency as forceful as a "God" house himself in a shape as puny and perishable as ours? Or were they addressing the consciousness of humankind—the brain of man, the mind of woman?

A vast majority of known deities are male in gender. This is understandable, as every religion and myth I know of (myths are extinct religions) was formulated and written by a man or men, but for Christian Science conceived by Mary Baker Eddy. But Mary formulated a new religion by decoding the words of Christ as written in the New Testament, which was penned by men. Did man create his multiple Gods and design them out of vanity to please himself? It is humankind alone that needs a mirror, though we seldom look into it with honesty and depth? Every religion, every belief system has a foundation, a story to preserve, and everyone believes in something, be it a legend, a belief system, a religion or science But regardless of belief, or lack thereof, people from around the globe experience similar anomalous occurrences, the only variables being the interpretations given to them, which usually reflect the belief system of the experiencer.

Many Eastern religions believe the past, present and future are all one. If the past, present and future exist simultaneously, the events related in this book could be more easily accepted, but not fully explained. So the question remains, how can one view the future, and what is the impetus for a near-death experience? What is the light? When we die, does some energy packet that is representative of us continue on? Is there an explanation for prescient dreams, precognition, extrasensory perception (ESP) and telepathy? Why does knowledge of the future come to us as flashes of reality? How and why? Though the vast majority are fake, do those who actually have the "gift" tap into that fast moving wave/plane to glimpse and see the future? Is the brain an interface between two worlds? How many of us have such powers? Researchers claim we all have it, though few choose to receive the information that is omnipresent. Buddhists believe that the Enlightened Buddha, who found truth beneath the bodhi tree (during an episode of sleep some equate with a near-death experience), lives within us all, but that we have forgotten his seminal knowledge. If so, what made us forget? And where do so-called paranormal powers come from? Did the dinosaurs have it? Do animals have it? Can your dog read your thoughts? Has the big bang or initial singularity happened over and over again like the flashing of a strobe light? Has the light, warmth and power of fire been found not a million times, but billions of times? Has this entire scene been played out before? Is it time to open up to the questions and experiences that have created every religion and belief since the beginning of human thought? Is there a dream dreaming us? Would I have ever traveled through hundreds of books on dozens of subjects if death and its strange attendants hadn't graced my life?

Not too long ago, all of humankind believed in prophecy and dreams often molded people's lives. Did we lose our metaphysical side when science proved the earth to be nothing more than a small roundish planet circling a mediocre star? Did we step away from the unprovable when the human eye looked through a telescope and saw the rings of Saturn? Did we set aside old wives' tales when doctors perfected the art of caesarean section so that mothers and babies once doomed to die could be given the gift of life, thus demolishing the myths of why a woman died in childbirth or a child found it impossible to enter the world? Did we move away from the unknown when microscopes proved the existence of germs, bringing forth cleanliness to surgical units and ways of improving health? Perhaps it happened whenever a more advanced culture punctured the myths of those living closer to nature, whenever beliefs or myths were proven to be false and nothing was offered to replace them.

Regardless of your own personal beliefs or answers, how do you explain the remote African tribe that sensed the exact time and cause of the death of a friend, an anthropologist, who had worked with them for many years and was on vacation hundreds of miles away?

Other anthropologists had arrived the day before the "knowing" after driving more than a hundred miles over trackless land and then trekking miles into uncharted mountains to reach the tribe's village. The tribe went into extreme mourning and performed many rituals in honor of their friend and mentor. They told the newly arrived anthropologists that their friend had been attacked and eaten by a lion. Weeks later, the anthropologists trekked back to their car and drove back to civilization where they learned that the female anthropologist who had worked with the tribe they had left the day before had been mauled and eaten by a lion. The day and time of her death meshed with the wails and mourning of the tribe she had known and loved.

How did the tribe sense the time and way of her death? How did Kim know she was going to die beneath ice water? And how did Kiera know she would die before her husband?

Perhaps the questions I'm asking are beyond answering, but validation of unexplained phenomena add strength to their existence.

Four years after Kim's demise, Dr. Leo Henikoff journeyed to Jackson Hole for the third time to fish with his friend, Dr. John Long. Serendipitously, I was invited to a small dinner party at the Longs' summer cabin, at which I was seated next to Leo to whom I am now married. Three years later, I was spending time in Chicago to be with Leo and lecture on death and dying. One evening there was a panel discussion on death and dying at the Skokie library (Skokie is a bedroom community north of Chicago). Of the many speakers were myself, Leo and Dr. Sherwin B. Nuland, author of *How We Die*, a very fine book that deals with the death of the body. When it was my turn to speak, I went to the microphone and told of Kim's dream, of her being thrown six weeks later and then dying according to her dream six weeks after the horse wreck. I didn't go past the event of her death. I spoke only of her dream and its content coming to pass.

When all speakers had spoken, the moderator opened the hall to questions. There were some 400 people in attendance. A woman towards the back stood up and asked that I go to the microphone. She said she wanted to tell a short story as she wanted to know if, within the framework of my research, I had heard of anything like what she was about to tell. "One night, a few years back, my husband suffered a heart attack. He was rushed to the hospital. While the doctors were working on him, I tried frantically to reach our daughter, a college student living in a dorm. The girls at the dorm said she'd gone to stay with friends for the night, but none knew where or a phone number. An hour and a half later, my husband suffered another heart attack and died. I tried again to reach my daughter, but it was impossible.

"I went home but, of course, I couldn't sleep. At 7:00 AM, the phone rang. I answered. It was our daughter. 'Oh, honey!' I said, but before I could say anything else she cut me off and asked, 'Mom, did Dad die last night?'

"'Yes,' I replied. 'He had a heart attack. Did someone tell you?'

"'No, Mom, I'm staying with friends, but last night something awakened me in the middle of the night and I saw this incredible rod of light not far from my bed. For some reason, it didn't frighten me and somehow I knew it was Dad. I don't understand why, but I felt, I don't know, calm.'"

If you have read all of the pages of this book previous to this one, I don't have to tell you how I felt. I looked back at the other speakers. Dr. Nuland wore a face of amazement and Leo's eyes told me that he had just become a believer. As far as I know, neither of us knew a single person in the hall. When I found my voice, I related my experience with the rod of light that had presented itself in my bedroom. You could have heard a pin drop.

DEATH

My father told me not to worry my little head about it; Dick said we had grieved enough and that I should get on with my life; my mother said everyone would understand but her parrot; and Kim's last tears were over the thought of others weeping for her. She must be very mad at me—I could irrigate the ranch with the tears I've shed.

That's another thing death taught me: many of my tears were for me as much as for those who had passed before me. After all, they are all right. If death is nothing but "a little sleep" they are all right. It was *I* who was lonely for them; it is *me* that misses them so much. During my odyssey, Kim's death, in particular, forced me to see life in different ways, to learn all I could, to be a part of life, to be kinder to others as well as myself. Death is always a teacher, oftentimes a harsh and demanding teacher that forces you onto higher levels of thinking, a teacher that pushes you through knotholes no one would ever approach on his own. Towards the end of my odyssey, I found, with the help of professionals, that I had grieved for everyone but myself, my mind having brushed my own agonies and mini-death aside. Another lesson, another climb to reach acceptance of all that had happened and the impact it had on my life.

Death is an unseen, but deeply felt entity that insists on growth. And the closer the death, the more you must learn. Only when you open to the lessons and find the courage to walk through the line of fire will you reach a true place of acceptance. But when acceptance becomes you, then, and only then, will your loved one(s) return to live joyously within your heart and mind for the rest of your days.

Psychologists, psychiatrists and grief counselors speak of coming to a point of closure, a point of acceptance. The word acceptance is a good word. In order to go on living your life, you must get to a place of accepting that which has occurred. You must acknowledge the fact that someone you love has died. I didn't say, "loved," but "love." Just because my father isn't here in the present doesn't mean I don't love him anymore. If anything, I love him more. I love him for all he gave me and for all the things he taught me. He is still a part of my life, as are all those who have traveled on before me.

But then there's the word "closure" I understand that the clinicians are talking about finishing your time of grieving, but the word elicits thoughts of closing a door and walking away. In reality, when you "finish" your time of grieving, a huge door opens and welcomes you into the next room of your life. All major events of our lives usher us into new rooms, be it marriage, the birth of a child, a life-changing disaster or death. But death, in particular, takes us into a room that is bigger, with higher ceilings and more windows through which one can see more of the world and its possibilities. Within that room, you will find your loved ones in the form of memories and the many ways their existence added to the shaping of your life.

As a person ages, more people who affected their life die. It's the natural way of things; it has always been the way of things. Eventually, or perhaps during the years of your youth, a person who hurt you in some or many ways will pass on. When such a person dies, grieving diverts from the norm. You won't miss the person who wounded you psychologically or physically, you may even sigh an "Amen." That, too, is part and parcel of natural grieving and it's all right. A woman described her late husband, telling me of his daily psychological beatings, "You know, when he died I didn't cry. It's been many years and I've never shed a single tear. He was one of those people who constantly hurt those closest to him through verbal abuse. I doubt he was aware of how he was, but I have never shed a tear and feel no remorse whatsoever." She was a healthy-minded woman. She accepted the reality that had been a part of her life and then went on with the rest of it.

In that next big room that opens following times of grief, people who hurt others—for me—exist as small books sitting on a remote shelf. By accepting their existence, and the part they played in my life, by processing their life as well as their death, I reached a place of healing that allowed hurtful memories to blow away with the wind. It's called forgiveness; it's called letting go. There is no need to dwell on sorrowful memories. Why would you want to? Most important is that you move on with your life. You need not carry the pains of the past as you journey on. Painful packages are best left in the room behind you.

I continue to wear Kim's best and most beautiful cowboy boots. Every time I put them on, I quietly say, "Okay, Kim, let's go dancing." Invariably, a feeling of lightness comes over me as a smile creases my face. We are the body electrochemical and somehow something that was or is Kim remains to fill my heart and mind with her voice, love and laughter, and sometimes, my eyes with tears. The tear times ease and become less frequent as the years go by, but "stuff" continues to clog my brain and then something will happen, someone will say something or do something or I will hear a particular piece of music and then the dam breaks and I am awash with renewed grief as if she had just left all over again. It's okay, I'm not diving back into a pit of grieving, just re-experiencing love and the memory of the initial loss. Besides, closets need to be cleaned out every once in a while and after a gulley washer you will find yourself stepping lighter . . . dancing, with or without cowboy boots.

Perhaps the most important thing to remember is that death belongs to those who are dying. Their death is not yours, it's theirs. Those in the process of dying should be allowed to maintain their dignity. Your desires, or intelligent concern, may not be what's best for them. Having been in close proximity to multiple deaths, I have learned that while you may think you know what you would do in their situation, you don't. The approach of death pushes one's ego aside, or clings to it with damning words. Nevertheless, every "last party" should be orchestrated by the guest of honor. You may not like it, you may not even wish to attend, but if you are close enough to be in on the action, then their death is a part of your life and you will, in time, learn from it. To a person, people approach death in individual ways. Many approach it as teachers or historians, sharing until their last breath, while others push you through an annihilating storm never to be forgotten. Either way, you will come away with things you never knew before.

Such hard-won lessons are seldom forgotten. One I had to learn was that death is not a failure. All living things die. Actually, all things die. Mountains push skyward only to crumble; oceans rise and fall; continents grow, twist, shudder, melt and diminish; stars are born, live, and then die to become brown dwarfs or black holes. Our galaxy whirls around a massive black hole like a merry-go-round, its star-horses going up and down as they go round and round. One go-round takes a mere 250 million years, but just think of the sight with a time-lapse exposure. We are nothing but stardust, and it now appears likely that the universe itself may eventually fade away via its increasing rate of expansion or when it clashes with another 11-dimensional universe, at which time a new universe will form from unproven strings. Or will it? Again, more answers we are looking for.

Without death, all would be in stasis. Nothing would change. This minute, as you read these words, would stand still and you would never experience another moment, another thought or emotion. Everything in the universe exists in a constant state of flux.

When I finished working through my grief, when I reached a place of true acceptance, I finally understood the words my father said to me when I picked him up from dialysis a few months prior to his death, "Dying is the most natural thing you will ever do."

As to life? Life is a party in continuum with a guest list that is constantly changing. More than 98% of all life forms that have ever lived on this planet are now extinct, having either died out or morphed (evolved) into forms more adaptive to life. Neanderthals no longer inhabit the earth, but they, like every form of life ever known, were invited to the party. For most (me included), the party is mesmerizing and much too brief. Few guests wish to leave but no one gets invited without accepting a ticket to exit. Death is not when the fat lady sings, but when the butler takes your ticket, hands you your hat and opens the door. When the door opens, sing your song . . . your way. And, on your way out, remember to say thank you for the invite.

The earth continues to turn, the sun to rise, the moon to orbit, the seasons to pass.

As do we. . . . Try to leave a good path for others to follow.

EPILOGUE

DEATH'S LITTLE HANDBOOK

We grieve every death that touches us differently in accordance to the relationship we had with the deceased, coupled with our perceptions of death.

In today's world, many seem to view death as an option. But the truth remains—we all die. Perhaps we suffer from a "medicine can fix anything" attitude. We read that "John" received a heart/liver/lung transplant and is doing well. What we don't read is the current quality of John's life or how he will end his days.

As to death itself? We don't talk about it, we don't learn about it and we don't discuss it with our families. Many see death as being someone else's fault. A man with a fatal illness dies—it's the doctor's fault. A child is born with a genetic abnormality—it's the doctor's fault. A person trips and falls down a flight of stairs, breaks her neck and dies—it's the property owner's fault. A person drowns—it's the pool owner's fault. Blaming others demonstrates a failure to accept life and the responsibilities that come with it. And if you can't accept life, you can't accept death.

Many of us refuse to write a will or protect their assets for future generations. When a death does occur, many survivors stand as novices with little knowledge of what to do, where to begin or how to proceed. Even the word "death" seems taboo: "Sam kicked the bucket." "Molly passed away." "Martha met her maker." "Tom bowed out last night." "Carla didn't make it." "Mr. Jones lost his battle with cancer." "We lost Dad last week."

Not writing an appropriate will or end-of-life directive is like letting others pick your wedding dress, your house or your car. Of all the times in your life when things should be done according to your desires, your last days are the most important. Having your wishes and thoughts written down and known by your doctor and family can make your life more comfortable, knowing that your last party will be the way you want it. You can't hide from death, it'll get you every time—you might as well plan your party ahead of time. Winston Churchill arranged the entirety of his state funeral, down to the choosing of the riderless horse that followed his flag-draped coffin.

For the novice—for everyone—I submit the following:

These things are beautiful:

Friends who arrive with love, food and hands to care for you.

Cards and/or letters that prove the love and caring of others.

Short phones calls expressing sympathy and love (but *don't* get maudlin).

Follow-up calls made a week, a month, a year later.

Offers to do errands, shop, mow the lawn or whatever. Some of these—just do it.

People who know when to come, when to call and when to go.

Cards containing an anecdote or picture of the deceased.

People coming through in a pinch.

Funeral and airline personnel moving mountains to keep you from falling.

And love. . . . Without love there would be no grief. Without love you would never know the difference.

From "Joy and Sorrow," by Kahlil Gibran:

Your joy is your sorrow unmasked
and the selfsame well from which your laughter rises
was oftentimes filled with your tears.
And how else can it be?
The deeper that sorrow carves into your being,
the more joy you can contain.

Grieving is difficult and painful. Many try to deny it, cover it, or bury it in the darkest depths of their mind, but denying one's grief can only lead to prolonged pain and internal suffering. Grief that is not expressed will surface through personality disorders or inner turmoil. It's something everyone should learn about. When the multiple possible processes of grief are known, pain and suffering are handled in a healthier manner with the knowledge that grieving always prompts emotional growth.

When someone dies, the emotional pain can be overwhelming, but after the initial battle, many find themselves in a place that is different, a place that still hurts and stings. It's just the backside of grieving.

Grief is a process of letting go, of allowing other people to be themselves, to be who they are, what they are, and where they are, even if their relative place in space and time is outside the dimensions of your mind—even if where they exist is a place we call death.

Letting go is key to successful grieving. It takes a lot of work. Fortunately, the pay-offs are worth the effort. Grieving forces a person to break with innumerable life habits. So many things cease to occur when someone close to you dies. Those who travel on before us are no longer present and therefore are no longer here to do the things they used to do. They don't build blocks with you anymore, or buy you wonderful books. They don't scold you with, "My dear girl . . ." They don't teach you something new every time you see them, or show you how to do something just right. They don't paint pictures, or carve wood, or create a feast for your daughter's wedding. They don't enhance your knowledge with mental games, or smoke up the house, or snore in your ear, or use you as a mental backboard. They don't flood you with presents at Christmas, or stand by you through thick and thin. They don't tell you how to hold your newborn baby, or what to do when he gets sick. They don't love you unconditionally, or babysit when you can't afford a sitter. They don't teach you life's ways or bake you waffles for dinner or tell you you're the best daughter in the world, or work with you through the day. They don't wash bushels of freshly picked spinach in ice-cold, artesian well water until their hands are numb, or cry with you when things are tough. They don't call to tell you of a dream or the latest book they've read. They don't raid your refrigerator or make you marvelous presents for Christmas that you may receive in February. They don't move in after their divorce or make you laugh when you're blue. They don't tell you their darkest secrets or worry you through the night. They just don't. And all those moments, when they would have been doing all those things, are times of intense grieving, as during those well-worn moments you are lost, wanting the phone to ring, wanting to be with them, to share a meal, go to a symphony, or know the warmth of a loving body—and it hurts.

No matter who leaves you via death's door, there will be habits that you will be forced to go cold turkey on, thousands of little life habits that are broken with a breath. Even if the relationship you had with the deceased was horrible, your mind will still have to get over the habits of your joint existence. So, grieving is a process of letting go of day-in, day-out habits, a process of realigning your life with new habits and going forth to a place where you can accept the whereabouts of your loved one. We call it death, paradise, oblivion, nirvana, utopia, netherworld, heaven, hell, the other side, bliss, beyond, kingdom come.

Experiencing your pain, crying your tears, expressing your anger, shedding your guilt, remembering the good times, letting go of the bad, learning to smile again, standing up and walking forth, loving them, remembering them forever, will get you through.

It's so important to have a life. The person who died had a life. Their life was their life, not yours. Their death was their death, not yours. Do not steal from others. You will have your own life, and your death will be a part of your life, a part of your story that others will tell.

THE LOSS OF A MATE

Widowers are wanted at all functions, anytime of the day.

Widows are wanted for lunch, but not after five.

There are good days and they get better with time.

There are bad days that defy description.

Loneliness is a bitch.

Every death carries a modicum of guilt. Shed it.

Possible deep depression lurks—fight it, ban it from your thoughts or get help . . . now, not later.

If you get up the spunk to go to a party and dance and laugh and some of your friends say terrible things about you, face the fact: they aren't your friends. They have no capacity for understanding where you are, where you've been or what you're going through. Remember that what they think has nothing to do with you. You need not live with their thoughts. That's their job.

Being a widow or widower moves you into another place socially. If friends fail you, don't look back; make new friends. Those old friends mean no harm, but they just don't know how to handle your situation.

For the friends who do stand by you, remember to give to them as they have given to you. You can have friends over, do things with them and share new experiences with them.

So, death forces change. A person you loved has left, taking with them innumerable daily habits; loving addictions that once filled your moments. Accepting that fact, letting go of old habits and readjusting to new ones is a large part of the process known as grief. (You will miss that open tube of toothpaste.)

As you begin to recover, do, at last, the things you have always wanted to do. The person who left would want you to do so, just as you would want him to do if you had been the one to leave. If you can't find enough self-love to fulfill your desires for yourself, then do it for him. If you truly feel the one you "lost" wouldn't want you to be happy, you will have to come to terms with the fact that he had some problems . . . or are they yours? Either way, take care of whatever problems arise, and again, do it now, not later.

When you are past sad and/or wish to be alone, read, expand your mind—but not your body! Stay away from the refrigerator. I know that carton of ice cream is calling you from the freezer. Give it to the kids next door. Fill your mind with something new. Filling it with joy and knowledge will promote understanding, which will aid you in your grief. And do something for someone else. Don't dwell on your misery.

If you work, keep at it. If not, take a job. If you paint, write or play an instrument do so—take classes, grow and get involved with life. Volunteer work works wonders.

And remember the old saying: Laugh and the world laughs with you. Cry and you cry alone.

DEATH ETIQUETTE

D o call the family. The call should be brief, unless the party expresses a need to talk. Don't worry about what to say. Simply call, announce yourself and say, "I heard the sad news. I'm so sorry." The rest of the conversation will take care of itself.

If death took a young person, or the death was very tragic, and you are simply a friend rather than a special friend or close relative, give the family a minimum of two to three days to themselves. Then make your call or send a card.

Even if the person who died was *only* the grandmother of a friend, try to understand your friend's loss and follow through with sympathy, a call or a card.

If you are a relative or very close friend, go to the home and give your condolences in person. If the family has no help and aren't cooking for themselves, see to it that they are cared for. Bodily needs are easily forgotten during those first days. But be sure to put up your antennae: don't do anything if you don't feel it's appreciated. This doesn't mean a flowery thank you, but the obvious gratitude shown through behavior. Don't do or stay if your presence seems to cause stress. It's a sensitive situation, but help is often needed so long as the "helper" helps, gives a hug and leaves.

Last, but most important: tell everyone! Tell everyone you know that so-and-so died. It's the one time when gossip is the nicest thing that ever happened. Why? Because the hardest thing in the world for a person who's grieving is to meet a person on the street who knew the deceased but doesn't know they died.

"Hey, how's Dick?"

It's hard to describe the pain such a question causes. It's like having your loved one die all over again. And what of the poor unknowing person who just put his foot in his mouth and now has to suffer under a weight of embarrassment mingled with shock and grief.

"Go tell it on the mountain, over the hills and everywhere."

And, should you be among those for whom recovering from the death of a loved one seems close to impossible and you have been trying to do so for a long time, ask yourself these two questions: If you had died, rather than your loved one, would you want that person to go through as much agony as you are going through? And, if you could live your life over again, would you have rather never met, birthed or loved the person who died so as not to experience the amount of pain you are experiencing? Tough but relevant questions—think on them.

The entire universe pulses with life and death, each being a vital part of the whole. Everything on this planet is a part of the universal ebb and flow—life and death. Everything is connected and everything that comes into existence ceases to exist. Everything transforms into something else. It's like some gigantic dance with particles constantly changing while whirling around to the strains of some cosmic orchestra. Some of us die at birth, some live long lives while others appear to leave in mid-stride, right in the middle of their dance—or so it seems.

One day, a few years after Kim's death, I was hiking in the high mountains when I came upon a small patch of wild flowers. Overwhelmed by their beauty, I sat down beside the tiny golden flowers and thanked them for their glorious color, for bursting forth with life in order that their species might continue. It was as though I had never seen wild, high-mountain flowers before; certainly my view of them had changed completely. Living in high altitude, surviving seven months of snow cover and through years of drought ranked them as strong and beautiful individuals, living their lives, flirting with insects, dancing in the breeze, scattering their seeds, then dying back in the fall of the year—all within the space-time continuum we call life.

Something to remember: Another person's death is *his* death; it is *not* your death—you will have your own. I hope there isn't a person in your closet who will deny you your death; I hope you will be allowed to pass on according to *your* wishes, as opposed to those of others. And do write down your wishes (preferably with the aid of a lawyer or hospice center), have the papers notarized and give them to your family, doctors, lawyer (if you have one) and anyone else who will work as an advocate for you when your time comes. And remember, you can change your mind and rewrite your desires at any time. The worst thing you can do to a dying person is destroy his dignity by taking away his control of the situation. Death is one's last party on this side, and being thus, the star of the party should write the script—and if they want to sit by the seaside, be plugged into every device known, have the doctor call hospice for a gentle passing or be tied to the mast of their sailboat and sailed out to sea—it's their party, don't take away their personhood, don't wound them as they are waving goodbye.

Journey forward; only look back with love. Always remember that life is a gift—treat it as such. Fill your life with love and learning. Work for the joy of accomplishment. Always do your best. When necessary, shed your tears—unabashed. . . . Kim did.

REFERENCES

Abbott, E. A. 1991. *Flatland.* Princeton, NJ: Princeton University Press. (Orig. pub. 1953.)

Allman, J.M. 1999. *Evolving brains.* New York: Scientific American Library.

Anderson, P. 1996. *All of us: The meaning of death.* New York: Dell Publishing.

Barley, N. 1995. *Grave matters.* New York: Henry Holt & Co.

Bauby, J. 1997. *The diving bell and the butterfly.* New York: Vintage Press.

Becker, E. 1973. *The denial of death.* New York: The Free Press/ Macmillan, Inc.

Biocca, E. 1996. *Yanoama,* New York: Kodansha International.

Blate, M. 1978. *The tao of health.* Florida: Falkynor Books.

Bolen, J. S. 1979. *The tao of psychology.* New York: Harper & Row.

Bouquet, A.C. 1956. *Comparative religion.* Great Britain: Penguin Books.

Boyce, M. 1983. Age of the world in Zoroastrian Mazdaism. In *Man and time: Papers from the Eranos yearbooks*, ed. J. Campbell. Bollingen Series XXX. Princeton, NJ: Princeton University Press.

Brill, A. A., ed. 1938. *The basic writings of Sigmund Freud.* New York: Random House.

Brook, S., ed. 1987. *The Oxford book of dreams.* New York: Oxford University Press.

Bruce, R. D. 1979. *Lacandon dream symbolism.* Mexico: Ediciones Euroamericanas.

Budge, E. A. W. 1986. *The book of the dead.* New York: Arkana Paperbacks.

Campbell, J. 1949. *The hero with a thousand faces.* New York: MFK Books.

——, ed. 1973. *Man and time: Papers from the Eranos yearbooks.* Bollingen Series XXX. New York: Princeton University Press.

——. 1987. *The way of the animal powers.* 2 vols. New York: Harper & Row.

——. 1987. *The way of the seeded earth.* 3 vols. New York: Harper & Row.

Capra, F. 1983. *The tao of physics.* Boston: New Science Library.

Carrington, D. 1995. *The dream-hunters of Corsica.* Great Britain: The Guernsey Press Co. Ltd.

Cartwright, R., and L. Lambert. 1992. *Crisis dreaming.* New York: HarperCollins.

Castaneda, C. 1968. *The teachings of Don Juan: A Yaqui way of knowledge.* New York: Simon & Schuster.

——. 1972. *Journey to Ixtlan.* New York: Simon & Schuster.

——. 1993. *The art of dreaming.* New York: Harper Perennial.

Cervera, J., J. L. Arsuaga, J. M. Bermúdez de Castro, and E. Carbonell. 1998. *Atapuerca.* Spain: Editorial Complutense.

Chagnon, N. A. 1992. *Yanomamo: The last days of Eden.* New York: Harcourt.

Chalmers, D. 1996. *The conscious mind.* New York: Oxford University Press.

Cheney, M. 1981. *Tesla: Man out of time.* New York: Dell Publishing.

Colt, G. H. 1991. *The enigma of suicide.* New York: Simon & Schuster.

Cotterell, A., and R. Storm. 2003. *The ultimate encyclopedia of mythology.* London: Anness Publishing Limited.

Damasio, A. 1994. *Descartes' error.* New York: Grosset/Putnam.

De Waal, F. 1998. *Chimpanzee politics.* Baltimore and London: Johns Hopkins University Press.

De Waal, F., and F. Lanting. 1997. *Bonobo.* Berkeley, CA: University of California Press.

Deacon, T. W. 1997. *The symbolic species.* New York: W. W. Norton and Co.

Delsemme, A. 1998. *Our cosmic origins.* New York: Cambridge University Press.

Dewy, B. 1989. *As you believe.* Inverness, CA: Bartholomew Press.

Donald, M. 1991. *Origins of the modern mind.* Cambridge, MA: Harvard University Press.

Dunn, P., and R. Eyre. 1976. *The birth that we call death.* Salt Lake City, UT: Bookcraft.

Ebon, M., ed. 1978. *The Signet handbook of parapsychology.* New York: New American Library.

Fernandez-Armesto, F. 2004. *Humankind: A brief history.* New York: Oxford University Press.

Ferry, D. 1992. *Gilgamesh.* New York: Farrar, Straus & Giroux.

Fossey, D. 1983. *Gorillas in the mist.* Boston: Houghton Mifflin Co.

Franz, M. 1986. *On dreams & death.* Boston: Shambhala Publications, Inc.

———. 1988. *The way of the dream.* Toronto, Canada: Windrose.

Gardner, J., and J. Maier. 1984. *Gilgamesh.* New York: Random House.

Goodall, J. 1986. *The chimpanzees of Gombe.* Cambridge, MA: Harvard University Press.

———. 1988. *In the shadow of man.* Boston: Houghton Mifflin Co.

———. 1990. *Through a window.* Boston: Houghton Mifflin Co.

Greenstein, G. 1983. *Frozen star.* New York: Freundlich Books.

———. 1988. *Symbiotic universe.* New York: Wm. Morrow and Company, Inc.

Groning, D., and M. Saller. 1999. *Elephants.* Hamburg, Germany: Konemann.

Groopman, J. 2000. *Second opinions.* New York: Viking.

Hall, C. S. 1953. *The meaning of dreams.* New York: McGraw-Hill.

Hadfield, J. A. 1954. *Dreams and nightmares.* Great Britain: Pelican Original.

Haw, R. C. 1981. *Mindpower and the spiritual dimension.* South Africa: Flame Lily Books.

Hawking, S. W. 1988. *A brief history of time: From the big bang to black holes.* New York: Bantam Books.

———. 1993. *Black holes and baby universes and other essays.* New York: Bantam Books.

Haywood, J. 1995. *Early man.* London: PRC Publishing.

Hill, T. P., and D. Shirley. 1992. *A good death.* New York: Addison-Wesley.

Hinnells, J. R., ed. 1984. *A handbook of living religions.* New York: Penguin Books.

Hobson, J. A. 1989. *Sleep.* New York: Scientific American Library.

Hogue, J. 1994. *Nostradamus: The new revelations.* Great Britain: Element Books.

Holloway, R., D. Broadfield, and M. S. Yuan. 2004. *The human fossil record.* New York: Wiley-Liss.

Jahn, R. G., and B. J. Dunne. 1987. *Margins of reality: The role of consciousness in the physical world.* New York: Harcourt Brace Jovanovich.

James, W. 1958. *The varieties of religious experience.* New York: The New American Library.

Jamison, K. R. 1999. *Night falls fast: Understanding suicide.* New York: Alfred A. Knopf.

Jung, C. G. 1958. *The undiscovered self.* New York: Little, Brown and Co.

———. 1961. *Psychological reflections.* New York: Harper & Row.

———. 1964. *Man and his symbols.* New York: Doubleday & Company, Inc.

———. 1974. *Dreams.* Princeton, NJ: Princeton University Press.

———. 1986. *The portable Jung.* New York: Penguin Books.

Kason, Y., and T. Degler. 1994. *A farther shore.* New York: HarperCollins.

Krippner, S., and J. Dillard. 1988. *Dreamworking.* New York: Bearly Limited.

Kubler-Ross, E. 1969. *On death and dying.* New York: Macmillan Publishing.

———. 1975. *Death: The final stage of growth.* Englewood Cliffs, NJ: Prentice-Hall, Inc.

———. 1975. *Life after life.* New York: Bantam Books.

———. 1981. *Living with death and dying.* New York: Macmillan Publishing.

Kunkel, R. 1981. *Elephants.* New York: Harry N. Abrams, Inc.

Lederman, L., and C. T. Hill. 2004. *Symmetry and the beautiful universe.* New York: Prometheus Books.

Lederman, L., and D. Schramm. 1989. *From quarks to the cosmos.* New York: Scientific American Library.

Lederman, L., and D. Teresi. 1993. *The God particle.* New York: Dell Publishing.

Lewin, R. 1957. *In the age of mankind.* Washington, D.C.: Smithsonian Books.

———. 1993. *The origin of modern humans.* New York: Scientific American Library.

Miller, S. 1997. *After death.* New York: Simon & Schuster.

Mims, C. 1998. *When we die.* New York: St. Martin's Press.

Moody, R. A. 1979. *Life after life.* Harrisburg, PA: Stackpole Books.

Morse, M. 1990. *Closer to the light.* New York: Ivy Books.

Moss, C. 1988. *Elephant memories.* New York: Fawcett Columbine.

Muller, R. 1988. *Nemesis: The death star.* New York: Weidenfeld & Wheatland Corp.

Neher, A. 1980. *The psychology of transcendence.* New York: Dover Publications.

Nuland, S. B. 1994. *How we die.* New York: Alfred A. Knopf.

Ornstein, R., and R. Thompson. 1984. *The amazing brain.* Boston: Houghton Mifflin Co.

Ostrander, S., and L. Schroeder. 1970. *Psychic discoveries behind the Iron Curtain.* Englewood Cliffs, NJ: Prentice-Hall, Inc.

Pagels, E. 1981. *The gnostic gospels.* New York: Vintage Books.

Parker, K. L. 2001. *Australian Legendary Tales; Dreamtime.* London: Folklore Society. (Orig. written 1878.)

Pearce-Higgins, J. D., and G. S. Whitby, eds. 1973. *Life, death and psychical research.* London: Rider and Company.

Peat, D. F. 1988. *Synchronicity: The bridge between matter and mind.* New York: Bantam Books.

Pinker, S. 1997. *How the mind works.* New York: W. W. Norton & Co.

Randles, J., and P. Hough. 1993. *The after life.* New York: Berkley Books.

Rinpoche, S. 1992. *The Tibetan book of living and dying.* San Francisco: HarperCollins.

Rybeck, D. 1988. *Dreams that come true.* New York: Doubleday.

Sabom, M. 1998. *Light and death.* Grand Rapids, MI: Zondervan.

Schiff, H. S. 1978. *The bereaved parent.* New York: Penguin Books.

Schwartz, G. E. 2002. *The afterlife experiments.* New York: Atria Books.

Seife, C. 2003. *Alpha & omega: The search for the beginning and end of the universe.* New York: Viking.

Siegel, B. S. 1986. *Love medicine & miracles.* New York: Harper & Row.

Singer, P. 1994. *Rethinking life and death.* New York: St. Martin's Press.

Stoddard, S. 1978. *The hospice movement.* New York: Vintage Books.

Time Life Books. 1957. *The world's great religions.* New York: Time Incorporated.

Tolnay, C. 1966. *Hieronymus Bosch.* New York: Wm. Morrow & Co. Inc.

Toth, N., and K. Schick. 2006. *The Oldowan: Case studies into the earliest stone age.* Gosport, IN: Stone Age Institute Press.

Watson, L. 1982. *Lightning bird.* New York: Simon & Schuster.

Wilson, E. O. 1998. *Consilience: The unity of knowledge.* New York: Alfred A. Knopf.

Vulliamy, C. E. 1997. *Immortality: Funerary rites & customs.* London: Random House UK. (Orig. pub. 1926.)

Also by Carole A. Travis-Henikoff

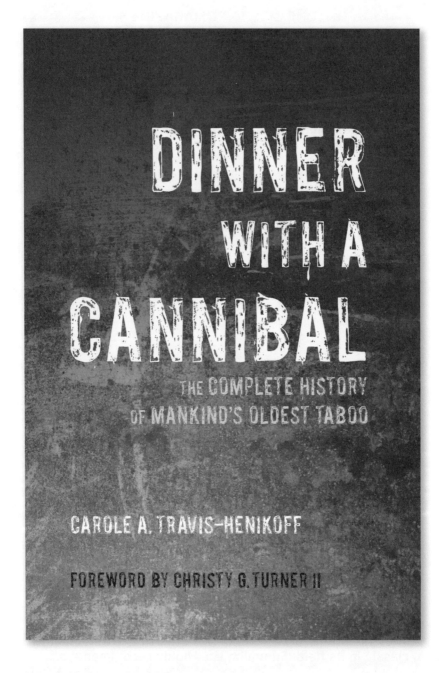

DINNER WITH A CANNIBAL

THE COMPLETE HISTORY OF MANKIND'S OLDEST TABOO

CAROLE A. TRAVIS-HENIKOFF

FOREWORD BY CHRISTY G. TURNER II

www.santamonicapress.com   1-800-784-9553

Praise for *Dinner with a Cannibal*

(STARRED REVIEW) "'The truth is, we all have cannibals in our closets,' writes Travis-Henikoff in her introduction to this meticulously researched, compulsively readable history of mankind's greatest taboo. As she eloquently illustrates, cannibalism has been around for as long as humans, and it's quite possible that its outlaw is a recent development in terms of recorded history. . . . Where Travis-Henikoff truly excels is in her sociological and anthropological analysis, offering thoughtful insights into the whys of cannibalism, lucidly explaining how cannibalism can begin in a society, as well as its historical employment in times of famine, war and even during a period of political witch hunting in Communist China. . . . Throughout, Travis-Henikoff maintains a thoughtful tone, free of judgment, that frequently challenging readers' beliefs. The result is an eminently enjoyable, albeit very dark exploration of a taboo topic that should give armchair anthropologists, sociologists and historians plenty to chew on."

—*Publishers Weekly*

"Travis-Henikoff, a scholar of paleoanthropology, covers the phenomenon's many raisons d'être, from survival to politically motivated terror. Her perspective as a gastronomist helps to situate cannibalism within a wide range of global culinary practices from the Amazon to the American Southwest to Polynesia. The book's range is impressive. Highly recommended."   —*Library Journal*

"Travis-Henikoff's lively and sometimes amusing anthropophagic romp shows that starvation and cultural patterns are often strong enough to counter moral taboos."

—*College & Resource Library News*

"Travis-Henikoff, an independent scholar who specializes in paleoanthropology, spent seven years researching and writing this fascinating book about the history of cannibalistic practices. Her writing engages readers to the point that one does not want to put the book down. . . . It will become a classic in its field. Summing Up: Highly recommended."

—*CHOICE*

Books Available from Santa Monica Press

The Bad Driver's Handbook
Hundreds of Simple Maneuvers to Frustrate, Annoy, and Endanger Those Around You
by Zack Arnstein and Larry Arnstein
192 pages $12.95

Calculated Risk
The Extraordinary Life of Jimmy Doolittle
by Jonna Doolittle Hoppes
360 pages $24.95

The Complete History of American Film Criticism
by Jerry Roberts
456 pages $27.95

Dinner with a Cannibal
The Complete History of Mankind's Oldest Taboo
by Carole A. Travis-Henikoff
360 pages $24.95

The Disneyland® Encyclopedia
The Unofficial, Unauthorized, and Unprecedented History of Every Land, Attraction, Restaurant, Shop, and Event in the Original Magic Kingdom®
by Chris Strodder
480 pages $19.95

The Encyclopedia of Sixties Cool
A Celebration of the Grooviest People, Events, and Artifacts of the 1960s
by Chris Strodder
336 pages $24.95

Faces of Sunset Boulevard
A Portrait of Los Angeles
by Patrick Ecclesine
208 pages $39.95

Footsteps in the Fog
Alfred Hitchcock's San Francisco
by Jeff Kraft and Aaron Leventhal
240 pages $24.95

Free Stuff & Good Deals for Folks over 50, 3rd Edition
by Linda Bowman
240 pages $12.95

Haunted Hikes
Spine-Tingling Tales and Trails from North America's National Parks
by Andrea Lankford
376 pages $16.95

James Dean Died Here
The Locations of America's Pop Culture Landmarks
by Chris Epting
312 pages $16.95

Just Doing My Job
Stories of Service from World War II
by Jonna Doolittle Hoppes
344 pages $24.95

L.A. Noir
The City as Character
by Alain Silver and James Ursini
176 pages $19.95

Led Zeppelin Crashed Here
The Rock and Roll Landmarks of North America
by Chris Epting
336 pages $16.95

Letter Writing Made Easy!
Featuring Sample Letters for Hundreds of Common Occasions
by Margaret McCarthy
208 pages $12.95

Mark Spitz
The Extraordinary Life of an Olympic Champion
by Richard J. Foster
360 pages $24.95

The 99th Monkey
A Spiritual Journalist's Misadventures with Gurus, Messiahs, Sex, Psychedelics, and Other Consciousness-Raising Experiments
by Eliezer Sobel
312 pages $16.95

Passings
Death, Dying, and Unexplained Phenomena
by Carole A. Travis-Henikoff
328 pages $24.95

Pop Surf Culture
Music, Design, Film, and Fashion from the Bohemian Surf Boom
by Brian Chidester and Domenic Priore
240 pages $39.95

The Quotable Actor
1001 Pearls of Wisdom from Actors Talking About Acting
by Damon DiMarco
360 pages $16.95

Rise and Shine
One Man's Extraordinary Journey from Near Death to Full Recovery
by Simon Lewis
312 pages $24.95

Roadside Baseball
The Locations of America's Baseball Landmarks
by Chris Epting
336 pages $16.95

Route 66 Adventure Handbook
by Drew Knowles
312 pages $16.95

Route 66 Quick Reference Encyclopedia
by Drew Knowles
224 pages $12.95

The Ruby Slippers, Madonna's Bra, and Einstein's Brain
The Locations of America's Pop Culture Artifacts
by Chris Epting
312 pages $16.95

Silent Traces
Discovering Early Hollywood Through the Films of Charlie Chaplin
by John Bengtson
304 pages $24.95

The Sixties
Photographs by Robert Altman
192 pages $39.95

The Third Tower Up from the Road
by Kevin Dolgin
336 pages $16.9

Tiki Road Trip, 2nd Edition
A Guide to Tiki Culture in North America
by James Teitelbaum
336 pages $16.95

Tower Stories
An Oral History of 9/11
by Damon DiMarco
528 pages $27.95